MAN-PUPPET O~~~~~~

The man in black picked up something which had been leaning beside him. A ring perhaps two feet wide ... yet when the man in black laid it down on the floor it was as large as he was tall.

The light went out. A bluish glow now emanated from the ring, revealing Bryda's face ghastly gray as she leaned forward, and Yarco's also, set and serious, and the conjurer's impassive.

And within the ring, where moments before there had been the bare planks of the floor, a shape that moved, and opened eyes glowing like coals, and spoke.

"What world is this?" the awful voice inquired.

Keith Woodcott's new novel is an epic adventure in cosmic terror and interstellar super-science.

Turn this book over for
second complete novel

Cast of Characters

KAZAN

Illiterate child of a line of thieves, he became master of unimaginable powers.

BRYDA

A prince's mistress, she was afraid to stake her own life—and hated the man she used as proxy.

YARCO

Lost on a bet before he was born, there was only one way he could become his own master.

CLARY

She scoffed at tales of devils, which stood her in good stead when they proved true.

SNUTCH

Nobody questioned his talent and intelligence—except for himself.

RURETH

Faced with events that seemed impossible, he kept his head and found that they were real.

?

A shapeless blackness with eyes like embers, its voice like a gale piping in a mountain range.

TO REBUILD A WORLD, FIRST TEAR IT DOWN!

An inexplicable murder and an equally improbable rescue brought research scientist George Gillian into strange company:

A great man five years dead.

A goat-eyed extraterrestrial.

A beautiful telepath.

And a gangster with weapons not yet invented—on Earth.

Gillian's investigations landed him dead center in a cosmic gamble, between an ape who dreamed of empire and an alien science infiltrating the Earth.

The future of the planet hung in the balance.

Turn this book over for
second complete novel

CAST OF CHARACTERS

George Gillian
Sworn to the search for knowledge, he held a planet's future in his fist.

Ape Abrussi
In his hands were forces that could mean doom to the human race.

Umbro
He considered man an inferior species, yet he would help them to survive.

Samuel Ronson
His own life meant little to him—that of the world meant a lot.

Sis Randolph
Behind her beautiful face lay a mind that could read others.

Hugo Strong
At his command—salvation or destruction.

THE DARKNESS BEFORE TOMORROW

by
ROBERT MOORE WILLIAMS

ACE BOOKS, INC.
23 West 47th Street, New York 36, N.Y.

THE DARKNESS BEFORE TOMORROW

Copyright ©, 1962, by Ace Books, Inc.

All Rights Reserved

Ace Novels by Robert Moore Williams:

DOOMSDAY EVE (D-215)
THE BLUE ATOM (D-332)
WORLD OF THE MASTERMINDS (D-427)
THE DAY THEY H-BOMBED LOS ANGELES (D-530)

THE LADDER IN THE SKY
Copyright ©, 1962, by Ace Books, Inc.

Printed in U.S.A.

Prologue

In the Galaxy called the Milky Way by some of its residents, and called other names by others, in that vast expanse of space where the stars sparkle like shining diamonds flung by some careless hand upon a black velvet rug, in the third spiral arm, out near its end, there is a sun. Some say it is a great sun. Others, more familiar with the truly vast suns of space, call it minor. Whether you call it major or minor depends on your viewpoint. Because it has no near neighbors, some say it is a lost sun. Others say it is an outlaw sun, thrust out near the edge of its Galaxy because of rebellious tendencies in its system. Others say that the reason it is so far away from the rest of the Galaxy is because of dangerous and delicate experiments in progress in this solar system, which involve the Life Force itself, its possible modifications and mutations—experiments with so great a potential for change that the history of the whole vast Milky Way, the whole Galaxy, may take quite a different course if they are successful.

But it *is* a big Galaxy. And other experiments are in progress in other solar systems in it. And experiments *do* go awry now and then, accidents *do* happen. There was an accident out toward Arcturus. This produced a vast scurrying among the planets of this minor sun, a great meeting at the highest policy-making level, decisions to act, and the orders necessary to implement these decisions, with far-reaching results.

One of those decisions sent the great ship into orbit around

THE DARKNESS BEFORE TOMORROW

the third planet. It stayed so far out that the possibility of a chance observation by a telescope was unlikely. To make doubly certain that it was unobserved, the great ship was put into an orbit which always kept it on the dark side of the planet, always sliding away into the darkness. As to the small ships that went down to the surface, experiments over centuries had indicated it was not too important if they were seen. The people who saw them were simply called crazy by the people who had not seen them.

From the bottom of the great ship, a round ball of crystal was lowered at the end of a chain—or was it a cable—that looked like silver. The ball was as big as a small house, the cable was perhaps a mile long. Inside the ship, a hidden mechanism began to operate, with the result that the ball slowly began a pendulum-like movement.

Forth and back, forth and back, like the pendulum of a gigantic grandfather's clock ticking time away in the void, the pendulum moved. Now and then the great ship shifted its position so that another section of the surface of the planet was directly under the swinging pendulum. At times the great ship dropped much closer to the planet, but always it stayed on the dark side and always the giant pendulum kept swinging, forth and back, forth and back, like a huge clock ticking away the seconds of destiny, ticking slowly away, as if it had all the time it needed to accomplish the aims of its operators. The great ship remained always near the planet but at ten year intervals new crews arrived and the old workers departed.

Chapter One

WHEN IT comes time to die, any place is good enough. This man had crawled into the doorway of a grocery store closed for the night and had cuddled his head in his hands and had died there. He had been in his mid-twenties, with an unruly mop of black hair and a thin pinched face. George Gillian shone his pocket flashlight on the body and made as fast and as complete an examination as he could without removing the man's clothes. There was no wound. Gillian had not expected to find one.

When they crawled into a corner like this, using the last desperate dregs of their strength, and cuddled up and died, neither a gun nor a knife had brought them to the end of their days. Gillian had seen three such bodies during the preceding month, two of them obviously criminals, inexplicably dead, the third a college student, also inexplicably dead. Dead bodies were getting a little too familiar to him. He was not accustomed to them, they were not his business, and he still felt a little squeamish around them. He had not expected to find a fourth here within a block of his own private laboratory.

Nor had he expected to hear the sounds of a fight in the street.

Nor did he now expect to hear the voice ask a question from right behind him.

"Did you kill him?" the voice asked, in broken English.

Gilliam got quickly to his feet to face the speaker. He held the flashlight down at his side so that its rays sprayed on the

THE DARKNESS BEFORE TOMORROW

sidewalk. This man might not like having a flashlight turned in his face.

The man was short in stature. He was wearing ordinary clothes, had a hat clamped awkwardly on his head, he had the tuft of a beard at his chin, and he had both hands in his pockets.

"I did not kill him," Gillian said. "I just found him here."

The man studied him for a moment. "All right. I believe you." he said. His voice had a strange quality in it, a foreign slurring of the words. "I go now." He turned to the right and moved away into the shadows of the night from which he had come.

As he turned, Gillian caught a glimpse of his eyes as seen from the street light on the left. The sight was startling. The eyes were not human. Instead they had in them something of the nature of the eyes of a goat.

A chill touched George Gillian as he stood in the dark entrance to the closed grocery store, with a dead man at his back and a stranger with a slurred alien accent in his voice slipping away into the street shadows on his right. Only after the man was out of sight did Gillian remember how heavy his breathing had seemed.

On Gillian's left, profanity and the sound of a blow showed that the fight still had some life in it. Far away in the night, he could hear a siren wailing. Perhaps the squad car was coming here, perhaps it was going somewhere else. The police were badly overworked. They had on their hands a vast increase in crime and juvenile delinquency. They also had found too many unwounded dead men in and around Los Angeles.

Looking at George Gillian, one would have had the impression that he might be a fullback on a professional football team. This impression would not have been correct. He was actually a research scientist, one of the finest of the young brains the Surging Seventies had produced in such large numbers. Even if this was true, he was still much too young, only twenty-eight, to have his private research laboratory. He had it, however, and so far as the public knew, he legally owned both the laboratory and all the equipment in it. Privately Gillian knew that this lab was

THE DARKNESS BEFORE TOMORROW

actually a gift, with definite and specific strings attached which required him to do any research the GRI required. The GRI—Group for Research and Investigation—did not mind spending its members' money for brains, for laboratories for the brains to work in, and for equipment for them to work with. In addition, some of the GRI members had a lot of money to spend. Gillian knew what he was doing when he accepted the GRI's gift.

From the left there came the sound of another blow. Gillian moved in this direction, then stopped as he saw the young woman lying between two cars at the edge of the street.

She was still moving. Gillian dropped down beside her. He slipped a hand under her head. She tried to bite him.

"Cut it out! I'm trying to help you!"

"Get lost. Nobody can help me. That goes double for anybody who works for Ape Abrussi." Her voice was taut with defiance and with her effort to suppress pain.

"I'm sorry," Gillian said. "I never heard of this Abrussi. The police ambulance will be here soon."

"The ambulance I'm going to ride in doesn't stop this side of hell!" The words grated at him. The speaker was about twenty-five, he guessed, with blonde hair and a dress that had once been stylish but now was badly torn.

"What happened?" Gillian asked. "Your dress looks like you were dragged along the street." Somewhere deep in Gilliam's mind, beyond the sorrow that he was feeling for this young woman, was the hope that she might be able to tell him something useful

"Terry ran over me with his buzz cart. He dragged me along the street," came the whispered answer. "My back's broken and I'm all chewed up inside."

"Who is Terry?"

"He and I were once friends. That was before Joe came along, before Terry went with Ape Abrussi. It was mostly my fault that he ran over me. I saw him coming and I tried to bluff him by jumping in front of him. He recognized me and tried to stop but the guy with him made him keep going. My name's Mary." So far she got, then she laid her head down on the concrete curb as if she needed to rest before talking any more.

THE DARKNESS BEFORE TOMORROW

"Who is this Abrussi?"

"He's an ape that looks like a man. God never gave him a human soul, so he thinks that everybody ought to be apes. He's strictly no good, big no good. His boys really weren't after me and Joe, they wanted Eck, who was with us. They don't really want Eck, but they think if they get him they can force Sis to give them something she's got. They want it—what she's got." Mary grew tired again and laid her head back down upon the curb.

Gillian made a quick mental note of these names, then, as a thought flashed through his mind, he asked an abrupt question, one he would not have asked if he had had time to think. "Did Joe have a lot of black hair and a thin, pinched face?"

"That's my Joe." Mary answered. "God how my insides do hurt! It's like they were crawling with fire. Say, mister—" Suddenly she was thinking about something other than the pain in her. "Say, mister, how do you know Joe? I don't know you, and I know everybody Joe knows."

Gillian, silent, wished he had not asked his question. There was no point in telling Mary that her Joe was dead not fifty feet from her. "Do you know anything about a new kind of weapon that kills without leaving a mark on the body?" he asked.

"Have they got that out tonight?" She was astonished. "From what we've learned, Abrussi almost never lets anybody else use that gun!" Suddenly she guessed the meaning that lay behind Gillian's question. She pulled herself erect. "Did they use that on Joe, mister? Did they, mister? Did *you* use it on him, mister? If you did, I swear I'll come back from hell and haunt you." Holding herself on her elbows, she stared at him as she intended to fix his face in her memory forever.

"I did not use anything on him," Gillian said quickly.

"Oh." She seemed to read in his eyes that he was telling the truth. "You look like you're all right, mister, so I'll tell you that Joe and I are going to be married, as soon as—" Her voice went into silence as she remembered where she was and realized that something had happened to her which might cause a change in her wedding plans.

THE DARKNESS BEFORE TOMORROW

"I try to be a right guy," Gillian said. "But sometimes it's hard to know how. About this gun that—about this gun—" He was not being indifferent to her pain, but he could not relieve it. Meanwhile, in the back of his mind, he was always remembering that there was a bigger pain—and a bigger problem—than even those which Mary faced.

"It's not really a gun, mister. As best we can get it, it's a crazy thing that looks like it is made mostly of glass." She lost the strength to hold herself on her elbows and settled back to the curb again. Her eyes went out of focus as a wave of pain passed through her.

Far in the distance still, the sirens wailed a little closer.

He eyes came into focus again. She gathered a little strength. "Go talk to Sis Randolph, mister, To Sis and to Eck. Sis—Sis knows something." The eyes went out of focus again. They seemed to look into some other world. Sudden happiness swept over the face. The voice had joy in it. "Joe! Joe! You were right here beside me all the time and I didn't see you! Joe, darling—" The voice went into silence, forever this time. But the glow remained for a little while on Mary's face.

Dying, she had seemed to see her man beside her. As he realized the meaning of her words, Gillian was a little dazed. Was this hallucination, or did she actually look into some other world where Joe waited? Gillian did not know, but he knew beyond any doubt that Joe's body lay in the entrance to a grocery store not fifty feet away. He looked down at the girl. Her body sagged into the street as if she had finally found the most comfortable resting place that Mother Earth had ever given her children.

Before Gillian could rise, feet pounded toward him along the street side of the parked cars. Someone screamed, "Get Eck!" Dodging between the parked cars, a tall young man with a baseball bat in his hand almost knocked Gillian down as the latter tried to get to his feet. Two hard-faced men with blackjacks in their hands tried to get at him from the street.

Crunch! The baseball bat took care of one of the blackjack wielders.

Smack! Gillian brought his fist up with him as he rose. It

THE DARKNESS BEFORE TOMORROW

landed on the side of the jaw of the second attacker. Probably unconscious before he hit the street, this man went over backward.

"Thanks, pal, whoever you are," Eck's voice sounded in Gillian's ear. "You think fast and you swing a real mean fist."

"I didn't really think about it," Gillian protested. "I just hit the closest one."

"If you can hit like that without thinking, what could you do—" Eck's voice went into silence as he stepped on the outstretched hand of the dead girl and looked down and saw what he was stepping on. His face froze. He called out a single sharp word, "Mary!"

"Sorry, but she won't answer, I'm afraid," Gillian said.

"How do you know she won't? Did you do her in?" Eck lifted the baseball bat.

"I'm getting a little tired of being accused of murders I did not commit," Gillian answered. "I found her here, dying. That's—*look out!*"

Two hard-faced men were coming from the sidewalk. Since Gillian was the closer, he went in ahead of Eck, hitting the first attacker solidly in the stomach. The man said, "Oof!" and lost all further interest in the fight. The baseball bat went over Gillian's shoulder and found the skull of the second man. He grabbed his head and spun in a tight circle before going down.

"You do a good job with that baseball bat," Gillian said, watching to make certain that neither man was showing signs of rising.

"No better than you do with your fist," the tall man said. He bent over and looked down at the body of the young woman, then looked at Gillian. "Where's Joe?"

"Down there in the entrance to a grocery store."

"Dead?"

"Yes."

The tall man looked appraisingly at Gillian. "I'm going to believe you," he said.

"Thanks." Gillian said. Standing fully erect, the tall man looked over the cars and down the street. His hand grabbed Gillian's shoulder, shoving him lower. "Down!"

Gillian went down without asking questions. "What is it?"

THE DARKNESS BEFORE TOMORROW

"The Ape is coming along the street," Eck hissed. "He's got the biggest little gun that ever was in his hand. I caught just a glimpse of him. I don't think he saw us but if he did, it will take more than your fists and my baseball bat to get us out of here."

"Is his last name Abrussi?" Gillian asked. "Mary mentioned somebody by that name."

"It is," Eck answered.

"Um." Gillian listened, then nodded in the other direction along the street. "Sirens are coming."

"They'll not get here in time if he spots us." The tall man peered around the fender of the car. "He's heard the sirens and can't make up his mind whether to run now or to look some more before running. He would like to get his bracelet boys out of here before the cops come, if he can."

"What are bracelet boys?"

"Slaves," Eck answered. He seemed to choose not to explain his statement.

"Why should he run if he has the biggest little gun?" Gillian asked. This was a question in the dark. He did not know enough about this weapon to identify it otherwise.

"Because he doesn't want to use it, if he can help it. He doesn't understand it, he's scared of it. He doesn't want to knock off a squad car full of cops with it, either, because nobody would ever believe they had *all* died of heart failure."

"Could he kill a whole squad car full of cops with it?"

"Just like that," Eck answered, snapping his fingers. He peeked around the fender again. "He's coming slowly in our direction. As he gets even with the car we're in front of, we'll sneak around it on the street side. We'll try to jump him from behind."

"If we fail?"

"Sis will bury us," Eck answered.

Gillian could glimpse the Ape now. He was short, stocky, with long arms. As the Ape reached the car, Gillian and Eck moved carefully around it on the street side. The sirens were getting closer, but they were still much too far away. Behind Abrussi, Gillian caught a glimpse of another man. The fellow was only a shadow but the way he had his hat

13

THE DARKNESS BEFORE TOMORROW

clamped firmly on his head told Gillian that this shadow had the eyes of a goat.

Was this second man following Abrussi?

Spotting the shadow, Abrussi stopped moving.

Gillian had the impression that Abrussi was a hunter but that there was another hunter in the act too.

Tires screamed on the asphalt. Abrussi must have assumed they were the tires of a squad car running without its siren on. He dodged between two buildings. The man with the hat firmly clamped on his head sauntered on as if nothing had happened.

All of this Gillian saw in a single glance. Then the tires screamed again. There was no sound of a motor but he turned to look. The car was one of the new models with a compact atom power unit generating electricity which directly powered a motor in each wheel. The ads said of these cars, with considerable truth, "All you hear is the whistle of the wind."

The car was a sport model with a slanting windshield, no top, and a single seat. In the trunk, however, a special seat had been built. On leash but straining at it was one of the biggest Great Danes that Gillian had ever seen. He was so startled at the sight of the great dog that he hardly noticed that the driver of the car was a woman. He did not know whether or not she was going to run over them. Spinning the car on two wheels, she careened toward them, then burned rubber from all four tires as she abruptly braked it to a halt.

"Don't stand looking," Eck said in Gillian's ear. "Get in."

Almost before Gillian realized what was happening, he found himself wedged into the seat of a car that had been built to hold only two passengers. It was not a comfortable position. Adding to his discomfort was the fact that the Great Dane was slobbering all over the back of his neck.

"Brutus likes you," the young woman said, calmly. "Otherwise he would be chewing your head off." The tires howled as she burned rubber, getting the car into motion again. Ahead, a flashing red light and a howling siren were coming toward them.

She braked the car to the curb and was getting a cigarette

from her purse when the two squad cars went past them. Gillian barely remembered enough of his manners to light the cigarette for her.

"Thanks," she said.

With a surge of power that almost took Gillian's head off, she put the car back into motion.

Chapter Two

"Sis—" the tall man leaned around Gillian to speak to the driver. "Sis, this is—" He blinked startled eyes as he realized he did not know his companion's name.

"Have you been picking up people on the street again, Eck?"

"He saved my life," the tall man protested.

"Oh." A flash of gratitude passed across the young woman's face, then was gone. She shrugged. "Well, perhaps he didn't have anything better to do at the time."

"Don't pay any attention to her," the tall man urged. "She really loves me but like all big sisters she feels she has to wash behind my ears and put me in my place ever so often. By the way, what is your name?"

Gillian gave his name. The tall man leaned in front of him again. "Sis, this is George," he called out to the driver. "Her name is really Kate but for some reason she prefers to be called Sis." he said to Gillian.

She glanced at Gillian out of the corner of her eyes, giving him a woman's quick appraising look that seemed to enable her to know more about him than he wanted her to, then hastily turned her attention back to the street. She was just in time to swerve quickly to the right and go between another car and the curb, a maneuver which left the driver of the other car shaking his fist at them.

"Are you two really brother and sister?" Gillian asked.

THE DARKNESS BEFORE TOMORROW

"Eck is my own sweet little baby brother," Sis answered. She nodded toward the rear of the car. "That's my other little baby brother just behind you."

"She means Brutus," Eck explained, when Gillian looked startled. "That's a very downgrading thing to say about a noble dog. What took you so long to get to us?"

"I wasn't sure exactly where you were. And by the way—" Alarm showed on her face as she braked the car to the curb again. "Where are Mary and Joe? How did they get away?"

Eck grunted tonelessly. The sound he made was absolutely flat and without meaning, so far as Gillian could tell. Apparently it meant something to Sis. Her face whitened.

"Do you really mean that, Eck?" Her voice was frantic. "Are they really dead."

"Mary is dead, this I know." Eck's voice was completely without tone. "I didn't see Joe myself, but George said—"

"I saw some man, with a thin face and a mop of unruly black hair, dead in the entrance to a grocery store." Gillian watched Sis as he spoke. "I'm reasonably sure that this was the man you are talking about. So far as I could tell, there was no wound on his body, no apparent cause of death." Sis' face went blank as he spoke.

She leaned forward and looked at her brother, either seeking advice on what to do next, or seeking added strength from him to face the blow that had hit somewhere inside her.

"It's tough, Sis. It's real tough." Sorrow was in Eck's voice, but strength was there too. "Don't let it throw you. They're not the first dead ones, and unless I miss my guess, they won't be the last."

"But they were such close friends—"

"Not as close as one other."

"I know." Sis' voice seemed to come from some far distance. Brutus, apparently sensing her feelings, tried to reach over Gillian's shoulder and lick her cheek. Her hand went up to caress the great muzzle. "It's all right, Brutus." She turned to look at Gillian. Her eyes flashed fire. "What was that you said about there being no wound on his body?"

Gillian repeated what he had said.

Her eyes flashed fire even stronger. "Why would you make a statement like that? Why would you notice there was no

THE DARKNESS BEFORE TOMORROW

wound on his body, and if you did happen to notice it, why would you think it important enough to be mentioned?"

Gillian did not try to evade the fire in her eyes. "I think it is important for several reasons, one being that Mary talked to me just before she died."

"Oh." Some of the fire went out of Sis' eyes.

"Mary said she thought I might be a right guy," Gillian continued.

"I agree with her on that," Sis said. "If I didn't, I'd turn Brutus loose."

Gillian chose his next words with great care. "Mary said I should find Sis and talk to her. She said Sis knows something." He looked straight into the eyes from which fire was still threatening to flash. They were the most disconcertingly candid blue eyes George Gillian had ever seen. Her hair was not blonde and it was not red but it was a mixture of the two colors. Her candid blue eyes weighed and measured him.

"Go on," Sis said.

"I assume you are the Sis that Mary told me about."

"I am."

"Then I would like to talk to you." Gillian said, gently. He was careful to keep all trace of threat out of his words and out of the tones of his voice. If he asked her, she might talk to him. If he threatened her, or tried to use force on her, he would find himself standing in the street watching her little car vanish silently in the distance.

Sis leaned forward and looked past Gillian at her brother. Between them, they seemed to be making up their minds. They said nothing. It was Eck who nodded and spoke. "George saved my life. He's all right. So get this buggy rolling."

Nodding, Sis stepped on the accelerator. Rubber burned from all four wheels.

"Besides," Eck continued, "A guy who can hit like George can, with either fist, I want to know better."

Sis nodded again.

"Besides, I have to find you a husband." Eck said.

"I'll take care of the solution to that problem myself." Sis

THE DARKNESS BEFORE TOMORROW

said, her cheeks crimson and her voice hot. Eck grinned. Brutus licked the back of Gillian's neck.

Gillian knew he was in.

For some time afterward, the only sound was the hiss of the tires on the asphalt street and the whistle of wind passing the sloping windshield. Sis drove so fast that Brutus put his head on Gillian's shoulder. She was a good but fast driver; she paid close attention to red lights and to the possibility of squad cars. Gillian had the impression that her fast driving resulted in part from her desire to keep her mind off something she did not want to think about. Maybe what she did not want to think about were Mary and Joe, but there was something even bigger than dead friends, something so big that two lives made no difference in comparison to it. Looking at her out of the corner of his eyes, he guessed she was about twenty-seven. With the ripeness of mature womanhood upon her, she was beautiful.

"Twenty-eight," Sis said suddenly, without taking her eyes off the street.

"Eh?" To Gillian her comment made no sense.

"I'm twenty-eight instead of twenty-seven," she answered. "And thanks for thinking I'm beautiful."

"What?" Gillian gasped.

Beside him, Eck grunted critically. "She's reading your mind, George."

"What?" Gillian repeated.

"She's reading your mind," Eck explained. "Sometimes she can make it work, sometimes she can't. You will have to learn how to stop her from doing it or she will boss you around something awful."

Gillian hastily put his mind under better control. He was aware of the existence of the psi functions; he also knew that millions of dollars had been and were still being spent on investigation of them, without any really clear or satisfactory results having been obtained. The GRI had poured millions of dollars into such work. It was not the fact of mind reading that startled him, it was the unexpectedness of it. Then as he realized how it had been possibly just been used. "You said something about picking up Eck's SOS—"

"That's the way to handle her, George," Eck said approv-

THE DARKNESS BEFORE TOMORROW

ingly. "Keep her off balance with unexpected questions and she'll be so busy trying to answer that she won't be able to read your mind. Don't let her get quiet or she'll tune to you like you tune a TV set to the channel of a transmitter. Yes, she picked up my mental SOS and burned rubber getting to me. This doesn't mean she knows everything, or can do this every time, but you and I can be thankful she did it tonight."

"Eck, I'm going to give you a knock on the head if you don't stop talking too much." Sis said. She rammed down even harder on the accelerator, which stopped all conversation for the time being. Cutting into an alley which ran at a lower level behind a row of old mansions that had once been called Millionaire's Heaven, she did not reduce speed. She seemed to be going full speed when she spun out of the alley and headed full tilt toward the huge double doors of a big garage dug into the face of the slope above. She touched a button on the steeering wheel as she made the turn.

Gillian was frantically trying to duck what he was certain was an impending crash when the doors swung upward and inward ahead of them and Sis, applying powerful brakes, brought the little car to a halt with its front bumper not more than six inches from the concrete rear wall of the garage.

"You have my sympathy, George," Eck said. "Every time she heads at full jet blast into this garage, I think certain we're going to crash. But the radio doors work every time. Only Brutus is able to take this landing without flinching. He doesn't have enough sense to duck."

"Brutus is a very intelligent dog, with complete confidence in my driving. He knows he doesn't have to duck." Sis unhooked his leash. Brutus fell all over himself getting out of the car, and led the way up a flight of steps. They followed him.

Upstairs was a garage apartment converted out of what had once been quarters for servants. In front was a great mansion. Enough light came in from the street to reveal untrimmed shrubbery in the remains of a formal garden.

"The place up front is actually a rooming house. Gramps is probably turning in his grave at the thought of the use

THE DARKNESS BEFORE TOMORROW

being made of his mansion." Sis said. At the question in Gillian's eyes, she continued. "Our grandfather built this place, around the turn of the century, for his bride. Eck and I now rent this little apartment. We don't live here all the time but it's a convenient place to stay for a few days."

"When we don't want to be found by anybody we don't know," Eck explained. "Come into the living room."

The living room was average size. The back windows looked out over the alley through which Sis had brought them at jet speed. Below, sloping away into the far distance, the lights of Los Angeles danced in a glow of bright color. To the left, a door led to a hall with a bathroom at the far end. Bedrooms opened out from the hall. In the living room was a duo-sound rig with a great stack of music tapes beside it. On top of it was the photograph of a smiling-faced man who looked to be in his early thirties. Riding on one shoulder was a small boy. Held with easy skill under the man's opposite arm was a larger girl with her bottom turned toward the camera. Struck by a resemblance, George turned to look at Sis.

"They always recognize Sis first," Eck said. "By her bottom."

"I'm going to have Brutus eat you alive."

"Brutus is already asleep," Eck said. The Great Dane was resting on the floor with his head between his legs.

"Your father?" Gillian asked, pointing to the photograph.

"Yes," Sis answered with a twinge of pain in her voice.

One wall of the living room was completely covered with autographed, framed photographs. Gillian turned his attention to these. He blinked in surprise when he saw that these were photographs of the world's great scientists. "They belonged to Daddy," Sis said. "They were his friends."

"Oh," Gillian said. His eyes went on to the last picture on the wall. He looked at it, looked again, then stood frozen.

"Inside, you're emotionally upset," Sis said. "What is there about this picture to make you act like you're seeing a ghost."

"Eh? Oh—" Gillian brought his voice, and his emotions, he hoped, under quick control. "That—that's Samuel Ronson."

"So it is. Did—do you know him?"

"I never had the good fortune to meet him," Gillian answered. "But he was—ah—" He quickly changed his mind

THE DARKNESS BEFORE TOMORROW

about what he was going to say as his throttled emotions threatened to erupt on him. "Ronson was a hero to me. More than—"

"How can anyone be more than that?" Sis asked quietly. "Particularly since you never met him?"

"When I was fourteen years old, and trying to make up my mind what I wanted to be, a copy of that picture of Ronson appeared in a magazine. I cut it out and pasted it on the wall of my basement laboratory. This was one of those little, seemingly unimportant things that may actually be very large to a boy and which may mark the turning point of his life. At this time, some of my friends had just joined a teen-age gang. They wanted me to join too. Every time I looked at the picture of Samuel Ronson it reminded me of something that I wanted to do more than anything else on earth. Instead of joining this teen-age gang, I became this other thing."

"This other thing was a scientist, wasn't it?" Sis said, real sympathy in her voice. "I know you have a doctor of science degree from Cal Tech, also that you have your own experimental laboratory, also that you are regarded by men who know about such things as one of the bright younger minds in the world today."

Gillian stared blankly at this remarkable woman.

"I told you that you will have to learn how to blank your mind or she will be reading it and then bossing you around something awful," Eck said. "She'll read your mind then use everything she learns against you if you don't walk the chalk line."

Gillian let go his breath. Up until then, he had not realized he was holding it.

Laughing softly and gently, Sis leaned forward and straightened an imaginary wrinkle in the lapel of Gillian's coat. "I'm not as bad as Eck makes out. Anyhow I like what I find in your mind. There's honesty there, and great integrity, and a yearning hunger for truth." The candid blue eyes had a soft mist in them.

"Watch her when she starts straightening your lapel," Eck warned.

Sis laughed softly and took her hand off Gillian's coat. "So

THE DARKNESS BEFORE TOMORROW

the picture of a great scientist was the turning point in your life. What happened to the boys who went on with the gang?"

"One was killed by a cop in an attempted holdup, one got out and is running a service station, the others are still around somewhere, just running." Gillian answered.

"Where is Ronson now, George?" Sis asked.

"Gone, vanished, dead for five years." Gillian answered. "Or so the papers say." Suddenly, he reached forward and grabbed her shoulders. She did not flinch away from the grip. "Do you have any reason to believe he isn't dead? Speak up or I'll shake an answer out of you."

Her face went white under the pain of Gillian's fingers. But she did not answer.

"Easy, George." Eck said, in Gillian's ear. "You'll wake up Brutus."

"Damn Brutus!"

"You're hurting me. Please let go." Sis said.

Not until then did Gillian realize what he was doing. Hastily he dropped his hand and began to apologize. Sis rubbed her shoulder and waved away his apologies. "I know how you feel. To some degree, Eck and I both feel the same way. Samuel Ronson was Daddy's best friend. He was Eck's godfather."

"He was?" Gillian looked at the tall man with suddenly increased respect. Eck was not only a good man with a baseball bat, but he had been touched by a great man. Gillian suddenly knew that this man and this woman, whom he had met so unexpectedly, were his kind. "Your father was also a scientist?"

"Yes, but not nearly as great as Ronson, though Eck and I thought he was mighty wonderful just the same." Again Sis' voice had pain in it.

"Do you know where Ronson is?"

"No. But this much I know—he isn't dead." She shook her head as questions started to form on Gillian's lips. "This is a psychic impression. I have no facts to back it up. I can be wrong but I think I'm right."

Gillian sighed. If Ronson was actually alive, he had to be found. So far as anyone knew, the man had simply vanished.

THE DARKNESS BEFORE TOMORROW

What had happened to him had been one of the great mysteries of the Surging Seventies.

"And your father—"

"Yes, George." Sis' voice was only a whisper. "We're sure about him. He *is* dead."

"I'm sorry. Don't tell me—" He stared at the woman in growing horror.

She nodded in response to his unspoken question. "He was found dead without a wound on his body. Ever since that day, Eck and I have been trying to find out who killed him; and how. That's why we are interested in Ape Abrussi. We know he has at least one weapon that kills without leaving a mark on the body of its victim. We don't know where he got it or how it works, but we're going to find out." Resolution was firm in her voice as she spoke. Looking from Sis to Eck, Gillian knew that these two people would never give up their search. Gillian liked this. He was another of the same breed.

"I think you know a lot, George, about this weapon and about a lot of other things. You belong to some kind of a group—"

"The GRI." Gillian said.

"I've heard of it." Sis said. "But what I was going to say was that Eck and I may know something too. Certainly the interests of all three of us go in the same direction, though our motives may be different. Perhaps if the three of us pool our knowledge, our abilities, and our resources, we may reach the goal we are seeking. Perhaps the whole human race, without knowing it, is seeking this same goal."

"I agree on all counts," Gillian said. "I'm with you on all counts." He meant every word he said. Sis and Eck both understood his meaning.

"Even if we've lost Joe and Mary, we've got you in exchange." Sis said. "Nothing can ever take the place of lost friends." Her blue eyes were close to tears which she was trying to blink away. "But we have a new friend. For this both Eck and I are grateful."

"Thank you," Gillian said.

She looked at her brother and nodded. As if he understood exactly what she meant, Eck went directly to the picture of

Samuel Ronson. He slid it aside. Behind it, the wall seemed blank, but, at the touch of a hidden spring, a section of the wall slid aside, revealing a small safe.

From the safe, Eck took a small package of papers, which he laid on the coffee table and beckoned to Gillian to examine.

Chapter Three

THE DRAWINGS looked a little like the doodling of a person talking to a persistent telephone salesman; they looked a little like sketches drawn on the walls of madhouses; perhaps they even looked a little like the frantic efforts of a new arrival from one of the outer planets trying to establish communication in a hurry with a human moron. At the top of the page was a drawing of a pendulum. Gillian understood this much. He frowned as he studied the rest of the drawings. He could see nothing about them to warrant the importance that Sis and Eck obviously placed on them.

The drawings were plans of something. A network of fine lines that looked like spider webs described an energy flow. A device that looked like a lens seemed to have the purpose of bending or focusing light, or some other radiation.

The pendulum was at the top of the page. It looked a little like the plumb bob on a surveyor's transit. However, arrows drawn from it seemed to indicate it was in motion.

"Where did you get these?" Gillian asked.

Eck nodded toward Sis. She was curled up on the sofa and was trying to pretend to be calm as she smoked a cigarette. This pretense of calmness was fooling nobody and she knew it.

"Sis drew them. She got them out of her head—or some place."

She leaned forward and tapped the drawings with the point of a carefully manicured nail. "There are the drawings

THE DARKNESS BEFORE TOMORROW

of a death ray, of the biggest little gun ever invented. I made them while watching a technician take such a weapon apart, repair it, and put it back together again."

At her words, Gillian felt a touch of chill run up his spine. "Where did this happen?"

"Right here in this room. I made the drawings right there on that coffee table, in a kind of semi-trance. But don't ask me where that technician was, because I don't know."

"Oh," Gillian said. He understood now that the drawings were the result of one of the cluster of psi functions. To one part of his science-trained mind, this threw a cloud on their reality. However, another part of his mind could not see this cloud. She had read his mind closely enough to prove it could happen! Who knew how the mind really functioned; who knew what its limits were?

"I had been alone here all day, thinking about Daddy and wondering who had killed him and what kind of a weapon had been used." Sis' voice had picked up a monotone and she related the experience. "The image of the technician came into my mind. To some degree, I looked through his eyes. This is hard to put into words, but it felt as it I was seeing what he was seeing, feeling what he was feeling, understanding what he understood. I saw both through his eyes and from some other, different viewpoint. He was working on this weapon. He understood it and I understood it, then. I drew what I saw. The meaning was completely clear to me then. However, when the semi-trance collapsed, I was left staring at some very foolish-looking drawings which I could no longer understand. However, I did know they were drawings of the death ray that had been used to kill Daddy."

She sank back on the couch as if exhausted. Eck looked worried. On the floor, Brutus suddenly awakened. He got to his feet, climbed up on the couch, and licked her face. She pulled his great head down into her lap and reached for a tissue to wipe her face. "One thing I can say for sure, when a Great Dane kisses you, you know you've been kissed."

"About this technician—" Gillian said.

"His body looked human," Sis answered. "But he had the yellow eyes of a goat."

THE DARKNESS BEFORE TOMORROW

"How on Earth—" Eck began.

"I didn't say he was on Earth," Sis answered. "He may have been in a space ship, he may have been on some other planet, he may even have been on a planet circling some other sun."

"The eyes of a goat," Gillian said, sombrely. "I saw a man with the eyes of a goat tonight. I was bending over Joe and he came up behind me and asked if I had killed him."

Sis sat up on the couch. "What happened to him? Where did he go?"

"I . . . the last I saw of him, he was following Abrussi."

"Then there are such people here on Earth!" Eck said, excitement rising in his voice. "We're on the trail of something. But why was he following Abrussi?"

"I don't know," Gillian answered.

"Damn!" Sis said. "He'll turn up again, though. I'll bet he will."

"I hope I have something better than a baseball bat if he does," Eck said. "Did he have one of those death rays?"

"He kept his hands in his pockets," said Gillian.

"Can you make that gun?" Eck asked.

"I don't want to make it," Gillian answered.

Sis looked pleased at his answer; she seemed to understand why no man, of his own free choice, would want to build a weapon that dealt in death; but she looked worried too.

"We need it if we are going to stay alive," Eck continued, patiently. "You know and I know that one or more of these weapons are on Earth today. They are in the hands of killers, of gangsters. The thugs who have them want more of them. Their purpose is to gain power."

"That purpose is as old as the planet," Gillian answered. "Through all history men have tried to find new weapons to gain more power."

"Now the weapons are coming from non-human sources," Sis said. "And that is a big difference."

"I agree with you," Gillian said. "That is a big difference. As long as we were fighting with weapons we could invent and make here on Earth, it was a kind of family quarrel; it involved only one planet. If one tribe invented a better bow, it wasn't long until the other tribes had this bow too. But if one tribe of humans—or one gang—gets this thing . . ." He tapped the drawings on the table. ". . . the other tribes will never have a chance. The scientific knowledge required to build this thing is so great that the other tribes will either all be dead, or will be in slavery, before they have a chance to develop such a weapon."

"Then you will build it, George?" Eck asked again.

"There is a tremendous gap between these drawings and a working model," Gillian said.

"You can bridge that gap. If you need help, Sis and I will give you all we have."

"Thanks," Gillian said, smiling. "There are others who will also give me all they have. The question is whether the best brains on Earth, pooled, know enough. What you ask is not easy."

"Will you try?" Eck persisted.

"I will if I have to," Gillian answered.

On the table, the telephone buzzed softly. Eck glanced at his sister, then lifted it and spoke into it. He clamped one hand over the mouthpiece. "It's Terry. He wants to come over and talk."

"Ask him where he got this number," Sis said. "It's not listed," she explained to Gillian.

"He says Mary gave it to him a couple of years ago," Eck answered. "And—he's crying, Sis."

"Then I guess he knows Mary is dead. Let him come over."

Gillian leaned back and lit a cigarette. He was annoyed because his study of the drawings was going to be interrupted. Eck took the plans and put them back into the safe, carefully putting Ronson's picture back into the exact spot it had occupied before he had moved it. Gillian was also annoyed because of what he had to say next. "I think I should tell you," he said slowly, "that Mary told me before she died that she had been hit and run over by a car driven by somebody named Terry."

The room got so quiet when he had finished speaking that he could hear the flutter of the wings of a heli-cab somewhere in the sky overhead.

"She also said that she had jumped directly into the path

THE DARKNESS BEFORE TOMORROW

of the car, trying to bluff Terry, and that he had done his best to avoid her. I don't understand this relationship; I don't understand why Terry should be crying, and I don't understand why he should be coming here now."

A little of the ice seemed to go out of the room at this explanation. Sis and Eck both looked sick but they also looked a little relieved. It was Sis who spoke. "Terry and Mary were friends a couple of years ago. They were also our friends. When Mary fell in love with Joe, she stopped seeing Terry. He took this pretty hard and, as a result, started running with the bunch around Abrussi. We tried to tell him not to do this, but he had been hurt. Even if it had been unintentional—Mary simply didn't love him—the pain was just as real. Terry faced the same choice you had long ago, only he had been hurt, and, in addition, he didn't have Samuel Ronson's picture to remind him of what he really wanted to be."

"I see," Gillian said.

"I guess he didn't know that Mary was with Eck and Joe tonight. When he discovered this, he realized that he still loved her and he did his best, in his way, to keep from hurting her."

"She also hinted—"

Sis nodded again. "They really were trying to capture Eck tonight. Then they could use him to force me to do what they want. But they don't want me, either. What they want are those drawings." She nodded toward the picture of Samuel Ronson.

Later, when a soft knock came on the front door, Eck went to answer it. The man who entered was short and stocky, with black hair, brown skin, and dark eyes. He spoke to Sis with evident embarrassment and nodded to Gillian when the latter was introduced. Sitting on the edge of a chair, Terry tried three times to light a cigarette.

"I'm sorry about Mary." The words were agonized. "I didn't know who we were after tonight until we got there. Mary jumped in front of my car and I couldn't turn fast enough to avoid hitting her. I knew she was killed by the way she went down. Later, I tried to find her but they

THE DARKNESS BEFORE TOMORROW

hustled me back to drive the getaway car before I could locate her."

Eck and Sis were silent, their faces blank. Their thoughts seemed to be far away. In spite of the fact that a cigarette was burning in the ash tray in front of him, Terry lit another one.

"I would like it very much if you would tell Joe for me that I'm sorry," Terry continued. "Also tell him that I am going to turn myself in to the police on a hit-and-run confession."

"Why turn yourself in, Terry?" Eck questioned. "That would mean two or three years in the penitentiary."

"I hope so," Terry answered.

"Do you mean you want to go to jail?" Eck asked.

"Yes," Terry answered. The agony deepened in his voice. "By that time, the Ape may have forgotten about me."

The room was silent. This man's suffering was obvious. He shook his left wrist as if something pained him there and Gillian caught a glimpse of metal under the coat sleeve. Terry got awkwardly to his feet. "You tell Joe for me I'm sorry," he said to Sis.

"Sorry, Terry." She shook her head. "I can't do this for you. You don't seem to know that Joe is also dead."

"Joe dead?" Terry gulped at this news.

"Mr. Gillian found him. He said there was no wound on Joe's body."

Terry turned to look at Gillian. The room was quiet.

"I didn't know," Terry said. He shook his left hand again. "No one told me. No wound, you say?" His mind seemed to wander. "There must have been a third car tonight, one I didn't know about. The Ape must have been in it."

"Where did he get that weapon, Terry?" The tone of Sis' voice indicated she was asking a question of no importance. Only her eyes, fixed on Terry's face, indicated how important it really was.

"I don't know," Terry answered. "I'm a little guy. I just drive a car now and then. I don't know anything important. I heard some of the boys say he had found it near a place called Mad Mountain, but I've never been there. I do know

THE DARKNESS BEFORE TOMORROW

he has several of the boys looking around near Mad Mountain for something most of the time."

"Where is this place?"

"Off that way, about fifty miles." Terry pointed toward the southeast. He scuffed the toe of one shoe on the rug. "I'm sorry about Mary and Joe." He moved toward the door.

"Don't go yet," Sis said. Terry stopped and looked at her. "How would you like a real tough job, Terry, one that will give you a chance to pay off for Mary?"

"What could I do?"

"You could go back to the gang and act as if nothing has happened. There are no witnesses who saw you run over Mary, so the police won't be after you. If anything happens, you could telephone us."

Terry turned this idea over in his mind. He didn't like it. "A dirty spy!"

"A spy on the side of decency, a spy on the side of the future," Sis answered. "But I want to warn you—"

"I know." His voice dropped to a whisper. "I'll be dead if they catch me." His gaze went around the room, searching for something. His eyes found Gillian's pen on the coffee table. He picked it up, then found a piece of paper. "Don't say anything aloud," he wrote. "But, for Mary's sake, I'll do it."

When all of them had read the message, he crumpled the paper in his hand and stood up.

"You're not making any damned spy out of me!" His voice grated harshly.

"But—" Gillian began. He stopped speaking as Eck dug him in the ribs.

Terry was holding up his left arm. Well up under the sleeve on the forearm was a metal bracelet that looked to be an inch wide and perhaps half an inch thick.

"Don't any of you try to follow me, either. I just came over here to say I was sorry about Mary, because I knew her."

Terry's voice snarled at them, but as he left the little apartment, his walk was that of a man with a new lease on life.

"He's wearing one of Abrussi's bracelets," Eck whispered. "Poor devil. I wonder if that bracelet has a radio trans-

THE DARKNESS BEFORE TOMORROW

mitter in it. I wonder if that's why he wrote his final message instead of speaking!"

"You know it is," Sis answered. Not until then did both realize that Gillian was staring at them in complete bewilderment.

"We don't know what these bracelets are, George," Eck tried to explain. "Abrussi's boys have just started wearing them and we haven't had a chance to get one into our possession so we could find out what it is. But whatever they are, they're no good for the guy who is wearing one."

"Mad Mountain?" Sis whispered. Abruptly she rose and left the room. When she returned a few seconds later, she had an atlas of maps in her hands and was rippling through them. "These are Daddy's old maps. He kept them for some reason which he never told us. I have kept them too, because they once belonged to him. Here's a map of the area Terry was talking about."

She laid the atlas on the coffee table. The point of her finger nail went over the map. "Here's Mad Mountain. There is such a place. It's even got a red circle drawn around it." Her voice took on a puzzled tone. "Did Daddy draw this circle? He must have. Why would he draw a red circle around this particular mountain?"

Gillian bent over the map. A faint dotted line led from the red circle off to the edge of the map. On the margin there, tiny figures had been written.

"That's Daddy's writing," Sis said, excitement mounting in her voice.

"These figures give a compass course and an altitude," Gillian said.

They stared at each other in bewilderment.

"I wonder why Daddy drew this circle around the mountain Terry has just told us about?" Sis' voice was a whisper in the room. "I wonder if this means that he knew there was something important in this place, knew it even before he died?"

"I know only one way to find out," Gillian said.

THE DARKNESS BEFORE TOMORROW

Chapter Four

AT THE controls of the helicopter, which his credit card and pilot's license had gotten from a rental service, Gillian watched the altimeter. Eck had a powerful telescope glued to one eye. Sis had a pair of 10 by 50 binoculars. Brutus, on the floor, was apparently bored with the whole thing, particularly with some supersonic note from the rotor vanes that was keeping him awake.

Mad Mountain was a flat-topped mesa perhaps fifty miles away. The time was mid-morning; there wasn't a cloud in the California sky. When he wasn't watching the altimeter and wasn't looking at Mad Mountain, wondering how it had got its name, Gillian was keeping an eye on this sky, to be on the safe side. Miles away another whirly-bird was visible but it seemed to have no interest in them. Sightseers, he supposed, or people taking pictures, or perhaps prospectors using magnetic detection equipment to probe the earth for mineral deposits that other prospectors had presumably missed.

"I'm looking," Eck spoke without taking his eye away from the telescope. "This side of the mesa has a talus slope leading down from the top. There's also a big cliff with an overhang on it which forms a natural cave. I've seen cliff houses built in similar spots over in Utah and Arizona. I don't see anything here." A note of disappointment sounded in his voice.

"There's probably not much to see. Whatever it is we're looking for, it doesn't stick out like a sore thumb. If it did, somebody in a helicopter would have spotted it long before now."

"How do we know they haven't?" Sis asked. "Maybe they saw it but didn't live to tell the story."

"What a cheerful sister I have!" the tall man grunted.

"I'm only telling the truth, and you know it. There is danger here." She looked at Gillian. "My guess is that we have to be at exactly the right spot and at exactly the right altitude to find this thing."

"I see a hole under the overhang of the cliff," Eck called out. "Can this be what we are looking for?"

THE DARKNESS BEFORE TOMORROW

Gillian swung the ship in until less than a mile separated them from the granite escarpment of Mad Mountain. Taking the binoculars from Sis, he studied the place. A hole leading down into the mountain was all he could see.

"I have the oddest feeling that we had better not get any closer in the air," Sis said. "I think it would be best if we landed on top and came down the slope."

"I agree with you," Gillian said.

"Do we want to look into a hole?" Eck questioned. "Probably it's nothing more than an old prospect tunnel."

"We want to look into this hole," Gillian said. Circling, he lifted the helicopter above the top of the mesa. Seen at close range, the flat top was mainly a illusion of distance. The top was actually a mass of boulders that offered few chances of a safe landing. Picking the best spot, Gillian set the ship down. Outside the windows, a few stunted cedars and forlorn cacti were the only visible signs of life. It was hard to realize that so desolate and so forlorn a spot existed so close to the teeming population complex that was Southern California in 1980. Lifting the high-power sporting rifle, equipped with telescope sights, from its resting place, Gillian levered a long cartridge into the firing chamber, and opened the door. Brutus was the first out.

"It doesn't look like much, but the nearest tree is that way," Sis said to the Great Dane. He went to explore. The three humans were slower.

They picked their way cautiously down the talus slope and reached the ledge that led to the overhang under which the mysterious hole was located. As they neared the hole, Brutus began to hang back. Sis had to coax the Great Dane to accompany them.

"Maybe Brutus has more sense than I gave him credit for," Eck said.

They reached the hole. Deep under the overhang, and at such an angle that spotting it from the air was almost impossible, about twelve feet in diameter, with smoothly polished sides, the hole went down into darkness, into mystery, perhaps into some lost world that lay below the surface of the earth. Coming from the hole was some radiation that made humans a little uncomfortable and which badly upset the nervous

THE DARKNESS BEFORE TOMORROW

system of a dog. Refusing to come within ten feet of the place, Brutus sat down and howled. They ignored him.

"Maybe this was once a mine shaft," Eck suggested, again.

"There are no tailings," Gillian said. "The miners would have to dump the rock somewhere."

"What do you think, Sis?" Eck asked.

"I think I agree with Brutus," she answered. "I wish we were all back in Los Angeles having a late breakfast." Her voice grew grim. "But this doesn't mean I'm going to run. It only means I'm scared."

"You're not the only one," Gillian said. "Do you pick up any ESP impressions?"

"I feel a heavy vibration here but it is so powerful that it blots out everything else." Sis was silent for a moment. "Now I'm *hearing* a sound. It's coming from that hole."

Listening, Gillian was aware that a low-pitched moan was coming from this hole. His startled imagination pictured some great beast in pain charging from its lair. He knew these ideas were untrue, however Brutus, beginning to howl, seemed to think they were real. Rising in crescendo, the moan became a howl. Sis grabbed Brutus and hugged him to the ground. Eck and Gillian, the latter with his rifle ready, hit the dust beside her.

The moan became a shriek.

George Gillian saw something come out of the hole that slanted under Mad Mountain. It was an aircraft of a design that had never come from a human drawing board. It seemed to be made either of condensed light or of some strange metal through which light rays could pass. The result was that while Gillian could not see the outside of the ship very clearly, he could see its interior fairly well. He could see the pulsing of radiations flowing in shifting, glowing colors from its energy source, he could see the steering mechanism, and he could aso see the only passenger in the ship, the pilot.

The pilot was dressed in a simple garment of shining cloth that fitted snugly against his body like close-fitting metal armor worn by knights of old. In height and build, he was about average for a human being. However, his head was oddly shaped, with knobs on top that looked a little like

THE DARKNESS BEFORE TOMORROW

very short horns. He had a tuft of whiskers at the end of his chin.

As the ship came out of the hole, the pilot turned his head and glanced at the three humans on the ground.

Gillian saw quite clearly that this pilot had the yellow eyes of a goat.

As the pilot saw the humans, a flick of surprise passed through those yellow eyes. But the pilot was not much surprised. The expression in the yellow eyes said he knew all about such lowly creatures, including what to do about them if they escaped from their cages.

Then the ship was gone. Moving with growing speed, it vanished almost instantly into the cloudless California sky above Mad Mountain. A little later the throbbing echo of a sonic boom came floating back.

Brutus stopped howling and began to whimper. George Gillian sympathized with the great dog. He knew just how Brutus felt.

Sis tugged at his elbow. "There was another one, George. Just like the one I saw repairing the gun when I made the drawings. He was right in that ship, piloting it."

Now, more than ever, Gillian sympathized with Brutus. Like the Great Dane, he knew how it felt to be lost and alone in a world he had not created and did not understand at all. Now he could no longer pretend to himself that the man who had asked him if he had killed Joe had not had goat eyes. Now he could no longer even think that the drawings Sis had made had no real source. While psychic material was often false and often misleading, in this case the source was in.

Getting to his feet, Gillian walked silently to the lip of the tunnel and looked down. Sis and Eck came to stand beside him. He ignored them.

The air coming from the tunnel was hot. A slight glow on the walls was fading away. Gillian wished he had a radiation counter. Looking down, he could see nothing.

From his pockets, he took a pen and a memo pad. Swiftly he wrote a number and a name. Tearing off the sheet of paper, he handed it to Eck.

"If I don't come back within an hour, you return to the

ship and use the radio to put through a call to this number. Give my name and your name. You will need no other identification than my name. Explain exactly what happened to me, and to you, and where you are. Don't try to fly the ship. You're not a pilot. Stay with the ship and help will reach you within an hour after you make the call."

"You talk like you're going down this tunnel," the tall man, his voice grim, took the note.

"I am," Gillian answered.

Sis started to speak but Gillian interrupted. "No, Sis, don't tell me it's like walking down the barrel of a loaded cannon. I know that. I want both of you to stay here for two reasons. First, to watch for another ship like the one we just saw in the sky. Second, I want somebody to get information on this place back to that number I gave Eck. If I don't come out, you two are to do this."

"But—" the tall man said.

"If it's my time to die, that's all right," Gillian continued. "Others have already died, as you have told me. Others will die. It is not too important if I die, but it is very, very important that two people I can trust will get this information back to the number I gave you."

They were silent. The expression on their faces indicated their rebellious feelings. He took the binoculars from Sis. Brutus came up and licked his hand. Turning, Gillian ran down the tunnel.

The frequency that had shaken his nervous system outside seemed to have died away. Had it come from the launching of the ship? Light ahead of him indicated the end of the tunnel. Coming to an abrupt halt, keeping as far out of sight as he could, he looked at what lay before him.

A monkey wandering into a radiation research laboratory would probably wonder about the meaning and purpose of all the junk it was seeing. It would not understand what it saw at all. It would have no grasp of meaning or purpose of any of the equipment. Waves on a pool of jungle water it would know about from experience. But waves vibrating uncounted millions of times faster than the waves on the jungle pool would simply not exist to the monkey.

George Gillian knew intimately the waves that vibrated

THE DARKNESS BEFORE TOMORROW

uncounted millions of times each second. He knew how fast they moved. He had equipment in his laboratory which could count both rate of vibration and speed of motion.

Were there waves as far beyond these as these were beyond the waves on the pool of the monkey? Gillian suspected that such waves existed, but he could not offer instrumental proof of what he suspected. No instrument had as yet been built which would measure such waves. They laughed at the traps of all known instruments, sped through the traps uncaught, and danced on and away. Yet all scientists were beginning to suspect that these waves were real also that they played a tremendous part not only in the ESP phenomena but also in all life, including the lives of humans.

Looking into this cavern, Gillian felt like the monkey that had wandered into the radiation research laboratory. A gulp came up in his throat. Wonder rose in him. He had to choke it down.

Off to the left several small ships similar to the one he had seen were sitting in a line. Here they seemed a little more real, a little more substantial than had the one he had glimpsed as it leaped from the launching tunnel. A number of technicians were working around one of the ships, moving it, possibly preparing it for launching. Putting the binoculars to his eyes, he saw that these technicians had short knobs like blunt horns on their heads. He passed this by to look up.

The cavern was several stories high. It had small openings with balconies at several levels.

Then he saw the ball that was made either of light or of glowing metal. At first, he thought it was floating unsupported in the air, then as he realized it was moving very slowly, he saw the long linked chain carrying the heavy cables upward, and he knew that he was seeing the pendulum Sis had tried to draw when the magic had been on her and she had seen into far distances. It was gigantic! The ball of glowing metal was at least ten feet in diameter, the chain that supported it was hundreds of feet long. Its motion was very slow, very majestic like the pendulum in some truly tremendous grandfather's clock keeping the time that ruled the world.

THE DARKNESS BEFORE TOMORROW

George Gillian could not even guess at the purpose of this pendulum.

He saw that in its downward sweep it would pass very near to a platform raised above the floor of the cavern. A great many instruments were on this platform. Apparently their purpose was to determine, to check, and to control the operation of the pendulum.

A man, or what looked like a man from this distance, was on the platform. He had a round, fat stomach that made him look like Friar Tuck. As the pendulum moved slowly past the platform, he inspected the instruments very closely and made minute changes on some of them.

Gillian put the binoculars on what looked like a man on the raised platform. He fully expected to see a creature with short knobs on his forehead, and as the powerful glasses brought him close, he expected to see that this creature had the yellow eyes of a goat.

Shock passed through him at what he did see. The man on the raised platform was—a man.

George Gillian at this moment simply did not believe his eyes. He had no time for further observation. A rising roar in the cavern pulled his attention elsewhere.

He saw that the technicians had put the ship they had been moving directly on the launching ramp that led to this tunnel. The roar was coming from the ship as it warmed up for flight.

Turning, Gillian raced up the tunnel as fast as his legs could carry him. Behind him, he heard the roar grow louder, he felt the pressure of rising air in the tunnel, and he knew the ship was starting up.

Light was ahead of him. He raced for it. And reached it! He threw himself on the ground and rolled over and over. A split second behind him the ship *whooshed* as it leaped from the launching tunnel, then roared past him. Eventually the sonic boom came back. George Gillian hardly heard it. He was content to lie still and pant to get his breath back, also to know that he was still alive. He knew he was being kissed but he didn't know whether Brutus or Sis, or both of them, were doing it. He knew Eck was trying to help him to

THE DARKNESS BEFORE TOMORROW

his feet. He was glad to accept this help. Once he got to his feet, he knew exactly what he was going to do.

"Come on. We're getting out of here."

Eck and Sis had dozens of questions they wanted to ask. He ignored all of them. Led by Brutus, they scrambled up the talus slope. Vanes whistled as Gillian lifted the helicopter into the air. As soon as they were safely launched, he reached for the radio telephone and gave a number to the operator.

"That's the number you gave me to call if you didn't come back out of that tunnel," Eck said.

"I know it is," Gillian answered, then spoke into the phone as the connection was completed. "This is George Gillian. Yes. That's my name. Get this message through to Mr. Strong immediately." With Eck and Sis listening, he gave a terse account of what he had seen. If the person on the other end of the phone had any doubts, he did not express them. "What I am going to say next has top priority. I don't care where Mr. Strong is or what he is doing, this information is to be passed on to him within ten minutes after I finish speaking. This is the message." Again he paused. "*Samuel Ronson is alive. He is in Mad Mountain.* Tell Mr. Strong he is not to disturb the situation in any way until he talks with me. *Yes, I said Samuel Ronson. I also said he is alive and that he is in Mad Mountain.* You can find this place on any map. Goodbye."

The man on the raised platform, the man inspecting the operation of the gigantic pendulum, was Samuel Ronson.

Slipping the phone back into place, and setting the helicopter on a straight course for Los Angeles, he patted Sis on the cheek. "Sometimes your ESP proves very, very accurate, my dear. Yes, Samuel Ronson is alive. The pendulum you drew also exists, a huge thing. And the technicians with the goat eyes are very plentiful down below."

Sis looked grateful.

"But what's this all about?" Eck asked.

"I don't know," Gillian answered. "I didn't think it would be smart of me to stick around down below and ask the boys what they were doing."

"I sure agree with you on that," the tall man answered fervidly. "But—"

THE DARKNESS BEFORE TOMORROW

"I guess the whole human race is asking, in one way o another, what something that is happening is all about." Gillian paused, wondering how to present the history o fifty years in a few words. "That something is happening i obvious. What it is nobody knows. Here are some of the symptoms of it. First, in sports, performance has steadily and consistently improved. Records have continously gotten better In the last Olympic Games only one record that was over twelve years old was left unbroken. Perhaps better training methods account for part of this improvement, but not for all of it. Some other factor is in operation that seems to be producing better athletes than have ever existed since we started keeping records in sports. To go from muscles to minds—in the field of pure science, the same thing has happened. Most of what scientists thought they were most sure of is in the junk bin today. Nobody dares predict what the science of tomorrow will be. Ideas are changing so fast that no one dares freeze the model. Did the same unknown factor that produced the improvement in the sports records also account for the gains in science? If so, how does it work? What is it? Is some unknown frequency impinging on the genes, the units of heredity, producing changes there? Are these changes in their turn resulting in more competent human beings?"

On the horizon, Los Angeles was a blur that was rapidly coming closer. Not satisfied with this, Gillian tried to set the throttle forward another notch. There was no other notch.

"Here is another aspect of the situation which most people just don't know exists. All the psi functions have also been accelerated. This includes all the meanings of clairvoyance, telepathy, clairaudience, precognition, telekinesis, and some others that nobody is yet sure enough about even to name. We have more and better sensitive individuals today than ever before, and most important of all, they are learning to accept themselves and we are learning to accept them, to work with them and their abilities, and we even hope some day to understand them." He looked at Sis as he spoke.

She smiled at him. "I would have felt a lot better if you had said this sooner. I was afraid you would just think I was crazy."

THE DARKNESS BEFORE TOMORROW

"Never, my dear. I admit I don't understand it, but I have seen this stuff turn out right a little too often to doubt that it exists. Many competent scientists have some of the psi functions themselves. You can bet they are investigating this field as thoroughly as they can, just to prove to themselves what was worrying you, that they're not crazy—if for no other reason."

"Well," Eck said. "It's good to know that my big sister is not going to be taken off to the nuthouse just any day now."

"I wouldn't worry any about her if I was you," Gillian said.

"Oh, I'm not, not really," the tall man answered. "I'm just making jokes, part of the time to keep from admitting how scared I really am."

"You are right in knowing that there is something to be scared about," Gillian said. His voice took on a somber tone. "This picture had its bad side. We have more and bigger and fuller mental hospitals; we have more neurotics and psychotics running around loose; we have more teen-age gangs, more adult gangs, more crime, more divorce, and more general law-breaking than ever before in all human history. Humanity seems to have lost all concept of moral codes and of ethical conduct."

Gillian inspected the throttle again. There still was no other notch. But they were over the city now and the rental landing field was fairly close. The tall man and his sister were very quiet.

"What does all this mean?" Sis asked wonderingly.

"It means conflict which may be the biggest in human history too, conflict between heavily accelerated growth and those who are trying to stop this growth or hold it back. It also means bitter conflict between individuals who are trying to take advantage of this very confused worldwide situation to grab power and wealth for themselves. Of these, I take it, the man whom you call Ape Abrussi is one. At present this conflict is in a state of very precarious balance. I don't suppose anybody on Earth today knows how this balance will eventually tip. If it goes to the bad side, if the Ape Abrussis really get into the saddle, well, we certainly have enough hydrogen warheads to blow the whole human race off the planet. If it goes to the good side, well, perhaps we are

THE DARKNESS BEFORE TOMORROW

entering the golden age of true humanity." Hope, though dim and far away, sounded in Gillian's voice.

He set the ship down at its landing field and signed the charge for it. As they got into her car, Sis still had questions to ask. "What part do you personally play in all this?" she wanted to know.

"A very minor one," Gillian answered promptly. "As you know, I happen to belong to a group of public-minded people, the GRI, the Group for Research and Investigation. This group financed my laboratory. In a sense, I work for it. When I signed that charge slip back there, I was spending this group's money. This group is legally and properly incorporated. It is doing its very best with the very large means in money and men at its disposal to find out what is going on, and if it agrees with the purpose that is behind this world situation, to do everything in its power to cooperate. If it disagrees, it will fight with every available resource. This group has real power at high military and political levels in this country, clear up to the president. It can get things done—but up until now, it has not known what to do." He dodged involuntarily as the doors of the garage swung up and in ahead of them.

Sis brought the car to a halt with its front bumper not three inches from the concrete wall of the garage.

Brutus was first up the stairs.

They heard him growl ahead of them.

"Brutus!" Sis called sharply.

They entered the living room. And stopped moving. The place was almost completely wrecked.

A hole in the wall revealed where Samuel Ronson's picture had once hung.

But Brutus had not been alarmed at any of this. He had growled at the man sitting quietly on the couch and was now sniffing at his toes and was looking up at his mistress as if this was something he did not understand.

The man was Terry. His head sagged forward on his chest, Terry looked like he was asleep.

Terry did not look up when they entered; he did not rise to greet them.

They knew instantly that Terry would never rise again.

THE DARKNESS BEFORE TOMORROW

They also knew that no undertaker would be able to find a wound on his body, that no autopsy would reveal a cause of death other than heart failure.

A growl sounded in the Great Dane's throat as he turned to the door that led toward the bedrooms.

The door was opening.

A man stood there. He was short and swart, with hot, angry eyes. In his hands he held a small weapon that looked as if it was made of glass.

"Just stand still, all of you," he said.

"Abrussi!" Eck whispered.

"Yeah. Just stand still. And keep your damned dog—"

Teeth bared, great forepaws swinging, the Great Dane went after the intruder.

The gun in Abrussi's hand snapped at him.

Brutus did not make a sound as he died. He simply collapsed and crumpled to the floor.

Abrussi looked from the dead dog to the live humans. A grin was on his face.

"Terry revealed a little more than he realized when he was here talking to you," Abrussi said. "My equipment picked it up. Terry saw that his best interests lay in coming back here with me, but when I found the safe behind the picture, he lost his head."

Abrussi shrugged. Terry had lost his head. Probably he had tried to swing at the Ape. Terry was no more.

"Don't any of you lose your heads," Abrussi said.

The little glass weapon in his right hand covered them.

Chapter Five

ABRUSSI SEEMED to know Sis and Eck Randolph. But he had never seen Gillian before. His hot, black eyes fixed on Gillian's face. "Who the hell are you?" The tone of his voice said he wanted an answer, fast.

THE DARKNESS BEFORE TOMORROW

At the sight of this man, Gillian felt strong feelings of revulsion rise in him. He controlled them. "Just a friend," he answered politely.

"That answer is not good enough," Abrussi snapped at him. "What's your name and your address."

Thinking they would mean nothing, Gillian gave his correct name and address. "Never heard of you." The way Abrussi spoke, the fact that he had never heard of this man made Gillian of no importance whatsoever. "But I will." He lifted his left wrist to his mouth. Revealed on the wrist was a bracelet similar to the one worn by the dead Terry, except it was wider and thicker. "Get the car up here right away," he spoke into the bracelet.

"Yes, sir," the bracelet answered.

Abrussi changed a setting on the bracelet, then spoke into it again. "I want the dope on George Gillian, 2131 Columbine Street. Get the lead out of your pants and get through those files in a hurry. I'll wait."

Abrussi did not have to wait long. The bracelet emitted a sharp whistle. "Nothing on a George Gillian, sir."

"All right, check further," Abrussi answered. "Get back to me with the dope. There's something on him somewhere. I want it."

"Yes, sir," the voice from the bracelet answered.

Tires squealed on the asphalt in the alley. Down below, motors whined as the garage doors swung open.

"We're going to take a little ride," Abrussi said to his three captives.

A man with a receding chin came up the stairs and entered the apartment. He looked at Abrussi, who nodded toward Terry. "Wrap him in a blanket and stuff him in the trunk." He nodded again, toward the Great Dane. "Put the dog in another blanket." His eyes darted to Sis as she moved and the little glass weapon shifted to cover her. "Stand still, Sis."

"When he was just a tiny puppy, I used to wrap Brutus in a blanket, so he would be warm at night," Sis answered. "Wherever he is now, I want him to be warm. It's my right to wrap him in his last blanket."

Ignoring the weapon, she moved past Abrussi and into the hall, Abrussi followed her. She disappeared into a bedroom.

44

THE DARKNESS BEFORE TOMORROW

His face grew grim. She reappeared carrying an eiderdown quilt. Refusing assistance from anybody, she wrapped the body of the Great Dane in this. Standing up, her eyes were moist but her chin was high and firm. She looked Abrussi in the eye.

"All right, Ape," she said. "We'll go for a ride with you. Some day we will repay the favor—and take you for a ride."

Abrussi blinked at her. His eyes had fire in them. Then he shrugged. "Anybody who takes Ape Abrussi for a ride, has to get up early in the morning," he said. "Go down the steps ahead of me. And don't try to run out the back door. I've got a couple of boys in the garage." He gestured with the little glass weapon.

Sitting beside Sis' little sports car, making it look like a very small bug, was a long, seven-passenger sedan. A chauffeur was at the wheel, another man waited to open the door. Abrussi motioned for his captives to get into the back seat. When they obeyed him, the man who had opened the door got into one of the raised seats in the rear and sat facing them. Abrussi got into the front seat and sat half-way turned around so he could see any move they might make.

"Don't anybody in the back seat lose his head," Abrussi said.

The man with the receding chin came down the steps carrying a heavy bundle wrapped in a blanket. He placed this in the trunk, then went back up the stairs. The next bundle was wrapped in an eiderdown quilt. Sis watched him from smouldering eyes. The trunk slammed heavily. The man with the receding chin got into the front seat and sat beside his boss.

"Get going," Abrussi said.

Tires squealed as the car was backed out of the garage, then squealed again as it started down the alley. A sharp whistle came from the front seat. Abrussi lifted the bracelet to his ear. "Good," he said. "Off." He turned to the back seat and looked appraisingly at George Gillian. "So you're one of the bright young minds?" he said to the latter.

"That is not my idea," Gillian answered.

"It's the idea of somebody who knows," Abrussi answered. His manner suddenly became friendly. "Glad to have you with me. I can always use bright young minds."

45

THE DARKNESS BEFORE TOMORROW

Gillian, looking at Abrussi's short, thick neck and wondering if he had the strength in his hands to break it, did not answer.

The car dropped them at a small, private airport. Here they were transferred to a large helicopter and put into a private cabin. Abrussi, not concerned about any effort to escape now, and with other business at hand, rode with the pilot. Meanwhile, he was busy on the radio set obviously hidden in the bracelet. The ship lifted and headed toward the range of mountains that lay toward the east. Gillian sat in silence. Eck clasped and unclasped his hands. Sis's chin stayed firm but the moisture in her eyes was still clearly visible.

The ship was set down in the landing area adjoining a large, rambling house that occupied much of the top of a mountain. Looking out, Gillian could see no road leading to the house, nor did the building of a road appear to be practical. He knew then that this was another mountain-top hideout that could be reached only by helicopter.

"This is one of my places," Abrussi said expansively, as they stepped out of the ship. The little glass weapon had disappeared into a holster inside his coat. With servants hastening to open doors for him, he took them inside, led them to a small room, told them very politely that he would see them as soon as possible, waved to the telephone and told them to order anything to eat or drink they wanted, but not to try to escape, and left them alone.

"Sis, he was only a dog," Eck said, sympathetically.

"He was my dear and trusted friend," she answered.

Gillian patted her on the shoulder. "Go ahead and cry if you want to."

"T—thanks, George." Borrowing Gillian's handkerchief, she blew her nose.

"Where does the money to pay for this place come from?" Gillian asked.

"Dope, gambling, and girls," Eck answered.

Gillian was slightly abashed at his own naïveté. "Perhaps, in some ways, I have led a secluded life."

"Did you think that dope, gambling, and girls have gone out of style here in this modern world of 1980?" Eck asked. He shook his head. "I suppose that dope, gambling, and

THE DARKNESS BEFORE TOMORROW

prostitution are other parts of the bad side of the picture you painted for us when we were coming back from Mad Mountain. At least, we have more of them than ever before."

Gillian went to the telephone and picked it up, hoping vaguely that he would hear a dial tone, but not really expecting it. There was no dial tone. A girl's voice said, "Yes, sir." While Sis and Eck looked hopeful, Gillian said, firmly, "I want an outside line."

"Yes, sir," the operator said.

While Gillian held his breath, he heard clicking sounds, then the operator came back to tell him, very politely, that all the outside lines were busy at the moment. "When can I get one?" he asked.

"I'm afraid you'll have to clear with Mr. Abrussi first," she told him.

Gillian sighed. Sis and Eck, reading the expression on his face, lost their hopeful looks. "Mr. Abrussi said we could order anything we wanted," he told the operator. "Send up a gallon of orange juice, a huge pot of coffee, steak, scrambled eggs, and hash browned potatoes, for three."

"I can do that for you," the operator answered. "Right away."

Gillian tried the doors. They were locked. He checked the windows. They could be raised six inches from the bottom and lowered six inches from the top. Looking out, he decided it would do no good to get them open all the way. Below was a drop of at least a hundred feet. The room they were in was on the edge of the mountain top.

"What about the GRI—" Eck began. As he spoke, the door opened silently. A six foot Negro, with a serving tray in his hands, entered. He looked sharply at Eck, but if he had heard the GRI mentioned, his face gave no indication that he knew anything about it. As he set the tray down, the bracelet glistened on his left wrist. "Your orange juice and coffee," he told them. "Your steaks, scrambled eggs, and hash browns will be along as soon as the cook can whip them up." He grinned at them. "My name is Washington Moses. If you want anything, just tell the operator to send me up. I'll take care of you right away."

"We do want one thing, Washington," Sis said hopefully.

THE DARKNESS BEFORE TOMORROW

"Yes, miss," he said, politely attentive. "What is it?"

"Out of here," Sis told him.

His dark face suddenly somber, he shook his head at the question. "To lead you out of this land, I'm afraid you will need a bigger Moses than I am." The smile gone from his face, he left the room. Later he returned with steaming platters of food. They had finished eating when he returned for the third time.

"The boss is ready to see you," he said. "I'll show you the way."

Alone in a huge office that sat on the edge of the cliff, giving him a breathtaking view of Southern California, Abrussi was all smiles. Dismissing Washington Moses with a curt nod, he turned to them. There was no mistaking that Abrussi was a powerful man in many ways, including physically, or that he had a most magnetic, winning manner, when he chose to use it. He chose to use it now.

"I'm taking you all into my organization," he said. His tone of voice conveyed the impression that this was the biggest opportunity they had ever had. "I'll start each of you at fifty thousand dollars a year. Of course, there will be an *up* on that. When we really get going, there is no top." His smile was very expansive.

Gillian mentally estimated his chances of breaking Abrussi's thick neck. Eck, thinking of strangulation, was clasping and unclasping his hands again. It was Sis who spoke.

"What is it you want us to do to earn our money?" she asked.

"Trust a woman to be practical," Abrussi said, beaming. He opened a drawer of his desk. From it he took the package of plans that Gillian had last seen going into the wall safe behind Samuel Ronson's picture. "These are what I wanted all along." He looked at Sis and Eck. "If you had been reasonable when I first asked for them, it would have saved everybody a lot of trouble." He sounded as if he was blaming them for putting him to the inconvenience of killing Joe and Terry. "I want you, Sis, to explain these in detail, and I want you, Gillian, to aid her in the development of all the scientific angles.

"Um," Gillian said.

THE DARKNESS BEFORE TOMORROW

"I want you to get started right away. A lot depends on this and I don't want any time wasted. You can have anything you want in the way of equipment. You will have quarters, full maid service, and full service from my own chef. To show you that everything is on the level, I'll pay your first month's salary in advance."

Another desk drawer was opened. From it, Abrussi took stacks of hundred dollar bills. Starting counting, he gave up. "It's too much trouble to count. For the first month, I'll make it an even five thousand dollars for each of you." He made three piles of bills and pushed them across the desk top.

The smile on his face was a most expansive thing.

"That's a lot of money," Sis said.

"Yeah." Abrussi grinned.

No one stepped forward to pick up his stack of bills.

Slowly the smile died on Abrussi's face. Hard, glittering lights suddenly showed in his eyes, as the ape looked out of them. It was not pure ape. Lurking somewhere in the background, was a hint of the king cobra.

Cobra fast, Abrussi's hand went inside his coat. It came out with the little glass weapon in it.

No one moved.

It seemed to George Gillian that an infinity passed while he was waiting for the sudden *snap* he had heard from this same weapon when it had been used to kill Brutus in mid-charge. He knew that Sis and Eck were feeling the same slow drag of time while they waited for death to come to them. Then, slowly, Gillian realized that Abrussi was bluffing. Sis realized this too.

"You can go to hell!" she said.

Abrussi exploded into violent rage. "Do you three punks think you can bluff me?" he shouted.

"If you shoot us, you won't have anybody to explain those drawings to you," Sis said, calmly.

Abrussi had known this all along. When he realized that his victims knew it too, the hot anger faded from his eyes. Cold rage came up. When he spoke, the hiss of the king cobra was in his voice.

"All right, if you want it the hard way."

Lifting his voice, he said, "Get Doc Muzzy in here, fast."

THE DARKNESS BEFORE TOMORROW

From a hidden speaker, a voice answered. "Right away, sir."

Abrussi eyed the three people standing in front of his desk. "If I was you, I'd take it the easy way," he said. "Doc Muzzy is a psychiatrist. He went on the hot stuff and couldn't get enough to satisfy him. He works for me now. He knows ways to make people talk that make even me shudder."

He looked expectantly at the three.

Again it was Sis who spoke. "As I said before, dead people explain no drawings."

"You won't be dead," Abrussi answered. "You will just wish you were!"

The door opened and two men entered. Between them, they had the third man by the elbows, supporting him. Bracelets were visible on the wrists of all three. The man in the middle held their attention. Wearing an apron that once had been white but which was now spotted with many stains, he was partly bent over. From this position, through thick-lensed spectacles, he seemed to peer out at a world that had lost most of its meaning for him.

"This is Dr. Muzzy," Abrussi said. Contempt that he did not bother to try to conceal was in his voice. He nodded toward Eck, Sis, and Gillian. "They're yours, Doc."

"Yes—ah—sir." Muzzy peered around the room until he located the persons his boss had indicated. He stared at them as if he could not quite make up his mind about them. "What—ah—sir—do you want done with them?"

"Give them your silent treatment," Abrussi ordered.

"Yes—ah—sir." A grimace that apparently had been intneded to be a smile crossed Muzzy's face momentarily, then faded as he thought of some difficulty. "But—we—ah—sir—only have two cells. There are three here. The whole purpose of the—ah—experiment—would be defeated if we put two in the same cell."

Abrussi thought about this. It was a problem he could solve. "Let the woman watch through the windows," he ordered.

"Yes, sir," Muzzy said. "Bring them one at a time." He turned and walked out of the room without help.

Gillian found himself placed in a small cell that had no

THE DARKNESS BEFORE TOMORROW

furniture and except for a small window up near the ceiling, it had no openings. Light came from some source concealed in the ceiling. Walls, ceiling, and floor were covered with some material that seemed to absorb sound. This material was scuffed and scarred near the floor. Gillian regarded these scuffed places with great doubt. They looked as if they had been made by some previous occupant who had tried to kick his way out.

"When you change your mind and decide to cooperate with—ah—Mr. Abrussi, just nod your head toward the window," Muzzy said. "But don't give in too soon, or I may think you are not sincere."

The door closed behind him and his two helpers. It made a soft sucking sound as it was pulled shut. When it closed there was no mark to reveal where it had been.

Except for the lack of furniture, the room seemed harmless. It was, however, rather silent. He called out sharply to the psychiatrist. The room seemed to absorb his voice, which became a thin whisper. At this point, the meaning of Abrussi's words *silent treatment* became clear. He tried to remember what he had read about such rooms as this—and about what happened to the people who had stayed in them a few hours, for experimental purposes. He could not remember all the details but he was very sure the results had been unpleasant, extremely so. Accustomed to hearing sounds all day and to some degree during sleep, the human ear would begin to behave very strangely when no such sounds were present in its environment.

Now Gillian realized the reason for the scuffed places on the walls near the floor. Some previous occupant had tried to kick his way out of this silent room. But first he had gone crazy.

Shock came up in Gillian, stronger than what he had felt on Mad Mountain.

Movement at the glass panel near the ceiling caught his eye. Looking, he saw that Sis was there. She made signs at him. He interpreted these to mean that Eck was in another cell and that she was going to be forced to watch both of them go crazy.

THE DARKNESS BEFORE TOMORROW

Her face had horror on it. But it also had resolution in the set of her jaw.

"Don't give in!" Gillian screamed at her. His words were whispers in the soundproof room. He saw her face disappear from the glass panel.

Outside, in the short corridor on which the doors of the soundproof cells opened, Sis was talking to Abrussi.

"You can make it easy on yourself," Abrussi said. Two bodyguards stood behind Abrussi. Wiping his hands on his spotted apron, Dr. Muzzy stood beside him.

Looking at Abrussi, Sis Randolph knew, for the first time in her life, the meaning of hate. She hated this man. She hated all he stood for. She hated what was happening to Eck and to Gillian. She hated what was happening to her. But more than any of these, she hated what would happen if Abrussi gained greater power, particularly if he gained it through her.

"You can still go to hell!" she told him.

Abrussi laughed at her defiance. In his own mind, he was sure she would weaken. Meanwhile, why not enjoy teasing her? He jerked his head toward the two panels in the wall. "Your brother is in one cell. Your boy friend is in the other."

"He's not my boy friend," Sis answered. "He is a very fine and splendid man, also something you don't understand, a gentleman!"

"Before Doc Muzzy gets through with him, you will see what kind of a gentleman he is," Abrussi answered, amused.

"I'll watch both die before I explain those drawings to you." Sis said. Her voice was firm with resolution.

"Will you watch both of them go crazy?" Abrussi asked.

She caught her breath. She had not thought about this side of the picture, she had not understood the real purpose of the cells. The shock wave that went through her nervous system left marks on her face.

Abrussi grinned again. "When you change you mind, just let Doc know," he said. He turned to leave, then stopped as Muzzy clutched at his arm in an effort to detain him. "No, Doc. No more of the hot stuff. Later, when you finish with your job here, you can have all you want."

THE DARKNESS BEFORE TOMORROW

Helplessly, Muzzy let go of Abrussi's arm, to stare after him as Abrussi went out the door.

The face that Muzzy turned toward Sis as the door closed had complete hopelessness on it. On his left wrist, the bracelet gleamed.

Turning away from Muzzy, she moved to the second panel. Inside, Eck looked up at her, waved, and grinned. A choked feeling rose in her throat. He, who would soon be needing courage so desperately himself, was trying to give her courage.

She moved to the other glass panel. Gillian was sitting on the floor. He also grinned and waved. The choked feeling came up in her throat again, stronger now.

She turned back to Muzzy, fully intending to choke the life out of him, if necessary, to get the keys to the cells, but the psychiatrist had slipped through the door.

A key turned in the lock to the outer door. She braced herself to leap at Muzzy. It was Washington Moses. She held herself in check. His dark face was expressionless as he looked at her.

"I came to see if there is anything you want, Miss—" He paused. "I never did get your last name."

"Randolph," Sis said.

"And the gentlemen in there?" He nodded toward the glass panels.

"One is my brother, Eck Randolph. The other is George Gillian. Washington—" She hesitated as she tried to decide how to word an appeal to this man who wore Abrussi's bracelet. "Washington, you loook like an honest man."

"I try to be honest, Miss Randolph. Is there anything you want to order from the kitchen?"

"I'm not hungry." He turned to the door as she spoke. She knew she had to speak now, or never. "Washington—" Desperation came into her voice. "Are you willing to help us?"

He glanced down at the bracelet on his left wrist, then spread his hands in a helpless gesture. His dark eyes studied her. Did she detect sympathy somewhere in their depths?

"We're innocent people! We have to get out of here." The desperation grew stronger in her voice.

53

"So many of us are innocent people, Miss Randolph." He opened the door.

"Wait a minute, Washington." She gestured toward the cells. "They're hungry in there."

"I have instructions to bring you anything you want from the kitchen. But I have no instructions to bring anything for them. Sorry, Miss Randolph." The door closed behind him. Washington Moses was gone.

Sis did not feel her body fall. Later, when she found herself on the floor, she knew she had fainted.

Chapter Six

WHEN HE was first alone in the soundproof cell, Gillian thought that the absence of sound was a little thing. Hours later, he knew better, and liked what he knew much less. He discovered that his ears, over his whole lifetime, had become accustomed to hearing sounds. Now large, now small, now noticed, now unnoticed, now the chirp of a bird, now a distant whistle, now the sound of a jet in the sky, now the impatient honk of an automobile horn—always there had been a background of sound which his ears had heard.

Cut off from this background for the first time, the ears reacted at first with a sort of puzzled bewilderment. Gillian's nervous system translated this lack of a familiar stimulus as something missing. Then what was missing became important. Then anxiety began to grow.

The ears began to grow hungry for sound.

When it was not forthcoming, they began to reach for it.

When this failed, they began to manufacture it.

The result was hallucination.

The ears began to hear sounds that did not exist in their immediate environment.

The nervous system became more and more alarmed.

THE DARKNESS BEFORE TOMORROW

Eventually the sounds that the ears were not hearing were converted by the alarmed nervous system into voices. As this happened, the whole neural structure began to try to go into action on the basis of hallucinated voices: the vocal chords tried to answer what the ears claimed they were hearing, the mind tried to think in terms of what it thought the ears were hearing and what the vocal chords were saying in reply. Since some of the things being heard were frightening, the adrenal glands went into action, manufacturing the fear hormone and pouring it into the bloodstream. The heart began to pound. Then the breathing picked up, eventually becoming more and more labored as the lungs fought for air.

As this whole vast complex developed, the individual would eventually go into wild panic. How far this panic could go, Gillian knew from looking at the scuffed places on the walls near the floor. Some poor devil had tried to kick his way out of here. Gillian tried to keep his nervous system under better control. He found, however, that no matter what he did, he still had to listen to the hallucinated voices. The fact that he knew they were hallucinations made absolutely no difference. He heard them anyhow.

He listened to the voices for a long time, recognizing them as memories becoming audible. Voices of friends long gone out of his childhood, including those of his parents. Some of the voices seemed to come from his infancy. He wondered if he had any right to be remembering these.

If he grew tired of listening to the voices, he could look up at the glass panel and see the wan face that occasionally appeared there. At first, he knew that the face belonged to Sis Randolph. Then he began to wonder about its identity. Whoever the woman was at the glass panel, she did not look happy to him. When he remembered that she was Sis, he felt very sorry for her, knowing that her ordeal was greater than the one he was undergoing. He was sure she would die before she gave Abrussi the information he wanted. She had something called *principles*. She was willing to die for them.

He also had the impression that she was trying to give him courage. He blessed her for this, and then, as some freak of memory gave him back a recent scene, he recalled that Mary,

55

THE DARKNESS BEFORE TOMORROW

dying, had seemed to find Joe waiting for her. If he died here, would he find Sis waiting for him on the other side? Or would he have to wait for her?

This thinking gave him no comfort. To get it out of his mind, he concentrated on the voices again. It was much better to hear the voices than to look at Sis. Looking at her hurt too much.

Time passed. Gillian did not know how much time had passed. Perhaps hours had gone by, perhaps a day and a night had passed, perhaps time had stopped altogether. He tried to sleep. His ears, hunting for sound with greater and greater hunger, stepped up the volume of the hallucinated voices. The harder he tried to go to sleep, the wider awake he was. He was in a condition that was neither sleep nor waking. He wondered vaguely how much he could endure before he leaped to his feet and began kicking at the wall.

The hours passed.

Occasionally he turned his eyes to the glass panel. Did he know the woman whose face he saw there? Trying to wave at her, he found he hardly had the strength to lift his arm. His breathing was labored. Had they shut off the air into the cell? Were they mixing some subtle gas with the air? Alarmed, he got to his feet. His heart began to pound as if it were about to burst from the rib cage. Panic came up in him. He screamed. The sound of the scream was lost in the silence of the room. He screamed again. He had to get out of here! *Had to!* Where was the door? Not finding a door, he began to kick at the material on the walls. At the exertion, his heart beat became alarmingly fast. Sweat covered his body.

The woman at the glass panel was motioning to him to lie down. What foolishness was this? *He had to get out of here!* Again he kicked at the wall.

This effort exhausted him. He fell. Again the half-state that was neither sleeping nor waking came over him. The voices started up once more. He listened to them.

The language the voices were speaking intrigued him. He did not know what tongue was being spoken but it was not English. Perhaps it was Spanish. Perhaps it was Italian. Perhaps it was French. It was not German. The harsh gutturals

THE DARKNESS BEFORE TOMORROW

of the German tongue were absent. Instead the language had many sibilances. He tried to remember if he had ever heard this tongue spoken in his life before, decided that he had not.

Some segment of rational thinking returned. He wondered why he should be hallucinating in an unknown tongue. This problem puzzled him but he was too weak to think about it. If the voices wanted to talk some foreign language, there was nothing he could do to stop them. If his ears wanted to invent sounds and his nervous system wanted to distort them into some tongue he had never heard, there was nothing he could do about it. Both his ears and his nervous system seemed to have minds of their own. He let these minds work as they wished. So subtly he did not realize when it began, he became aware that he was beginning to see.

This was strange. His eyes were closed. He knew they were closed. But closed or not, he was seeing something. Then he recognized what it was.

It was a cable that seemed to be miles in length. At the far end of it was a huge ball. This was moving so slowly that he was not certain it was moving at all. As he watched, he realized that the cable and the ball were parts of a gigantic pendulum.

This pendulum seemed to be in motion in some void. He did not know where it was. It was not on Earth. It was out in the sky somewhere beyond the Earth but it was not as far away as the Moon. As this thought came into his mind, he realized he could see both the Earth and the Moon.

The Earth was a gigantic dark mass that obscured most of the sky. The Sun was not visible. He assumed it was behind the planet.

Like a vast grandfather's clock, the pendulum seemed to be keeping time in the void. Old time or new time? Past time or future time?

Very vaguely and dimly, he was aware of a feeling of horror. This seemed to be coming from the dark mass of Earth so far below him. It seemed to be a definite radiation leaping upward through the sky. Even at this distance, he could feel it. It seemed to him that Earth was groaning as it turned. The whole planet seemed to be suffering.

THE DARKNESS BEFORE TOMORROW

Fantastic ideas came into his mind. He thought that the whole planet was a gigantic boil. Excruciatingly painful to the touch, the boil that was the planet was being lanced. The Earth writhed and twisted at the pain coming from this celestial surgery. In his nightmare world, Gillian decided that the pendulum was a knife cutting into the boil that was a planet.

He could not see the fulcrum of the pendulum. He seemed to be at the fulcrum, looking down. Hissed voices were around him, talking their unknown tongue. He was not listening to what they were saying. He was adjusting the pendulum, making minor changes in its sweep, so it would cut into the boil of the planet quicker and cleaner.

Or was the pendulum creating the boil?

This thought startled George Gillian. It almost make him wake up. Then the horror of real sounds broke into his nightmare. To his overstrained, hungry ears, real sound had the impact of a sudden, painful blow.

A voice was shouting to him. "Wake up! Wake up!"

To shut out the horror of the sound, he tried to cover his ears with his hands.

A woman's voice frantically told the first voice to be quiet. It went into grumbled silence. Then the woman's voice was also asking him to wake up but was doing this much more gently. He tried to cover his ears tighter. Even a gentle voice sent painful shocks through a nervous system too long without sound. He did not want to wake up. He wanted to stay where he was and watch the pendulum keeping universal time in the night sky. Gentle hands pulled at his hands, trying to get them away from his ears. He would not permit it.

Other sounds came, so violent they blasted through his hands. Oddly, they sounded like the fire of an automatic weapon, perhaps a submachine gun. Then came a blast like the explosion of a hand grenade, hurting his ears and his nervous system so badly that he flinched. It shocked him into opening his eyes.

Sis' face was directly above him. It was Sis who had spoken to him, it was Sis who was still trying to get his hands away from his ears.

THE DARKNESS BEFORE TOMORROW

Above her, bending over her, was a man in a dappled green garment. His head was covered by a helmet and he had a rifle in his hands. The helmet had three bars on it. Gillian thought vaguely that this made the man a sergeant. The sergeant was looking bewildered.

"What's wrong with him, Miss? There's not a mark on his body. I checked."

"He's completely exhausted and in a state of shock," Sis tried to explain.

The door of the cell was open. Two men, also wearing helmets and uniforms, were coming through it. Between them, they were supporting a third man. Sis got to her feet and ran to the arms of this third man. He tried to hug her. When he got his arms around her, she seemed to collapse. Vaguely, Gillian recognized this man as Eck. The tall man had a thick crop of whiskers on his face. He was trying to grin but the effort was not very successful.

From the distance came more sounds of automatic weapon fire. Gillian clapped his hands over his ears again. He tried to sit up. The effort was not much more successful than Eck's effort to grin. Sis slid out of the tall man's arms and abruptly sat down on the floor beside him. She was laughing and crying at the same time. She waved her hand at the three men in uniform.

"They're Marines, George. Marines!"

"Marines?" Gillian's own voice hurt his ears. "How—how did they get here?"

"I don't know and I don't care," Sis answered.

Another man in battle dress, with an eagle on his helmet, came into the cell. He glanced at the sergeant, who stiffened to attention, then his eyes went on to Sis, Eck, and Gillian. "There should be two men and a woman, sergeant. Are these the ones?"

"I think so, colonel. At least we found them here in these cells."

"Are they all right?"

"I wouldn't say so, sir."

"Then get the first-aid and the stretcher detail in here on the double. As soon as first-aid okays moving them, get them out of here and into a ship and on their way to a hospital."

59

THE DARKNESS BEFORE TOMORROW

"Yes, sir," the sergeant said. He went out the door. Outside, his voice could be heard shouting for a stretcher detail.

The colonel bent over Sis. "Are you all right?" he asked.

"No, sir," she answered.

He asked the same question of Gillian and Eck. From each, he got stout answers that they were all right. The expression on his face said he did not believe them. He went around the cell, kicked at the walls, shouted and listened to the way his own voice vanished even with the door open. "Who made this? Who put you in here? How long have you been here?" He shook his head as Gillian tried to talk. "No, don't bother to answer. When we catch the man who did this, I'll personally make him wish he had never been born!" The colonel's face looked very grim as he spoke.

A man with a red cross on his helmet came through the door. He bent over Sis first. Men carrying stretchers were following him.

"This place is full of dangerous men, colonel," Gillian said.

"It's full of dangerous rats, you mean," the colonel answered, as more automatic rifle fire sounded outside. "They're on the run with my boys right after them. We're after papa rat."

"You must mean Abrussi," Eck said. "I want to warn you—"

"We already know the kind of gun he has." The colonel's voice grew very grim. "We want that gun. I have orders to take this place apart clear down to the foundation, if I need to, in order to get that gun."

"Be damned sure you get it," Gillian said.

"They're okay to move, sir," the man with the cross on his helmet said.

"Then get them on those stretchers and get them out of here," the colonel answered.

Sis did not protest at being carried. However, both Gillian and Eck, sure they were all right, waved the stretchers away. They could walk. Each took one step and collapsed.

"That's enough," the man with the cross on his helmet said. "Just hold still."

Gillian hardly felt the needle slip into his arm. He saw Sis and Eck get the same treatment. All three of them were moved out on stretchers. Just outside the door of the corridor

THE DARKNESS BEFORE TOMORROW

a man in a dirty apron was lying on his back. Dr. Muzzy was looking up. He wasn't seeing anything. There was a hole in the middle of his head.

"He resisted," the sergeant said.

The expression on Dr. Muzzy's face said that this was the best thing that had happened to him in a long time.

As they reached the open air, the colonel suddenly began to swear. Gillian saw a helicopter lifting into the air. A Marine shouted something at the colonel, who grabbed the sergeant's weapon. The helicopter was already in the air. The colonel emptied the weapon at it. The ship kept going. The colonel grabbed an automatic rifle from another man in battle dress, ran to the edge of the mountain, knelt there, and began to fire. The helicopter dipped once as if struck, it lurched downward, but it was beyond the top of the mountain, and it righted itself before it crashed. The ship kept going. Looking as if he wanted to throw the rifle at it, the colonel got to his feet.

"Abrussi is in that ship. He's got away," the colonel said. His voice had the explosive violence of rifle fire in it.

On the way to the landing area, dead men in battle uniforms revealed the way Abrussi had gone. Gillian knew that an examination of their bodies would reveal no wounds.

"These are paratroopers, George," Gillian dimly heard Eck say.

"But who sent them here?" Gillian answered, drowsily. The needle that had gone into his arm was taking effect. He saw that Sis, on her stretcher, was already asleep. Then, without knowing it, Gillian was asleep too. If it was not a natural sleep, it at least had no nightmares of mile-long pendulums in it.

When he awakened, he was in a hospital. He knew it from the smell.

An intern with an expression of studied calm on his face was bending over him. At the foot of the bed a husky young man with a crew haircut was standing in such a way that the shoulder holster under his coat was revealed. Gillian coughed, then choked, then the bed seemed to try to turn over. He tried to tell the intern to catch the bed. Gillian coughed again. The bed righted itself. "Where's Sis?"

THE DARKNESS BEFORE TOMORROW

Bare feet scuttled on a plastic floor and Sis found her way between the white screens. The young man with the crew haircut looked startled. The sight of her even shook the intern out of some of his calm. Sis was wearing nothing but an abbreviated hospital nightgown. She leaned on the side of the bed and looked down at Gillian.

"George, are you all right? You and Eck were simply wonderful to stand up under all that torture." She glowed at Gillian as she spoke.

He was starting to glow back at her when the face of an angry nurse came between the screens. She took a firm grip on the abbreviated nightgown and Sis went away with her.

The intern cleared his throat and tried to resume his shaken expression of calm. "I'm Dr. Adams. You seem to be in pretty good shape."

"Thanks," Gillian said. "Who is he?" He nodded toward the foot of the bed.

The crew cut reached into his pocket and pulled out a small embossed card, with the letters GRI on it. "Mr. Strong is waiting to see you, sir, just as soon as you are able."

"I'm able," Gillian said. "If I'm not, it makes no difference."

At the nod of agreement from the intern, the young man with the crew cut found his way between the screens. He returned in a few minutes with a small, baldheaded man who looked like a gnome. But he was a benevolent gnome, and a real power in the world, not only financially but politically.

"I suppose we have you to thank for the Marines," Gillian said.

Hugo Strong showed signs of embarrassment. He had very real power but he was always embarrassed when anybody mentioned it. "Well—I—ah—suggested—"

"I know," Gillian nodded. "You just made a suggestion. How high did you have to go to get the Marines into action."

"Too high," Hugo Strong promptly answered. "The man I talked to issued specific orders that I was not to make the jump with them, darn him. He wouldn't even reactivate my commission temporarily." For an instant, Strong glowered at the memory of some strong injustice done him. The glower

62

THE DARKNESS BEFORE TOMORROW

came to focus on Gillian. "You are such a blunt young man. Such things as these are best handled with the utmost of tact and finesse. However, I would not have you any other way," Strong finished hastily.

"How did you know where we were?" Gillian asked, bluntly.

Hugo Strong looked at the crew cut. This young man promptly went away. Strong looked at the intern, who likewise took the hint. "We have had a man there for some time."

"Who was he? Did he escape? Everyone there wore those damned bracelets—"

"Yes, he escaped." The gnome smiled. "In fact, he is here now."

"Bring him in, so I can thank him," Gillian said.

It was Washington Moses who came between the screens. His dark face had a smile on it. "Those silent cells are no good. Are you all right?"

"Yes," Gillian said. "And thanks."

Moses smiled. "We all have to do everything we can to make the future a little better. No need to thank me. I'm glad to do my part."

"Including risking your life?" Gillian asked.

"Did you do any less?" Washington Moses answered.

As Gillian was suddenly silent in growing embarrassment, Hugo Strong nodded approval. "That's the way to talk to this brash young man, Washington. That kind of talk will make him shut up, fast."

"Yes, sir." Washington Moses turned and found his way between the screens. They heard Sis call him and knew from this that she had been listening. The murmur of her voice as she thanked Washington Moses was indistinct. Then Eck called to him. They could hear Eck thanking him too.

"Abrussi is now at the top of the list of wanted men. However, he did not escape with the drawings the young lady made. We have them," said Strong.

"Good!" Gillian said.

"Just as soon as you feel able, I would suggest that you take these drawings to your laboratory. We will provide adequate guards. We must know about this weapon, we

THE DARKNESS BEFORE TOMORROW

must know its source, and we must know the principles on which it operates," Strong said, in a whisper.

"At Mad Mountain—" Gillian began.

"Your report on this place was received. It is being investigated."

"Very cautiously, I hope. Samuel Ronson is there. Whether or not he is a captive, I do not know."

"We are being very careful not to disturb the situation. Now if the young lady and her brother are willing to go with you to your lab, and help you—" He looked up and blinked as Sis came between the screens again.

"The young lady is willing to do everything she can," she said. "I think I can also speak for Eck."

Eck himself came creeping between the screens. "I'll speak for myself," Eck said. "I'll be there, even if all I can do is run errands."

"Good," Hugo Strong said.

"And if you will consider a volunteer—" Eck continued.

Strong appeared alarmed at this idea. "We can't accept volunteers. Their backgrounds must be most carefully checked."

A dark face came between the screens. Strong blinked. "Do you mean that Washington Moses is this volunteer?"

"Naturally," Eck answered.

"Then everything is settled," Strong said beaming. For the first time, he seemed to become aware of the brevity of the hospital nightgowns that both Sis and Eck were wearing. He blinked at both of them.

"It's all right," Sis said hastily. "Eck is my brother and we're used to each other. Anyhow I have to go right back to bed before that nurse—" The nurse had discovered that her patient was missing again and was beginning to search for her. "I'm coming," Sis said, departing.

"A most remarkable young lady," Hugo Strong said, blushing.

"You can say that again," Gillian said, firmly. "Shall we say that we will start tomorrow morning at my lab?"

"That's fine," Strong said. "You will have available to aid you the best men I can find on such short notice. Are you sure, however, that you will be able to start so soon? You have been through a most harrowing experience."

"I'm able," Gillian said.

"And so am I," Eck said.

"Me, too," Sis added, from somewhere beyond the screens.

Hugo Strong smiled like the benevolent gnome that he was, and took his departure. The young man with the crew cut returned, to take up his position at the foot of the bed. The expression on his face said he had orders to stay there as long as was necessary.

"Good night, Sis," Gillian called out.

"Good night, George. Good night, Eck," she answered. Her voice already sounded sleepy.

Chapter Seven

LOOKING AT THE metal monster sitting on the floor of his laboratory, Gillian tried to pretend he was not in the least dismayed by his creation. They called it a Z generator. Eight feet tall, its circumference at the base was almost twenty-four feet. No one had checked its weight, which must have been almost two tons.

This monster represented the first attempt to translate Sis Randolph's drawings into constricting metal and expanding force. The best available brains had worked like slaves for over a month constructing it. They were grouped around it now in the late afternoon, looking at their handiwork, a little awed by the potential it represented, a little worried about what the result would be when they turned it on for its first test—and irked to the man because of the size of it.

It was Sis, giggling just a little behind Gillian, who put their thoughts into words. "After all, George, it *is* a little large to fit snugly into the palm of one's hand."

"Damn it, we all know that," Gillian said exasperated. "It's

THE DARKNESS BEFORE TOMORROW

the best we can do on our first attempt to translate the ideas of super-science into a model that the technology of Earth can produce. Also, it was *your* drawings we used as a starting point, and while you were willing, you didn't come forward with any new ideas as we worked out the plans."

"I couldn't help it," she said, contritely. "I can't turn higher perception on at will. I have to take what comes. In this instance, nothing came."

She and Eck were living upstairs over the lab in the quarters that had once been occupied exclusively by Gillian. On the roof was a private solarium, open to the sky, which made a fine place for sun bathing. Sis had used it for this purpose but neither Eck nor Gillian had had time for such activities.

Outside were guards, in plain clothes. Washington Moses was in charge. As circumstances permitted, Hugo Strong came and went. If Strong had had a free choice, he would have spent all of his time here, but he had other duties, one of which was to prod all available law enforcement agencies to find Ape Abrussi.

Abrussi had vanished. Perhaps one of the colonel's bullets had found its mark and the Ape was dead, but Hugo Strong was not willing to believe this until Abrussi's body had been found and positively identified. As head of a hidden, worldwide narcotics ring, Abrussi had many places to hide.

Mad Mountain was under cautious 24-hour a day surveillance. It was obvious that this mountain and the creatures with the goat eyes were giving Hugo Strong much cause for deep concern. They were giving high military and political circles even greater concern. No publicity had been given to the goat-eyed creatures. None was likely to be given.

In a world as touchy as that of 1980, the authorities were admitting nothing that might give the public additional cause for alarm.

Glaring at the monster in his laboratory, Gillian wondered how the public would react if it knew this thing existed. Now that the first model was finished and ready for testing, he was a little scared of it. In the past, scientists had poked their noses into many strange matters. The results had occasionally

THE DARKNESS BEFORE TOMORROW

been disastrous. In creating this monster, science had poked its nose into another strange matter.

"Gentlemen, are we ready?" Gillian asked.

Around the monster, particularly at the instrument panels designed to meter both input and output, men suddenly looked alive.

Gillian pressed the switch that fed current into the monster. Heavy relays thudded. Every light burning in the laboratory dimmed. At least a hundred kilowatts were going in.

The output meter said that less than one watt was coming out.

As burning insulation assailed Gillian's nose, he hastily cut off the current.

He looked at the men in the laboratory. He did not need to see their shaking heads to know what the result had been.

The Z generator had burned up enough electric current to light a small town. It had not produced enough output energy to light a small bulb. The needle of the meter monitoring output had hardly moved.

"Something happened," Sis whispered, behind Gillian. "An energy, of some kind, was generated, but it went so fast it did not have time to stop on the meters.

Gillian felt a touch of wonder at her words. Theoretically, the speed of light was a limiting velocity. Her words hinted at the possibility that there might be some radiations which moved so fast that the speed of light was a slow crawl in comparison to them. Gillian wondered if perhaps something had happened on Mars when the Z generator had gone into operation. Had the Moon been startled, had Venus felt the passing of some energy originating in this laboratory?

"Something came out of this generator that leaped across the whole Solar System in—in—" She groped for a word to express a very small fraction of time. "It was almost there before it left here," she finished.

The men listened to her. They respected her. Her drawings had made possible the building of this generator. They gathered around her, asking questions. She tried to answer but her voice faltered. "There are no words to say what I felt when this generator was turned on. And the instruments

THE DARKNESS BEFORE TOMORROW

which will reveal what I can't say in words have not been invented yet. They will be invented, when—" Her eyes sought Gillian's face. "When some of the minds being born today work long enough and hard enough and in the right direction."

"We'll run a series of test checks in the morning," Gillian said. "In the meantime, you have all worked very hard. I suggest you all take the night off."

The assembled men looked grateful at his words. As they were leaving, Washington Moses came into the laboratory. He looked dubiously at the monster.

"Eck went to the local restaurant for food. I'm sure he brought enough for four," Gillian said. "Come on up to the roof and join us at dinner."

Washington Moses looked grateful at the invitation. Upstairs, in the dining room, Eck was waiting for them. "What happened?" he asked.

"Almost nothing, so far as the meters went," Gillian told him. "However, Sis thinks they may have felt our generator on Mars."

"Then I will expect a Martian to come calling on us," Eck answered.

After they had eaten, they went into the solarium to rest and loaf, but Gillian, mindful of the failure of the work on the Z generator, did more fretting than loafing. The sun had gone. The lights of the vast city twinkled into the far distance. In the sky, helicopters were moving lazily.

"Do you have anything on Abrussi?" Gillian asked Washington Moses.

"There's not even a whisper about him anywhere," the dark man answered.

"You sound as if that worries you."

"It does," Washington Moses answered. "The Ape hasn't quit, he's only in hiding. He will come out again, if for no other reason, because he wants more of those little glass weapons. He wants another one so he can have a spare for his personal use." A wry bitterness sounded in the dark man's voice. "He thinks the one he has was fully loaded when he got it, like an automatic pistol with a full clip. He doesn't know how many shells he has left in it."

THE DARKNESS BEFORE TOMORROW

"Where did he get it?" Eck asked.

"I'm not sure, all I know are the rumors I have heard. The story is that a strange ship crashed in the desert and exploded. Abrussi found this glass weapon on the body of the pilot. He's like a savage who finds a high-powered rifle in the ruins of an airliner that crashed in the jungle. He knows that his new weapon can be used to kill people. This is about all he knows, except that he wants more of them."

"I don't know that we know much more," Gillian said drily. "It is going to take a lot of improvement to get our Z generator down to a size that will fit inside a pistol that can be carried in one hand."

He twisted with impatience and annoyance. Was Earth science so far behind that it could not even grasp the fundamental principles on which the glass weapons operated?

The ship came straight down.

There was no roof on the solarium, so it came straight down inside the enclosure. Except for a slight hiss, like that of a distant airbrake in operation, it was soundless. Identical with the ships they had seen leaping into the sky from the tunnel into Mad Mountain, it came to a sudden stop a foot above the floor.

A pilot with the eyes of a goat looked out at them. He was not wearing the single garment of shining cloth that the pilots of the other ships had worn. Instead, he was dressed in an ordinary business suit. A felt hat was clamped firmly on his head.

As they came to their feet, he opened the door of the ship and stepped out.

In his hand, he had one of the glass weapons.

Gillian recognized the pilot. By the hat. The last time he had seen this pilot, after asking if Gillian had killed a man named Joe, he had gone up an alley where presumably Ape Abrussi was in hiding. This pilot had been the dark shadow in the night when Eck and Sis and Gillian had first met.

The little glass weapon covered Washington Moses.

"Throw ze veapon at my feet," the pilot said.

Reluctantly the dark man took from its holster the weapon he had started to draw. Carefully, his face a mask, he threw it on the floor. The pilot bent over and picked it up. He

69

THE DARKNESS BEFORE TOMORROW

glanced at it, sniffed at its clumsiness, and stuck it into his pocket. With great care, he looked the four humans over. They did not seem to impress him much more favorably than the weapon he had taken from Moses.

"Vere is it?" he asked. His voice had a slight hiss in it, like that of an angry snake about to strike.

"Where is wat?" Gillian asked.

"Ze ozzer one like zis, ze ozzer *jednar.*" A stubby forefinger pointed at the weapon he was holding. "You 'ave it. You just used it. I pick it oop on my—what you call *radar.* I vant it. I vant it right now."

His English was not good but his meaning was clear. Much too clear. He thought they had one of the little glass weapons. "I don't know what you mean. We have no—what you call *jednar.* We—" Gillian caught the words in time to keep from revealing that this was what they were trying to build.

"But you just used it," the pilot said, firmly. "I took what you called a *feex* on it."

"But you couldn't have taken a fix on it when we don't have such a weapon!" Gillian protested.

The glass weapon came very steadily to focus on him. "I vill kill you," the pilot stated. "Ezzar I 'ave ze *jednar,* or I vill kill you all. Then I vill find it myself."

He was very calm in making this threat. His manner indicated that he would think no more of killing four humans than they would of swatting four flies.

"But we don't have a *jednar!*" Sis burst out.

Her words got her the thoughtful attention of the goat eyes beneath the hat brim. "You must be a voman, a female. I have seen zem now and zen, as I vent among you." His tone indicated that he took a very dim view of the females he had seen, considering them to be of less value than mosquitos. "And you do 'ave a *jednar!*"

"We do not," Sis said. "We're trying to build one!"

"Oh!" The grunted sound conveyed comprehension but no approval. "You vant to build one? Before you even know how dangerous such a vepon can be in ze wrong hands, you vant to build zem?"

"That's the problem right now!" Sis answered. "One *is*

THE DARKNESS BEFORE TOMORROW

in the wrong hands. We have to build them, to protect ourselves."

"Oh." Did the goat eyes show a flicker of sympathy? "Someone else has one?"

"Definitely," Gillian spoke. "A man by the name of Abrussi. Were you looking for him the first time I saw you?"

"I vas looking for someone who had just used ze *jednar*," the pilot said. "I did not know his name. Where is zis Abrussi?"

"That's one thing we want to know too," Sis said.

The pilot seemed to consider the situation. He was a little confused, not quite sure what he should do. "That vill come later," he said. "For right now, I know I pick up radiations from *jednar*, from this place."

"They came from the Z generator," Sis said.

"Oh." Comprehension was now very clear in the pilot's voice. "Zen show me ze—what you call Z generator." He made motions with the little glass weapon. "Valk ahead of me and show me ze *jednar*—ze Z generator. Remember, please, I vill kill you if necessary."

Seemingly with no concern for it, the pilot left the ship on the roof. The walls of the solarium kept it from being seen from the street. Probably no one had seen it come down. It had landed too fast for clear observation in the darkness.

In the laboratory, the pilot studied the Z generator with great care. Without ever taking his eyes completely off the four humans, without ever failing to keep them covered with the glass weapon, without ever giving them an opportunity to jump him, he still managed to give the monster an adequate examination. when he had finished, he had one comment— a grunt heavy with contempt.

"This is only the first model," Gillian said, resenting this contempt.

"The youngest child of the *Tejani* would laugh at zis."

"We'll do better on later models!"

"I do not think there vill be any later models," the pilot said. "Stand back, please."

Reaching into one pocket, he took out a small rod that looked a little like a ballpoint pen. After making a careful adjustment on the rod, he laid it on top of the Z generator

THE DARKNESS BEFORE TOMORROW

"Up ze stairs, fast." he ordered them.

On the roof, he ordered them into the ship. With the *jednar* menacing them, they had no choice but to obey.

The little ship took off as it had landed, with a hiss. It went almost straight up. It was Washington Moses, pointing down and back, who called their attention to what was happening in the place they had just left.

The laboratory was already burning.

The little metal rod which the pilot had left on top of the Z generator had done its job thoroughly.

Even this glow of light was quickly lost in the vast carpet of lights of the city, so fast did the little ship move.

If those on the ground heard a sonic boom in the sky, it was so common an event that no one paid any attention to it.

The pilot looked at his four captives. "My name is Umbro," he said. "Your names, please."

He was quite calm, and now, very polite. He did not even keep the *jednar* in his hand now that the ship was in the air. It had gone back into a holster under his coat.

They gave him their names. He made no notes, apparently trusting to memory to retain this information, if it was of sufficient importance to be retained. When Sis mentioned that kidnaping was a serious offense, he shrugged the thought away. Millions of humans swarmed on the planet now far below them. What did four more—or four less—matter?

"Zis Abrussi—" Umbro spoke. "Where can I find him?"

"We don't know," Gillian answered.

"You mean zis man is a criminal and you cannot find him?" This idea seemed to astonish Umbro. "He has a *jednar* and you do not take it away from him?"

"You don't seem to have been able to take it away from him, either," Sis said, daringly. "I gather you have been looking for him."

"That I have," Umbro answered. "But I did not know who I was looking for."

"Is it any help to you now that you know his name?" Sis persisted.

Umbro shrugged this question away. "Sooner or later,

THE DARKNESS BEFORE TOMORROW

he vill use ze *jednar* again. Zen I vill find him." He tapped his finger on an instrument in the little ship. "Zis vill tell me when he uses it."

"Then that instrument told you we were using the Z generator?" Gillian said.

"But, yes," Umbro answered. "How else vould I have known to come see you?"

"I knew a Martian would come calling," Eck said plaintively.

"A Martian?" Umbro asked. He shook his head. "Oh, no. The *Tejani* do not come from Mars."

"Then where do they come from?" Gillian asked. "What are they doing here on Earth? What's the purpose back of—all this?"

Umbro seemed to consider these questions. "I am only what you call a cop, a detective," he answered. "I am given a job to do, I do it. I am not on the Council of the *Tejani*. I do not answer such questions."

"But you have to know," Sis protested.

The yellow eyes looked calmly at her. "Do you know what is on ze mind of your leader—what you call your *president*? Do you know his secrets? Do you know what he does and why?"

"Well, no," she admitted.

"It is ze same with me," Umbro said, shrugging. "All I know is that something very dangerous to all is maybe coming. So the *Tejani* come in close to your planet. My leader tells me go *here*, go *there*, find ze *jednar*. He does not tell me why." Something like a bleak grin appeared on the immobile face. "He tells me if I do not do ze job right, he vill cut off my horns." He pushed the hat back on his head so that the knobs were visible. "Of course, he is making what you call a joke. If I do not find the *jednar* soon, what he vill really cut off vill be my head."

The picture Umbro presented of himself was that of a small cog in a vast machine. It was a picture which his four captives could understand. They were also small cogs in a vast machine, in a vast culture complex. But what was the purpose of the vast *Tejani* machine? Umbro either did not know this purpose fully or would not reveal what he knew.

THE DARKNESS BEFORE TOMORROW

However, he was the pilot of this ship. He must know how it worked. Gillian began to question him about the ship, only to discover that Umbro knew very little about it either, except how to fly it, at which he was an expert.

"Do you know how—what you call your car works?" He looked at Sis as he asked this question. "You know how to start, to steer, and to stop. It is ze same with me. The ship I know how to fly. If it does not fly, I call someone to make it work."

"Where did you learn English?" Eck asked.

"In part, from your radio messages. Our language experts studied zese strange noises and decided they were talk, of some kind. They learned it. They teach it to those *Tejani* who have to go to Earth. I talk many times with humans on your planet. Always, ze think I am a foreigner. I do not let zem see ze knobs on my head. It is that simple." His shrug conveyed the impression that going among humans and being accepted by them as one of them was not difficult. Humans were on the stupid side.

"Zey are too busy making what they call *money* or what they call *love* to notice what is going on around them," Umbro said. He grinned again. "I could steal ze planet. Zey would not know it vas gone!"

As he spoke, he seemed to be swinging the ship in a fast circle in the sky. There was no feeling of acceleration—which meant the *Tejani* had already solved a problem that had baffled the best brains on Earth.

"Where are you taking us?" Eck asked.

"You vait, you find out," Umbro answered.

It was Sis who first realized their destination.

"He's aiming for that hole in Mad Mountain." Her voice was almost a scream. "He's trying to hit it in the dark. If he misses—"

"You shut up." Umbro said firmly. "Vill not miss!"

Although there was no feeling of acceleration, Gillian knew that the ship was picking up tremendous speed on its long slant downward. Washington Moses put his head down into his hands as if he could not bear to look at the great ball of the planet rushing madly upward. Eck tried to brace himself against the impact of a crash landing.

THE DARKNESS BEFORE TOMORROW

There had been at least one crash landing of such ships. Out of that crash, Abrussi had gotten the little glass weapon that his dark mind had seen as a source of infinite power.

Gillian and Sis both held their breath.

Whoosh!

The ship was in the hole that led downward into Mad Mountain. As automatic control devices operated in split seconds, the ship lost its speed and came to a gentle stop on the landing ramp in the cavern.

Umbro pushed his hat back on his head, clearly revealing the two knobs high on his forehead. Wiping away beads of sweat, he grinned. "See! Umbro do it!" As he stepped out of the ship, he was very proud of himself.

The shadow came from behind the next ship.

Crunch!

Darting up behind Umbro, it struck downward at him with a short piece of pipe.

Umbro went down without knowing what had hit him.

The shadow was a man. Bending over Umbro, the man jerked the *jednar* from under the coat of the *Tejani*. Holding it aloft, he shouted in triumph.

"I got me one of them too!"

Other men came running from behind the ship.

On the wrist of the man holding the *jednar* aloft, Gillian saw the glint of a metal bracelet. They had found Ape Abrussi. The men outside the ship were Abrussi's men. They were armed with submachine guns.

They discovered that this ship which had just landed had carried passengers.

"Come out of there, you!"

Covered by the *jednar* in the hand of the man who had slugged Umbro, covered by submachine guns, knowing that the slightest suspicious move would result in instant death, the four filed out of the ship.

They were searched. The empty holster under Moses' coat produced suspicion, which was somewhat relieved when the gun for the holster was found in Umbro's pocket

"Who are you and where did you come from?"

Gillian tried to explain that they were captives and that Umbro was a kind of *Tejani* detective. This produced laugh-

THE DARKNESS BEFORE TOMORROW

ter. "Him a dick?" It also got the unconscious Umbro kicked in the side, to show contempt for all detectives. In turn, Gillian asked who they were.

"We're Ape Abrussi's boys," the answer came. "Ape has been casing this place for a long time. He just took it over."

In one way, this produced relief. Gillian had been afraid that Abrussi and the *Tejani* were cooperating. In another way, it produced even greater concern. Instead of being captives of the *Tejani*, they were again captives of Abrussi. Gillian could not see that they had gained anything in this exchange.

Off in the distance, machine gun fire sounded.

"The boys are still mopping up," they were told.

At close range, a submachine gun was as deadly as the *jednar*.

"Take 'em to the boss," the order was given. "He'll know what he wants done with them."

With submachine guns at their backs, they moved across the cavern. Dead men—and dead *Tejani*—were huddled here and there on the floor. The *Tejani* had fought, but obviously they had been taken by complete surprise. Perhaps they had been a little over-sure of their own competence and had not realized the speed and the viciousness with which the human animals could and would attack them.

In the cavern, the huge pendulum was still in operation. It reminded Gillian of something he had seen in a dream once. Like a grandfather's clock keeping the time of infinity, the great ball at the end of the supporting chain-cable was moving slowly and ponderously in its rhythmic cycle.

Abrussi had already set up headquarters in the huge room that he had taken over. His elite guard of chosen men, each wearing a bracelet, was present. Other men were setting up radio equipment. Although the fight for the cavern was almost over, Abrussi was still directing his men like a field marshal on the scene of a battle that has just decided the fate of nations. For Ape Abrussi this was a moment of great glory.

Adding to his glory was the man with him. This man had the round stomach of Friar Tuck.

Friar Tuck was listening with great deference to everything

THE DARKNESS BEFORE TOMORROW

Abrussi was saying. More important, Friar Tuck was agreeing with him.

At the sight of this Friar Tuck deferring to Ape Abrussi, George Gillian was very sick deep down inside.

Friar Tuck was Samuel Ronson.

When Gillian saw the bracelet glistening on Ronson's left wrist, the sickness grew so deep that it seemed to reach the bottom of his soul.

Chapter Eight

ABRUSSI TURNED away from Ronson and saw the captives his men were bringing to him. Washington Moses was nearest. At the sight of the dark man, Abrussi's face became the face of an ape. As his hand went inside his coat, its movement was ape fast.

The little glass weapon spat at Washington Moses. The dark man crumpled to the floor without a sound, with an expression on his face of mild astonishment at finding death so easy.

"Damned double-crosser!" Abrussi said. His face was the face of an ape but his voice had the snarl of a tiger in it. His eyes went on to Gillian, to Eck, then came to rest on Sis.

"You!" he said, astonished.

"You can still go to hell!" Sis said.

It was Samuel Ronson, moving very fast to get his body between the muzzle of the *jednar* and Sis, who saved her life.

"What the hell, Ronson?" Abrussi said, recoiling. "You heard her insult me!"

"The child is overwrought, Mr. Abrussi." Sweat gleamed on Ronson's face. "She doesn't know what she is saying."

"By God!" The *jednar* covered Ronson now.

"Please forgive her, Mr. Abrussi. She and her brother are my godchildren."

THE DARKNESS BEFORE TOMORROW

"What?"

"Their father and I were very good friends. It is part of my duty to look after them." Ronson seemed to be completely unaware of the *jednar*. "I will guarantee their manners in the future. Besides, after you have enrolled them, there will be nothing to worry about on this score."

The dark suspicions of the cobra were in Abrussi's eyes as he looked at Ronson. Conflict was within him. It was better, it was safer to destroy this scientist, and the other three too. But he needed the scientist, he also needed the others. The greatest of good luck had given them back to him after they had escaped.

"I do need them," Abrussi said.

Ronson started to breathe again.

"Doc, you take them and have them enrolled," Abrussi said to Ronson. His eyes blazed. "And if there is even the whisper of another double-cross, none of you will ever have a chance to explain how it happened—because you'll be dead."

"Yes, sir," Ronson said.

"You go with them," Abrussi said to two of his men. "If they try to escape before they are enrolled, gun them down."

With two men behind them, they stepped around the body of Washington Moses. Ronson offered Sis his arm.

"If you weren't my godfather, I'd tell you to go to hell too," she said.

"Please, my dear," Ronson said, in a whisper. "I am doing my best to save your lives."

Again he offered his arm. This time she took it. "But what are they going to do to us?" she asked. "What does *enroll* mean?"

"Whatever it means, accept it—and stay alive," Ronson whispered.

Equipment of a very specialized kind had already been set up in a large room. Abrussi had come prepared not only for victory but with the means to consolidate it. This equipment was designed to install the bracelets. "Enroll" meant that a bracelet was fitted to the left wrist.

Several of the *Tejani* were already in the room. Their yellow eyes were dazed. A sudden assault which they had

THE DARKNESS BEFORE TOMORROW

not foreseen had overwhelmed them and their superior science. They could not understand how an ape could come out of the jungle and overwhelm them almost before they knew what was happening.

Ronson, with the three humans, moved to the head of the line. His face had sudden lines in it as he talked to Sis, Eck, and Gillian. "Please do not resist," he whispered. "Believe me, they will kill you if you do. If we submit now, we may live to fight another day." He was making a desperate effort to control his emotions. Suddenly he jerked his left arm and winced from pain as his bracelet went into action.

Gillian was fitted first. Slipped around his arm, the bracelet was snapped shut and then sealed. "Don't try to take it off," he was told by the wizened little man who was in charge of the operation. "You won't live long enough to get the job done."

Gillian's wrist was placed under a powerful electronic beam, which seemed to activate instruments built into the bracelet itself. The wizened little man picked up a powerful magnifying glass. "Records," he spoke into a microphone. "Serial number 1719." He turned to Gillian and asked his name, which he repeated into the microphone. "Test one." he called out sharply.

Gillian almost screamed in pain as a jolt of electricity shot from the bracelet up his arm to the elbow. Now he understood why Terry, and others, had winced. They had been getting such jolts of electricity. Before the pain had died away, the wizened little man was calling for the second test. This time the jolt of electricity went from the bracelet up to his shoulder with an intensity that was almost paralyzing. Grabbing his shoulder, he fought the pain.

"I want all three of you to listen to me," the wizened little man said. "I'm only going to tell you once. These bracelets contain radio receivers and transmitters. Anything you say will be transmitted back to our main installation. Monitors on duty there are listening. If they don't like what you are saying, they will give you the test one jolt as a warning. If this doesn't make you mind your manners, they will give you the test two jolt. If this doesn't calm you down, they will report what is happening to Mr. Abrussi. If he doesn't like

79

THE DARKNESS BEFORE TOMORROW

what you're saying, he will give you the test three jolt. You may live through it. You may not. It is certain to knock you out for two or three hours. The test three jolt will hit your heart."

Holding his shoulder, Gillian watched Sis and Eck go through the ordeal of being fitted for bracelets and the jolts of electricity as equipment inside the metal rings was activated. Samuel Ronson stood beside him. Agony was deep on Ronson's face.

"What are the *Tejani* doing on Earth?" Gillian asked quietly.

"There is a great emergency—" Ronson began, then was silent as he realized that monitors might be listening to what he was saying. "Although I felt it best to keep my connection with them secret, I felt it a great honor to cooperate with them."

"You cooperated with them willingly?" Gillian asked.

"Young man, you are asking questions unwisely—"

"So Hugo Strong thought," Gillian said.

"Do you know him? Do you know the Group—" Again Ronson stopped speaking, but his eyes were fixed on Gillian with sudden intensity.

Sis came to them. She was holding her arm but she was acting very brave. She waved aside Ronson's concern for her welfare. "I think I should introduce you two," she said. "Particularly so, since it was your photograph, godfather, that marked the major turning point in the life of George Gillian."

"Ah? And how was that?" Ronson said.

Sis explained to him. As he understood the situation, his eyes grew somber with hidden pain. "Then I am honored to have unknowingly influenced a youth to become the man you obviously are," he said to Gillian. "And in addition to my two godchildren, I bear in part at least the responsibility for your presence here. I will do my best to live up to the faith you put in me when you did not even know me." As if he again recalled the existence of the monitors, he spoke very quickly. "I am sure you will find cooperation with Mr. Abrussi to be as rewarding and as satisfactory as I anticipate finding it."

THE DARKNESS BEFORE TOMORROW

The bracelet on Ronson's arm emitted a sharp note. "Mr. Abrussi wants you," the tiny speaker said. "He also wants 1719, 1720, and 1721."

"1721, that's me," Sis said.

"In just a minute—" Ronson began.

"Get the lead out of your pants," the tiny speaker said. "When Mr. Abrussi wants anybody, he wants them right now!"

Chapter Nine

THEY FOUND Abrussi in the main cavern with four men acting as a bodyguard. He was looking at the gigantic pendulum.

"What's this thing, Doc?" he said to Ronson.

"It is a secondary resonator," the scientist answered.

"A secondary *what?*" Abrussi frowned.

"It moves in rhythm with a primary resonator. In doing this, it spreads certain radiations more intensely over a local area," the scientist explained.

"What does it do?"

Ronson looked a little bewildered at this question. "This is not easy to explain in a few words, Mr. Abrussi. I do not wish to take up your valuable time by going into unnecessary technical details. This resonator performs many operations, one of the most important being to impinge certain high frequency radiations upon human genes—"

"What's genes?" Abrussi asked.

"A gene is the unit of human heredity," Ronson explained. "In their totality, they carry within them certain tendencies which may appear in the next generation. According to the way they are paired, the genes determine what an individual will look like, what color eyes, hair, and skin he will have.

THE DARKNESS BEFORE TOMORROW

In a general way, they also control body height and size, and—it is thought—the formation of brain and neural tissue."

Abrussi shook his head. This talk was completely beyond him but he had no intention of admitting it. "Everybody knows all of that, Doc," he interrupted. "What I want to know is what good is the damned thing?"

Ronson sought for words that would reveal as little as possible but would give the impression of saying much. "So many factors enter into the situation that it is almost impossible to state the value of this pendulum. If the whole project succeeds—and there is no guarantee of success—then this pendulum will have had enormous value. If the project fails, then this pendulum will have had no value. I do not think I stretch my facts too far if I say that the whole future of the human race, perhaps the future of this planet, perhaps the future of the Solar System rests on this and similar pendulums. But to say what that future will be is impossible. It is like gambling, Mr. Abrussi, like playing with dice. No one can foresee what numbers will come up."

"They're shooting craps with us, huh? Is that the idea?"

"Not at all, sir. This is a gamble that must be taken. We have no choice in the matter—and not very good hopes of influencing the outcome. But the whole future of the planet—"

"It's that big, huh?" Abrussi looked at the pendulum with greater respect. He did not understand a tenth of what he had been told but he knew there was a nugget of truth in it somewhere. His jaws began to work as he tried to chew his way through what he had heard, seeking the one aspect of the situation that interested him. "If it's that big, somebody will pay plenty for it!"

"You would try to blackmail a whole planet for the sake of personal gain?" The words popped unintentionally out of the mouth of the astonished scientist.

"Who's talking about blackmail?" Abrussi demanded angrily. "It's not that way at all. If this thing is that big, we can work out a deal on it."

"You have changed the words but not the fact." Ronson was becoming angry. "You would try to make some group or some nation pay you off before you would permit a better future to come into existence! You—"

THE DARKNESS BEFORE TOMORROW

Abrussi lifted the bracelet to his mouth. "Teach Doc some manners," he said into it. "Give him the shoulder jolt!"

Before Ronson could protest the jolt of electricity had shot up his arm from the bracelet. His face turning white, Ronson grabbed his shoulder.

"Now get this straight, Doc!" Abrussi said. "I've got six ships. If more come down the tunnel, my men are ready to grab them. I've got almost a thousand of these little glass guns." He tapped his coat where the *jednar* was holstered. "What I've got is a lot. I can do plenty with six ships and almost a thousand little glass guns. My men are going to learn how to fly the ships. I'm going to learn myself. We can drop down out of the sky any place we please on Earth. We can raid Fort Knox if we want to. There's not anything on Earth that's going to stop me. And I'll tell you one other thing—*there's not any scientific plumber who is going to give me any back talk!* Have you got it, Doc?"

"Yes, sir," Ronson said.

"If I want to sell this thing," he gestured toward the pendulum, "that's my business. If I want any advice from any scientific mechanic on what to do with it, I'll ask for it. Got it, Doc?"

"Yes, sir," Ronson said. Some of the color was returning to his face.

"There's just one reason you're alive right now, Doc. It's not because you've got a big name as a hot-shot scientist. It's because you can find out how these little glass guns work. Got it, Doc?"

"Yes, Mr. Abrussi," Ronson said.

Abrussi jerked his thumb toward Gillian, Eck, and Sis. "There's just one reason they're alive. And that's because you said they could help you. Got it, Doc?"

"Yes, sir," Ronson repeated.

"Then all of you get the hell out of my sight and get busy!" Abrussi ended.

As they walked away, they saw Abrussi standing with his hands on his hips looking upward at the vast pendulum in its slow, majestic sweep across the cavern.

Ronson chose a room to use as a research laboratory, sharing his own living quarters with the three others. Always

THE DARKNESS BEFORE TOMORROW

at least one of Abrussi's men, armed with a submachine gun, guarded them. Apparently Abrussi did not trust his own bracelets or his own monitors too far.

To George Gillian, the days that followed were worse in many ways than the desperate hours he had spent in the cell of silence. His thoughts had been nightmarish there. Here, working to uncover the secret of the *jednar* for a man he despised, his thoughts were torture. Sis was undergoing much the same reaction. She became hollow-eyed and her body lost its curves. Eck seemed to have forgotten how to make jokes. The tall man was losing weight to the point where his body seemed to be little more than a skeleton clumsily draped in clothes. Samuel Ronson tried to keep up a show of hope, but this was so forced as to be painful, and he soon gave up the effort. They dared not express their real feelings. The transmitters in the bracelets promptly carried any treasonous ideas to unseen ears.

A *Tejani* technician by the name of Troon, an expert in the repair of the *jednars*, was discovered and was assigned to help them. Sis found much food for thought in the appearance of Troon.

"He is the—ah—person I saw when I made those drawings," she whispered to Gillian. "I watched him working on a *jednar*, though I didn't know what it was then."

"Your clairvoyance, or foreseeing of the future, whichever it was, was accurate," Gillian whispered in reply. She brightened a little at this. He wondered how much he could say. "Can you foresee a little of the future now, can you find out anything about all of this, how it will come out?"

She closed her eyes and was very quiet, then opened them and shook her head. "It's all confused. I'm not sure there is any future, either for us, or for anybody."

When he was silent, trying to grasp her meaning, she went on. "It feels as if the future hasn't been decided yet, that everything is still in the balance. *George, I'm so scared.*" Her voice was so low a whisper that he could hardly hear it.

In sympathy, Gillian took her in his arms and gently patted her. Her blue eyes had depths of pain in them that he had never glimpsed before.

THE DARKNESS BEFORE TOMORROW

"Take it easy, my dear," he whispered. "This will work out all right."

"You're a swell guy, George. But right now you're an awful liar. Right now you're as scared as I am there isn't going to be any future, for us or for anybody." She buried her nose in his coat, then looked up at him again. "However, thanks for lying. It makes me feel a little more secure."

Troon had been fitted with Abrussi's bracelet too. He seemed to find this exasperating beyond all comprehension. For five days he resolutely refused to cooperate in any way with any human. He understood almost no English and while he knew that Ronson had been present in the cavern when the *Tejani* controlled it, he seemed to feel that the scientist was now untrustworthy too. Troon hated the bracelet, he hated Abrussi. From the way he glared at Ronson, at Sis, at Eck, and at Gillian, he apparently hated all humans.

"From what I understand, he says he will not help us," Ronson said to Gillian. "He says he will die first."

When the jolts of electricity from his bracelet, intended to force cooperation from him, became unbearable, Troon was as good as his word. Dying did not seem difficult for him, nor was it something that he feared. Troon simply fixed his gaze on the nearest bright object—in this case a small piece of glass that reflected light from an overhead *Tejani* glow ball—took a deep breath, and closed his eyes. A few seconds later, his body fell off the stool he had been sitting on.

That was all. Other *Tejani* took the body away.

Ronson, very sorry but having more than one life resting in his hands, hastily advised Abrussi that Troon was dead.

"Catch another one," Abrussi told him. "And in the future, don't bother me when I'm getting ready to take a flying lesson in one of my new ships."

"We can learn something from the *Tejani*," Sis said slowly. "Where do they come from?"

"Mercury," Ronson answered. "Closest to the Sun, Mercury apparently has some of the highest evolved life forms in the Solar System."

"Don't be getting any ideas that you can close your eyes and stop breathing," Gillian said to Sis.

85

THE DARKNESS BEFORE TOMORROW

"I'm not, George," she said quickly. A faraway look came into her eyes. "But I think that I *could* do it. It's just a matter of intense concentration in the right direction."

"The right direction is to stay here and fight!"

"Do you think there will still be fighting?" she whispered.

"The GRI still exists. Hugo Strong still exists. I still exist. There will be something," Gillian whispered, warily watching the bracelet on his wrist.

Abrussi's men found another *Tejani jednar* technician. He gave his name as Telso but he was not willing to give anything else. After a few jolts of electricity from the bracelet on his wrist, Telso began to disassemble a *jednar* that had stopped working. Ronson and Gillian watched the process very carefully. Abrussi added another guard to the one who was constantly with them. The two guards also watched. Telso worked very slowly. Ronson and Gillian regarded him with deep sympathy—and hoped fervidly that he would not decide to die too.

As the weapon was taken apart, Gillian began to plot mathematically the components thus revealed. He soon covered several pages with equations. Ronson followed the development of these equations with the keenest interest. When they were finished, he looked at Gillian with great respect.

"What you have just done is a most remarkable accomplishment," the scientist said. "I would consider it a great honor to have on my lab staff the man who developed these equations—if I had a laboratory."

"Thanks," Gillian said. Coming from Samuel Ronson, this was high praise.

"Under other circumstances—" Ronson glanced from the bracelet on his wrist up to the faces of the two guards. "However, the circumstances are what they are."

"These equations do not describe the energy discharged from the *jednar*," Ronson continued. "They describe the field that contains this energy, that holds it in bounds, that gives it direction. They are like the barrel of a rifle, which holds the violent explosion of the power within bounds and gives it direction. Without the barrel, the powder would explode in every direction. Without the field described by these

THE DARKNESS BEFORE TOMORROW

equations, the energy of the *jednar* would be dissipated in all directions and would kill the user rather than the person he was aiming at."

"I know," Gillian said.

Behind them, a guard cleared his throat. "What's all this double-talk about?" he demanded.

"We are discussing these equations," Gillian said, pointing to the sheets of paper.

"They look like hen tracks to me," the guard said, squinting. "How do I know that's not some kind of secret writing?"

"Mathematics is the language of science," Ronson said. "There is nothing secret about it. Complete courses in mathematics are given in every university."

The guard grunted. Inside, Gillian grinned. He reached for the pen and quickly wrote another series of equations. Ronson studied them carefully, then grunted and reached for the pen himself. "You are wrong here and here," he said. Meanwhile he wrote another series of equations. Although he was careful to keep any expression from his face, inside Gillian grinned even broader. Samuel Ronson had understood his meaning perfectly and had answered in kind. Right under the noses of the guards, they had established a private means of communication, via the symbols of higher mathematics. The guards could see what was being written but they could not understand. The monitors listening through the bracelets could hear nothing except the scrape of the pens on paper.

In this way, Gillian got part of the true story of the *Tejani*. He already knew they came from Mercury but now he learned why they were on Earth. It was a story that awed him. Implicit in it was the knowledge that life was not restricted to one planet, to Earth, but existed all through the planets of the whole System. The Sun was the great central generator that gave life to all within the range of its radiation. In some strange and incredible way, the Sun and the planets were also expressions of the Life Force, though here Ronson's mathematics began to fail.

The *Tejani* had not come as conquerors. They had come as secret saviors of the Earth and of themselves as well. They

THE DARKNESS BEFORE TOMORROW

had stayed hidden and would continue to stay hidden until the inhabitants of Earth were prepared to receive them. To come openly might well set off extremely dangerous political, economic, and religious repercussions, which the *Tejani* wished to avoid at all costs.

As they interpreted the story flowing from the equations Ronson was writing, George Gillian was completely certain that every moment of hero worship he had spent on this scientist as a teen-age youth, was here being repaid, full measure, heaped up, and overflowing.

Then Gillian began to develop his own equations, with results that startled both him and Ronson.

"There is a definite correlation between the confining field of the *jednar* and the force field around the *Tejani* ships. These equations prove it. This means we must examine the drive mechanism of one of the ships," Gillian said.

"They are Mr. Abrussi's pride and joy," Ronson said.

"We can at least ask him," Gillian pointed out.

"Why do you need to do this?" Abrussi demanded, when they went to him.

"Because there is some correlation between the field of the *jednar* and the field generated by the ships in flight." Gillian explained.

"*Field?* What's a field?" Abrussi asked. When this was demonstrated to him by means of iron filings dribbled over a sheet of paper held above a small magnet, he had a ready answer. "What good is that?"

"As part of the electro-mechanics of this universe, it is very important," Ronson interposed. "Science has begun to suspect that the whole universe is made of enormously complex fields of different kinds."

"All right, Doc, if you say so," Abrussi grudgingly yielded to their request. "But you'll have two guards with you all the time you're monkeying with my ships. And if you try to escape—"

Umbro was at the ships. He had a bandage on one side of his head and a bracelet on his left wrist. His yellow goat eyes hardly admitted their existence until he saw that they, too, were wearing bracelets, then his manner softened.

"I have been put in charge of pilot training," he explained.

THE DARKNESS BEFORE TOMORROW

His manner indicated that on one of his flights, preferably while he was teaching Abrussi, there would be a case of pilot error. But he showed them the working mechanism of the ship's drive. Gillian, excited, wrote page after page of equations. Ronson examined these with great care.

"Yes," he replied, in mathematical symbols. "There is no question but that the field of the ship will stop radio transmission from the bracelets. But what does this mean?"

"It means that if we can get into one of the ships, and can get it started, the bracelets won't work," Gillian answered, via written equations.

"Um," Ronson said, aloud.

Throughout the cavern, Abrussi's men were busy. Television cameras had been installed on top of the mountain. These were wired directly to the big roon that Abrussi was using as command headquarters. Other men were being trained in the use of the *jednars*. A military organization was coming into existence, with the men grouped into squads and with a regular chain of command upward from the squad to Abrussi. Always he had a special squad hidden but alert at the end of the landing ramp, in anticipation of the arrival of more ships. His intention was to capture both ship and occupants. But no more ships arrived.

Gillian tried to talk to Umbro, but the *Tejani* was very depressed. "I'm afraid he is going the way of Troon," Gillian reported.

Ronson shook his head in silent sympathy. "Many of us may go the way of Troon before this is over," he whispered.

Breaking the silence of the vast cavern, over the recently installed loudspeaker system, came the sudden blare of a siren.

This gave way to Abrussi's voice yelling commands.

"Attention all units! Attention all units! Put plan A into operation at once. *At once!*"

There was an instant of silence during which the startled cavern seemed to try to catch its breath. Then Abrussi's voice came again.

"Marine paratroopers are landing on top of the mountain!"

THE DARKNESS BEFORE TOMORROW

Chapter Ten

"Doc Ronson, I want you and your whole crew in here right away!" Abrussi's voice came over the loudspeaker. "On the double!" he added.

The siren was blaring again as they hurried to obey this order. In the vast cavern, the military organization that Abrussi had built was coming to life. Files of men armed both with *jednars* and with sub-machine guns were racing toward their battle stations.

As if completely unimpressed by any of this, the vast pendulum was continuing to measure infinite time. It seemed to say that animals who thought themselves to be men might fight their lives away if they wished. It was not going to be disturbed. It measured a greater time than the life of one man.

In the room which he had fitted up as a private command center, Abrussi was busy being a field marshal. Around him was a semi-circle of television screens. In front of him was a microphone. Another circle of loudspeakers gave him reports from his fighting units.

"I want you to watch this, Doc," Abrussi shouted as they entered. "I had a hunch they'd try to use paratroopers again. This time I'm ready for them." The ear-to-ear grin on his face revealed that the real reason he had called them in was to be witnesses to his military genius.

Behind him, his honor guard was drawn up.

The screens revealed large planes dropping low over the mesa top. As each plane came down, it spewed out a flutter of many parachutes, each with a man in battle dress swinging from the end of the lines.

Abrussi's men, armed with *jednars*, had already reached the mesa top.

Before they reached the ground, many of the chutes were carrying dead bodies.

THE DARKNESS BEFORE TOMORROW

"Give 'em hell, boys!" Abrussi screamed encouragement.

The pilot of one of the troop carriers was hit. His ship spun out of control and crashed. A second pilot was also struck. His ship went into a dive that ended among the boulders on top of the mesa.

The attack was a massacre. Perhaps a dozen paratroopers reached the top of the mountain alive. A vicious manhunt immediately began to kill these as they tried to hide among the rocks or to find their way down the sides of the mesa.

Apparently a hasty order to stop the attack went out from some commander in a ship in the sky overhead. The troop carriers stopped coming.

"Did you see me lick 'em, Doc?" Abrussi shouted.

His triumph was short lived. The initial onset of the paratroopers had been planned as a surprise attack. A sudden heavy explosion on top of the mesa indicated the second phase of the attack.

One of the screens revealed smoke and debris flying upward.

"Heavy artillery shells landing!" the speaker said.

Abrussi looked startled. "What have they done—brought up a division?"

As if in answer to his question, TV cameras at the edge of the mesa, covering the rugged approaches, showed foot soldiers moving cautiously forward. Taking advantage of every bit of cover, running forward and dropping to run forward again, men in battle uniforms were moving up the rugged, rocky approaches to the mesa. The cameras did not catch the battery of field artillery that was shelling the top. It was out of sight.

"They can shoot shells at the top or the sides of this mountain from now until doomsday!" Abrussi said. "They won't do any damage. When they lift the barrage to let their men attack, my boys will be waiting for them."

"He's right," Gillian whispered to Ronson. "Coming up the sides of this mesa against *jednar* fire will be suicide. And if the attack should show any signs of succeeding, all he has to do is go up in his ships. Then he can either escape or

THE DARKNESS BEFORE TOMORROW

continue his slaughter from the air. There's not a fighter plane on Earth that can defeat the little *Tejani* ships.

Ronson's eyes had questions in them.

"If we are ever going to escape, now is the time," Gillian continued, in the lowest possible whisper. "I think the battle noise will keep the monitors from understanding us. If we can reach the ships—"

"We don't know how to fly them."

"Umbro is there. If we can go to him and tell him we wish to inspect the drive mechanism on the ship that is on the ramp—We did this once before, remember?" Gillian said.

"But Mr. Abrussi needs an audience—" Ronson seemed to make up his mind in a split second. "I'll try," he said. He moved forward and stood in a respectful manner near Abrussi.

"What the hell do you want, Doc?" The barrage on top of the mesa had stopped. The attacking soldiers were moving forward again. At any second, the *jednars* would begin to reach them. Abrussi was watching the scene unfold.

"Very well planned and executed, Mr. Abrussi," Ronson said.

"I'll say it is! Am I going to jolt the military high brass in this country!" Abrussi said, gloating. "But that wasn't what you came up here to say to me, Doc."

"No, sir," Ronson said. "I merely felt that with your military genius in charge, there is no question of the outcome of the battle. However, in my department a very pressing matter had just come up when you called us. I am quite sure you will not want us to delay the development of the *jednars* unnecessarily. After all, you have bigger plans than this skirmish."

"What do you want, Doc?" Abrussi interrupted.

"It is essential that we have further data on the drive of the ships," Ronson continued. "I would suggest that we go now."

"The ships!" Abrussi was startled. "What do you want to poke around in my ships for? You already did it once."

"But that was merely preliminary, sir." Ronson was nothing if not respectful. "And time is pressing, sir."

"Fire!" Abrussi screamed into the loudspeaker. The screens

THE DARKNESS BEFORE TOMORROW

revealed soldiers beginning to go down on the slopes of the mesa as the *jednars* went into action. The soldiers out there did not know what was hitting them. There was no sound of a bullet, no explosion. All they knew was that their comrades were going down and were not rising.

"With your permission, sir, and with your authorization, I will take my staff to examine the drive of one of the ships immediately."

"Okay," Abrussi said.

Ronson turned away. Watching, Gillian took a deep breath, and suddenly realized he had stopped breathing.

"Hold it, Doc!" Abrussi shouted.

Ronson turned quickly. "But you gave your permission and your authorization—"

"Your staff can go, Doc," Abrussi answered. "You stay here!"

Only a split second did Samuel Ronson hesitate. "Of course, sir, if you wish it," he said to Abrussi.

"Carry on," he said to Gillian.

"But—"

"I said to carry on!" Ronson's voice had a note of command in it that Gillian had never heard before. Gillian obeyed it without questions. As he moved to the exit, he spoke to Sis and Eck.

"Come on with me. And don't look back." His voice had the same tone of command in it that had been in the voice of Samuel Ronson.

They obeyed him. But Eck's face was bleak and Sis' eyes were pools of despair.

As they moved away, the loudspeakers suddenly roared with the sound of heavy explosions. Glancing back, Gillian saw that jets were bombing the top of the mesa.

In the main cavern, they saw that the great pendulum had slowed markedly in its majestic sweep.

"Probably the bombs jarred its operating mechanism," Gillian said.

"I think it's stopping because time is standing still for us—and for the human race," Sis whispered. "I think the battle going on right here may decide the future of all humanity for generations, perhaps for centuries."

THE DARKNESS BEFORE TOMORROW

Her eyes had changed from pools of despair to pools of haunted horror. "I'm seeing things I don't want to see," she continued. "I'm seeing worlds smashed to pieces, whole planets disintegrating. I'm looking into—into a possible future."

She was keeping pace with Gillian and with Eck as they moved toward the ships but she seemed to be walking in a trance. Gillian caught her arm. Her skin was cold.

"My dear—" he whispered.

"I don't know that this future will come into existence. It's possible but it doesn't have to happen." She did not seem to be aware of Gillian's hand on her arm, or even of his presence. Her voice had changed from a whisper to a monotone. "An ape came out of the jungle. He saw men and he thought it would be great to be a man. He built himself the body of a man and he went among men as a man. They thought he was a man. They didn't know that inside he was all ape. He found a powerful weapon. With it, he went forth to conquer."

"Wake up, Sis! Wake up!" Eck whispered, sharply.

She looked at her brother as if she did not recognize him.

Gillian tightened his grip on her arm. Slowly, she recognized him. Slowly, she became aware of where she was. She clutched at Gillian's arm.

At the ships, a guard stopped them.

"We're making another examination of the drive on the ships," Gillian said. "Umbro is to help us."

"Yeah?" the guard said.

"We have Mr. Abrussi's permission," Gillian added.

"All right," the guard said. "Just wait right there."

"But—"

"I'll have to check this with Mr. Abrussi," the guard said. "Those are his orders." He lifted his bracelet to his lips. "With the fight going on outside, it may be some time before I can get through to him." He looked more closely at Sis. "What's the matter with the dame? Is she drunk?"

"She's a little upset by the bombing," Eck answered.

In Abrussi's command headquarters, Samuel Ronson also waited. The screens revealed that the attack by the ground troops had stopped. He sympathized with the confusion of the commanders outside. Their men were being killed. They

THE DARKNESS BEFORE TOMORROW

didn't know how this was being done. The screens revealed that the troops were being pulled back.

Out of the corner of his eyes, Ronson watched the cavern. He saw that the pendulum was slowing, saw also that Gillian, Sis, and Eck had been stopped by a guard at the ships. At this distance, they looked like toy figures.

If he had a warm regard for them in his heart, Ronson kept all sign of this off his face. Sis and Eck were his godchildren, and as for Gillian—if he had ever had a son, he could not have wished for a better one than this.

At this thought, Ronson felt a choked feeling rise inside him. As a boy, Gillian had saved his picture. Ronson had never said how much this simple act had meant to him. All his life, he had been so immersed in science that he had almost forgotten what warm personal relationships were. The three standing talking to the guard had given this knowledge back to him.

"My boys have got 'em licked, Doc!" Abrussi screamed at him. "They've got 'em backed clear away from the mesa!"

"My congratulations, sir," Ronson said. "You have proved your military genius this day."

"They'll have to come to terms with me now," Abrussi continued. "When they learn about my ships, they'll have to make a treaty with me, just like I was a foreign government."

The ape was tasting triumph. He was finding it a heady drink. The command bracelet which he wore on his wrist whistled for his attention. "I'm busy," he shouted back.

"If you will excuse me now—" Ronson said.

"Naw, Doc, stick around," Abrussi answered.

The bracelet whistled again. This time he answered it. "Huh? At my ships?" He appeared startled. "Oh. Yeah, I told them to do it. It's okay. But you go with them and make double-sure."

He looked at Ronson. "It's your gang, Doc. My boys stopped them."

"Your staff is very efficient, sir," Ronson answered. He looked out through the opening that led into the main cavern.

The toy figures were moving again. Going away, going toward the ship on the launching ramp, they seemed to be getting smaller. The guard following them made a fourth.

THE DARKNESS BEFORE TOMORROW

A radio technician entered the command room. "Somebody is trying to reach you on the radio, sir, from outside," he said to Abrussi.

"Huh? Who is it?"

"He refuses to identify himself, sir. Shall I switch him to your unit?"

"All right. I'll talk to him." In Abrussi's mind was the thought that probably the commander of the attacking forces was trying to reach him, to arrange a truce. How he would tell this brass hat what was what!

The technician hurried from the room. One of the speakers suddenly came to life with a new voice.

"Abrussi?" this voice said.

"That's me," Abrussi answered. "Who in the hell are you and what do you want?"

The voice started to answer, then coughed instead, as if somewhere somebody was changing his mind about the words he was going to use. "This is Hugo Strong," the voice came again. "And what I want from you is unconditional surrender!"

At the tone, at the name, and at the demands, Abrussi's eyes almost popped out of his head. He knew who Hugo Strong was. Everybody knew this much. Abrussi needed only a split second to gather his wits. Then he exploded in rage.

"All right, so you're Hugo Strong!" Abrussi shouted into the microphone. "Just exactly who do you think Hugo Strong is to be giving me orders? And by what right are you trying to lay down the terms of surrender?" The more he thought about the words Strong had used, the angrier Abrussi became.

"Personally, Hugo Strong is nothing." The voice coming from the speaker was quite calm, quite sure of itself. "But right at this moment, Hugo Strong holds a commission from the President of the United States as a general in the armed forces."

"So they've given you a commission!" Abrussi screamed. "So they've made you a temporary general. So what?"

"So this!" Hugo Strong answered. "Right at this moment I am sitting in a bomber 30,000 feet above you. We're ready to

THE DARKNESS BEFORE TOMORROW

begin a bombing run at any minute. Mad Mountain is our target!"

"So you've already bombed Mad Mountain!" Abrussi screamed. "So bomb it again and see what good it does you!"

"You don't seem to understand the situation, Mr. Abrussi." The voice was still quite calm. "The preliminary bombing, the paratroopers, the ground attacks, were merely to draw you out. If they succeeded, well and good. If they didn't succeed—"

"They didn't succeed!" Abrussi's voice became even shriller. "My boys have licked all of your toy soldiers! We can lick ten times as many!"

"But can you lick an H bomb, Mr. Abrussi?" Hugo Strong asked. "Because this is what we have, right here in this bomber, and we're ready to drop it unless you agree to unconditional surrender!"

Abrussi, his face suddenly white, snapped off his microphone. Mad Mountain would stand up against any amount of ordinary bombing but an H bomb would turn it into a lake of lava. Or so Abrussi believed.

"Get over here, Doc!" he yelled at Ronson. "And stall Strong until I can get a ship into the air and knock that damned bomber down!"

"Yes, sir," Ronson said.

Out of the corner of his eyes, he looked across the cavern. There he could see four toy figures talking to two more toys at the door of the ship on the launching ramp. At this distance, he could not be sure, but he thought one of the two toys was Umbro. The other was probably a guard at the ship itself.

Two guards now!

Abrussi was out of his chair and was starting toward the ships when Ronson called to him.

"I would suggest most strongly, sir, that you stay here with me," the scientist said.

"Stay here and get bombed?" Abrussi screamed.

"The danger is not immediate," Ronson urged. "They will need several minutes to launch the bomb."

"Doc—"

"I need you here not only to establish my identity so I

THE DARKNESS BEFORE TOMORROW

can stall Mr. Strong, but also to add your voice of authority to the talk," Ronson said. His voice was as calm as that of Strong had been. He closed the switch that opened the microphone.

"Yes, sir, Mr. Strong. This is Samuel Ronson. Yes, Mr. Strong, I know you were talking to Mr. Abrussi. He is right here with me, sir." He cut off the microphone again and turned to face Abrussi. When he spoke a tone of command was in his voice.

"Yes, Mr. Abrussi. As commander-in-chief, your place is right here, directing your fighting forces."

Abrussi hesitated, then came back to his command post. He was shaking, his face was white. No one could predict how long he could be kept here. But at this moment, he was here.

Looking across the cavern, Samuel Ronson saw that the parley of the toy figures was still going on outside the ship. Would they never get into the ship!

Opening the microphone, he prepared himself to talk to Hugo Strong.

Chapter Eleven

"Vaht you want?" Umbro said. While he was still wearing an ordinary business suit, he had stopped wearing his hat. The horns on his forehead were clearly visible. The impression he gave was that he wanted to gore somebody with them— he didn't much care who.

"We want to talk to you," Gillian said, persuasive. Since he had forbidden Sis and Eck to look back toward the command room where Ronson was with Abrussi, he felt he should not look back either.

"Not time to talk," Umbro answered. "Big booms overhead. Too much noise. Can't even think."

THE DARKNESS BEFORE TOMORROW

"There's a little battle going on overhead," Gillian said. "But we can't let this stop us when we have work to do."

"Battle? *Tejani* come?" Hope flared in the yellow eyes, then faded. "No, not *Tejani*. Vhen they come, it is not a battle but already a victory."

"Humans are fighting," Gillian said.

"Heh!" Umbro put disgust in to his grunt. "Let 'em fight. Let 'em kill each other. All they good for!"

"All humans aren't bad, Umbro," Eck tried to say.

"Show me vun good vun." Umbro answered. "Just vun." He turned away. "Get lost!" he said over his shoulder.

Gillian looked at Eck, then at Sis. He resisted the impulse to look over his shoulder toward the command room. Gillian turned to the guard who had accompanied them. "Mr. Abrussi said—"

"I get it," the first guard answered. He conferred with the second guard, who was on duty at the ship on the ramp. They turned to Umbro.

"We don't want any back-talk out of you," the first guard said. "When the boss says to do something, it gets done, see?"

"No talk," Umbro answered.

"We want you to open up the covering over the drive mechanism," Gillian said, pointing to the ship on the ramp. "We need to develop our equations on the correlation between the field of the drive and the restricting field of the *jednars*."

"Get lost," Umbro said. He was in no mood to cooperate with anybody who even looked human.

The first guard lifted his bracelet to his lips. "We've got a contrary monkey here," he said. "Give him a jolt up to his shoulder."

"Glad to," the voice of the unseen monitor answered.

Umbro grabbed his shoulder. His face went from a pale yellow to white. A blue radiance seemed to spring out from the nubs on his forehead.

"Are you going to do what the boss wants?" the guard asked.

"Vill do," Umbro said, with his lips. His yellow eyes said that if he ever had the chance, he would consider it a

THE DARKNESS BEFORE TOMORROW

privilege to have a few private words with this guard. He turned and entered the ship. Gillian, Eck, and Sis followed him.

The two guards followed them. Armed with submachine guns, they stood watching.

"Vhat you vant to talk about?" Umbro demanded.

"Open up the cover over the drive," Gillian said. He took a quick glance back across the cavern. Deep in his heart, he was still hoping that he would see Samuel Ronson coming.

"This is Samuel Ronson, Hugo," the scientist said into the microphone. "Of course, you remember me."

"I—ah—" the loudspeaker stuttered a little. "I remember *a* Samuel Ronson, with the greatest of respect and fondness. But I do not know that you are that person."

"Mr. Abrussi is right here with me," Ronson said. "He will identify me."

"Sure, it's Doc Ronson," Abrussi screamed into the microphone. "He's the greatest scientist alive on Earth today. If you drop that damned H bomb, he won't be alive. I guarantee you that."

At this threat, the speaker went completely silent. Apparently, somewhere in the sky, Hugo Strong had run into a situation that was stopping him cold. Strong would not willingly risk the life of the greatest scientist on the planet.

"Now where's your surrender terms?" Abrussi shouted into the microphone. "Now it's you will do the surrendering." Abrussi had seen his advantage. He was prepared to use it to the fullest possible extent.

Quietly Samuel Ronson turned his head so he could see across the cavern.

The toy figures had entered the ship on the ramp.

But the guards had entered with them.

The door of the ship was still open.

Ronson did not know when the door of the ship would close. But he had complete confidence in George Gillian and Eck Randolph.

The speaker came alive again. "This puts rather a different light on the matter," Hugo Strong's voice came.

"You damned right it does!" Abrussi shouted at him. "Now

THE DARKNESS BEFORE TOMORROW

I'm the one in the driver's seat. If you drop your damned bomb, you'll kill Ronson too. And you're not going to do this, are you, Strong?"

"I must—ah—" Strong's voice faltered. "I must have positive identification that the man in the cavern is actually Samuel Ronson."

"You fix him up with that identification, Doc," Abrussi said.

In the ship, Umbro slowly began to remove the covering of the drive mechanism.

"I hope you will cooperate fully with us," Gillian said to him.

"Huh!" Umbro answered.

"Do you want another jolt?" the first guard asked.

At this question, Umbro began to work faster. But it was obvious that he was still going much slower than was necessary.

Gillian wiped sweat from his face. "It's hot in here," he said.

"Just what I was thinking," Eck answered.

Sis was silent. As if she hardly had the strength to stand, she was supporting herself against the inner wall of the ship. "It's almost too hot," she said, fanning herself and moving a step closer to the door.

"It's not so hot you can't stand it, honey," the first guard said.

"Don't you call me *honey!*" she flared. "Don't either of you do it."

"Hard to get, huh?" the second guard said.

"Hard, but not impossible," she answered.

The first guard grinned at her.

Gillian's fist hit him just where his jaw blended into his neck. It was a smashing blow that had all of Gillian's strength behind it.

The guard did not know what hit him. As he went backward, Gillian caught the submachine gun. He turned to use it on the second guard, then hastily lifted the muzzle.

Eck had struck with flashing speed at the solar plexus of the second guard. This man doubled forward. Eck hit him

101

THE DARKNESS BEFORE TOMORROW

on the chin. He went backward. Eck snatched the submachine gun from his hands.

Sis calmly closed the door and locked it.

Gillian turned to Umbro.

"Kindly cooperate with us fully now," he said to the startled *Tejani*.

"Huh?"

"By turning full power into this job and heading it up the ramp, fast!" Gillian said.

For an instant, Umbro hesitated. Hope leaped into his yellow eyes. He glanced at the guards, then at Gillian and at Eck. Perhaps some humans were good for something after all.

Then his eye caught the bracelet on his wrist. Mutely he held it up.

"The field of the ship will cut off completely the radio transmissions through these bracelets," Gillian answered. "So kindly get the ship in operation, *fast!* Otherwise, I'll try to fly it myself!"

Now, as he grasped the situation, Umbro moved with real speed. A growl sounded deep in the ship as he turned the power into it.

When he saw the door of the ship close, a smile lit the face of Samuel Ronson. He had known he could depend on Gillian and Eck. He did not know what had happened to the two guards who had entered the ship with them but he was reasonably certain they were going to take an unexpected ride.

With the ship out of the cavern, three people for whom the scientist had a great fondness would be safe. This was the important thing. Knowing they were safe made life worth living—and worth giving up. They represented the future. They represented the hope of something better coming into existence within the human race. Their safety and their welfare were worth any sacrifice. Although neither of them seemed to know it, he knew that Sis and Gillian were head over heels in love with each other. Their children and their children's children would help lift the darkness that lay between today and tomorrow.

"Fix him up with identification, Doc," Abrussi repeated.

THE DARKNESS BEFORE TOMORROW

"Oh. Ah. Yes, sir." Samuel Ronson had to withdraw his mind from the future he was seeing before his mind's eye. He picked up the microphone but as he prepared himself to talk into it, he turned his body so he could watch the ship. The door was closed but the ship was still at rest.

He wanted this ship in motion.

"Hugo?" he spoke into the microphone.

"Yes, Samuel—if you are Samuel Ronson, that is," Strong's voice came over the loudspeaker.

"I'm Samuel Ronson, all right. I'm going to prove this to you."

"All right. I'm listening," Strong said. Coming over his microphone, subdued and in the background, was the hum of a great bomber in flight.

"I'm going to prove it," Ronson said. His eyes were still on the ship. Had it begun to move? If it had even started to move, those inside it would be safe from the killing energy transmitted by radio through the bracelets.

He saw the ship move.

"I'm going to prove I am Samuel Ronson by asking you to do me a favor," the scientist said. His voice was very calm. There was a smile on his face.

"A favor?" Strong sounded doubtful. "What kind of a favor?"

"Do me the favor of dropping that bomb, Hugo," Samuel Ronson said. "By dropping the bomb—"

"Dropping the bomb?" the startled speaker yelled. "We'll lose you. You're the greatest scientist on Earth. We need you."

Ronson's eyes were on the ship. It was certainly moving. "Better ones by far than I will be born," he said. *"Drop the bomb, Hugo! And wipe this nest of apes out of existence."*

Ronson knew that Abrussi, screeching like an outraged ape, was drawing his *jednar*. The scientist did not mind this. He had expected it.

But something happened that he had not expected. He saw an explosion take place between the nose of the ship and the entrance to the tunnel that led upward to freedom. Staring in consternation at this, he saw the ship stop.

"Drop the bomb, Hugo—" Samuel Ronson was repeating

103

THE DARKNESS BEFORE TOMORROW

mechanically as Abrussi shoved the little glass weapon that left no wound against his body and pulled the trigger. He did not feel the life go out of his body the way it had gone out of the body of Washington Moses, out of the body of a Great Dane named Brutus, out of the bodies of many others. If he had felt his life go, Ronson would not have cared. He had proved his identity. He had proved part of the meaning of the word *man*. And he had tried his best to save the lives of three whom he loved.

If his own life had been given, it had gone in a great cause. And it had been given willingly for things greater than he was.

In the great bomber in the sky, there was consternation. Then Hugo Strong, in a voice as terrible as that of an avenging angel, said. "He proved who he was. *And what he was*. Release the bomb!"

In response to his orders, the great bomber began to move into the approach to its bombing run.

Yelling to his honor guard to follow him, Abrussi left his command headquarters as fast as his legs could take him. He knew a bomb was coming. He wanted to be out of the cavern before it hit.

His destination was his ships.

Chapter Twelve

STARING AT the explosion directly ahead of him, Umbro stopped the ship.

As the drive was cut off, the bracelets went into action. The monitors did not know what was actually happening but they knew that something was wrong. Since they couldn't reach

THE DARKNESS BEFORE TOMORROW

Abrussi at this moment—he did not respond to calls—they acted on their own initiative.

In the pilot's seat, Umbro felt the pain lance up his arm to his elbow. His yellow eyes glittered.

Gillian, Sis and Eck felt it too.

"Keep the ship moving!" Gillian hissed.

Umbro pointed at the smoke from the explosion.

"That was a grenade," Eck said. He was only guessing about the explosion but his hunch was that his guess was right. "A paratrooper on his way down the mesa has found the opening to the tunnel. He's lobbing hand grenades down it."

"What if we start up and meet a grenade coming down?" Umbro asked.

"Serial number 1719," the voice of a monitor squeaked from the bracelet on Gillian's wrist. "Report!"

"Yes, sir," Gillian said. "Right away, sir."

"What's going on there?" the monitor demanded.

"A paratrooper is rolling grenades down the tunnel," Gillian explained. *"Get the ship moving if it's only an inch at a time!"* he hissed at Umbro.

"Oh," the monitor said. For a second, he seemed satisfied. Then another question came. "What are you doing at the tunnel? You've got no business there. Where is—"

A throb came from inside the ship as Umbro turned minimum power into the drive.

"Answer 1719!" the monitor demanded. "I'm going to jolt you up to your shou—"

The voice was fading away and was becoming garbled as the energy of the ship's field began to block radio communication. The jolt of electricity came, but it was only a mild shock.

George Gillian almost sobbed with relief. At least one problem was solved!

Umbro pointed up the launching ramp.

Another grenade had exploded there.

"Keep it moving some way!" Gillian shouted. He dug his fingers under the edge of the bracelet on his wrist. A yank that had all the strength of his arm in it broke the circle of metal. It spat blue flame at him as it broke. He flung it at the wall of the ship. Since Eck and Umbro were already

105

THE DARKNESS BEFORE TOMORROW

tearing frantically at the bracelets on their wrist, Gillian turned to Sis.

She looked at him as if she did not recognize him.

"He's dead," she said. "I felt him die."

Gillian grabbed at her arm. He slipped powerful fingers under the bracelet and yanked at it with all his strength. She winched at the pain and cried out, but the bracelet came free. It, too, spat blue flame at Gillian, like the fangs of a dying snake trying to strike as it died.

"My dear!" He caught her in his arms.

"He's dead," she repeated. "He died to give us a chance to live."

"I knew this was in his mind," Gillian said. "If I had been in his position, I would have done the same."

"Ape Abrussi killed him," she continued. "Like Washington Moses, for doing what Abrussi said was double-crossing him." Her eyes were far away. "Why is it that serving the highest is called *double-crossing* by the lowest?"

"I don't know, I don't know," Gillian whispered. Umbro, free of his bracelet, was still holding the ship in minimum motion. He was watching the smoke clear slowly away.

"If we start up, and meet a grenade coming down—" Umbro whispered.

"Before he died, he told Hugo Strong to drop the bomb," Sis continued. "Mr. Strong is going to do it. Up there somewhere, a bomber is moving into position." She glanced upward toward the far-away sky.

"Ape Abrussi will die," Sis said. "And so will we." Her voice went into silence, then came again as a wan smile lit her face. "I wonder if Brutus is waiting to bark a welcome to us over on the other side?"

In this mad moment, it was hard to know where fantasy left off and fact began.

She pointed across the cavern. "There comes Ape Abrussi now!"

Following the line of her pointing finger, Gillian could see Abrussi and his men running toward the ships. They were moving as fast as apes could run.

The giant pendulum had stopped completely.

"Time stands still for the human race," Sis said.

THE DARKNESS BEFORE TOMORROW

Abrussi pointed toward the ship on the ramp. He must have realized what was happening and shouted an order to his men to fire.

A sound like that of hailstones rattled on the hull of the ship. Guards at the other ships had opened fire with submachine guns.

"Take her up!" Gillian said to Umbro. "Fast!"

The *Tejani* pilot nodded. He was not wearing his hat but he seemed to give a mental tug at it anyhow, to settle it firmly over the knobs on his forehead, so that neither wind nor explosion could blow it off as he went up the tunnel. The symbolical setting of the imaginary hat on his head indicated the speed that Umbro intended to be making as he took the ship out in the face of a possible grenade coming down. He shoved the power control forward to the highest possible setting.

Whoosh!

The little ship did not fly into the launching tunnel, it leaped into it.

It moved so rapidly, it leaped so fast, that the paratrooper outside did not have time to toss the grenade on which he had already pulled the pin down the tunnel. He only had time to fling it backwards and over the edge of the cliff, where it exploded harmlessly.

"We sure stirred up a hornet's nest down below," he shouted to his companion.

Did you see the hornet that came out?" the second paratrooper answered. "We had better get down this mountain fast."

They had missed their recall orders. Going down the talus slope at full speed, they heard the sonic boom come back from the farther sky. This made them move even faster and probably saved their lives.

Umbro did not reduce speed and turn the ship until Mad Mesa was a dot on the Earth far below them. Then he swung the little vessel in a big circle.

From this height, the whole vast panorama that was the industrial and cultural complex of Southern California was spread below them. The land swam in a vast blue haze. Down there in that vast haze youths were in training to

THE DARKNESS BEFORE TOMORROW

break more records in sports. Others were preparing themselves to be better muscians, better painters, better scientists. Still others, not knowing what was happening but knowing only the pressures rising within them, were taking steps that would make them into something less. From this height, the giant tug of war was invisible. But it was real nonetheless.

Umbro pointed into the blue. Floating near them in the vast depths of the sky was a great bomber. Its bomb bays were open. It was coming in on its bombing run.

As they watched, something fell away from the belly of the bomber.

The object fell slowly, slowly, slowly. It was an H bomb going down. Its target was Mad Mesa.

Umbro, *Tejani* profanity on his lips, pointed again, this time toward the mesa. Leaping up from it were what looked like midgets from this height.

"*Tejani* ships!" Umbro said. "Abrussi is getting away!"

In the great bomber, Hugo Strong did not see the *Tejani* ships flashing into the sky, he did not know they were carrying Abrussi and many of his men to safety.

As he watched the bomb fall away and away and away, Strong's eyes were filled with tears.

The bomb struck.

Where Mad Mesa had been was now a mushroom-shaped cloud.

Many of Abrussi's men were killed in this explosion, as were many *Tejani,* including Telso.

From the little ship, Gillian and Umbro, Sis and Eck, watched the cloud form. Sis turned her eyes away from the sight.

Umbro shook his head. "No good," he said. "Fall-out raise hell all over your planet."

"Worst of all, it didn't get Abrussi," Gillian said. "Where will he go now?"

Umbro's yellow eyes glinted. "I not know vhere he go. But this I know—he vill use the *jednar* again. Then I vill know vhere he is. Then I vill find him!"

"Then *we* will find him!" Eck said.

THE DARKNESS BEFORE TOMORROW

Umbro's yellow eyes looked up at the tall man. What he saw there he seemed to approve.

"Ve vill find him!" he said.

"What I want to know is—where are we going now?" Sis asked.

Umbro spread his hands in a gesture that said this was an easy problem to solve. He turned to the controls and the little ship shot away at vast speed toward the infinite depths of sky.

"That way?" Sis said, doubtfully.

"That vay!" Umbro said, firmly.

Chapter Thirteen

THE NEWSPAPERS reported the story in detail and with what they thought was accuracy. The headlines said:

**BOMB DROPPED
DURING WAR GAMES**

—

**H BOMB FALLS
IN DESERT**

—

Sub-headlines added to the story.

Part of Training Program for Military and Civilian Forces, General Says—Test Successful—No Loss of Life

Later editions amended this statement to *small loss of life*. Buried deep in the news stories was additional information

THE DARKNESS BEFORE TOMORROW

which indicated that the fall-out was heavy in Arizona, that earth tremors had been felt on the east coast, and that the Earth's magnetic field had twanged like the string of a giant bow.

Helicopters carrying television cameras were buzzard-thick over the scene of the explosion. Mad Mountain had been a mesa. Now it was a mass of broken rock spewing across the desert. Curiosity seekers would have carried most of this rock away if the shaken division of paratroops had not been used to seal off the whole area, which was much too hot with radioactivity to be safe for humans. Mad Mountain itself, the scene of the explosion, would be too hot for safe examination for some time.

There were men who wanted to examine what was left of Mad Mountain. Hugo Strong was one of them. Hugo Strong did not know whether or not his bomb had destroyed Abrussi. He thought it had, but he wasn't sure. There was much else buried in the tumbled, broken rock of what had been Mad Mountain that Strong wanted to know about. High political and military circles also wanted to know what was there. If the biggest conference in all history was on in these high circles—and it was—this was a secret well kept from the public. No one in authority was willing to voice the suspicion mounting almost to a certainty that Earth was being visited regularly by creatures from some other planet. This was a great secret, to be kept from the public at all costs—though most of the informed public already knew or suspected the truth.

In the United States, in the whole world, was vast unrest. A vast new educational program was announced. A new crime wave broke out. What was happening on the planet? which way was the world going? No one seemed to be able to answer these questions.

Ape Abrussi read in newspapers flown to him the story of the bombing of Mad Mountain. This enraged him. He knew the bomb had been intended to destroy him but he was in no position to come forward with the truth of the matter. He was embittered at the loss of the great pendulum. He would have been able to sell this to somebody, he was sure. But he still had five ships, he had numerous *jednars*, and he

THE DARKNESS BEFORE TOMORROW

had the hard core of his own men. With these much could be done.

Abrussi was holed up on top of another mountain, this one located in the middle of Mexico, in a palace that a Spanish grandee had built centuries before. Although another man's name appeared on the deed—this to meet the requirements of Mexican law—Abrussi's money had bought the place. His men, both Americans and Mexicans, staffed it. The Mexicans Abrussi regarded with deep contempt, a feeling which they fully understood and reciprocated.

Abrussi hid his five ships in big sheds just below the level of the castle. The grandee who had built the place had used the sheds for curing tobacco. Abrussi had used them for treating poppies from which opium was to be extracted. Big and roomy, they made excellent hiding places for the *Tejani* ships.

This castle was remote, it was isolated, and most important of all, it was in Mexico. No paratroopers were likely to land on top of this place. If Hugo Strong ever learned he was alive and attempted action against him, such action would have to proceed first of all through diplomatic channels. Abrussi had good reasons to believe he could stall any such action for years.

Abrussi did not know where Gillian, Sis, and Eck had gone. He assumed they had flown the ship in which they had escaped to landing field in the United States and there had turned it over to the Air Force. Probably it was hidden in a hangar in some well-guarded experimental base, while amazed scientists tried to discover how it worked. Probably Gillian, Sis, and Eck were with Hugo Strong. Abrussi hoped they were in hell. He had had nothing but bad luck from them.

For three days after he arrived in Mexico, Abrussi cowered in bed. He was so badly shaken by his close brush with death from an H bomb that neither liquor nor his own opium could restore even a semblance of calm to his shaken nerves.

After three days, the fear worked itself out.

Then came anger.

As soon as he fully realized that the bomb had actually

THE DARKNESS BEFORE TOMORROW

missed, the anger turned to towering, murdering rage. He had almost been a king! If Ronson had not double-crossed him, if Gillian and the others had not run, if Hugo Strong hadn't dropped that bomb . . .

As he saw how close he had been to victory, and realized he had missed, Abrussi became a raging, mad animal. His eyes became so bloodshot and his whole appearance so menacing that a Mexican servant, bringing a fresh bottle of brandy, became frightened, clumsily dropped the bottle, and turned to run.

Abrussi pulled the *jednar*. The little glass weapon snapped its sound of death. If it did nothing else, this action proved to Abrussi how important he was. Summoning other servants to remove the body, he screamed at them that he had killed this peon and that he would kill them too if they didn't look alive. He defied them, or the government of Mexico, to do anything about his act. If he was mad with anger, it was the kind of madness that gave him back his lost courage. In this humor, he ordered his guard assembled, for review, in the inner courtyard.

Like most homes in Latin America, this structure had an inner patio. Since this was a castle, the courtyard was on a grand scale. It included a plot of grass big enough for a tennis court, flowering trees, several fountains, and flowers of every color.

After his honor guard had been assembled, Abrussi went forth to inspect them. He also intended to tell then his plans for the future now that his courage had returned. Each wore a bracelet, each was armed with a *jednar*. While they were few in number, the *jednars*, plus the little ships, would give them great striking force. They could hit any spot on Earth they chose and be gone in a few minutes. They could destroy the nerve center of a nation and escape before resistance could be organized.

Such a force as this, as small as it was, could become a pack of wolves preying at will upon the governments of the planet. As he looked at his men and realized again the potential in the ships, Abrussi knew again that he was a power on the Earth.

"We took a little setback," Abrussi told his men. "But we've

THE DARKNESS BEFORE TOMORROW

still got enough left to be top dog in any fight that comes along. They may think they're smart, dropping a bomb on us and making us run, but the day will come when we will drop something on them. Then we'll get to watch them run."

Like Hitler of an older day, he harangued his men, giving courage to them and to himself, giving them the will to be wolves. Abrussi did not need this will himself. He already had it.

"There are three people I want. George Gillian, Eck Randolph, and his sister," Abrussi said, in another vein. "They're hiding somewhere. I want them found and I want them brought to me here, one way or another!"

Out of the corner of his eyes, Abrussi saw the little ship flash down from the sky. His first thought was that it was one of his ships. "Who took out one of my ships without my—"

Coming from flashing speed to an instant halt in split seconds, the ship landed. Out of it leaped armed *Tejani* led by Umbro.

Abrussi started to draw his own *jednar*, started to shout to his men to do the same, then, as he saw the *jednars* covering him, he hastily changed his mind. A glance at Umbro's face told him that this particular *Tejani* would kill him without mercy.

Dressed in shining garments, two other *Tejani* moved ahead of Umbro. A second look told Abrussi that these were not *Tejani*. They were George Gillian and Eck Randolph. A third look told him that they were no longer wearing his bracelets.

At the sight of them, one thought entered Abrussi's mind. "Damned double-crossers!" In his mind, by escaping they had double-crossed him.

In his world, this had only one consequence. Abrussi's reflexes were very fast. He got the *jednar* out of its holster under his coat.

"Better think again," Gillian said.

Seeing Umbro behind them, Abrussi caught the reflex movement while the *jednar* was fully drawn but was not yet aimed. Facing the weapon in the hand of Umbro, he was afraid to complete the movement. He would be dead before

THE DARKNESS BEFORE TOMORROW

he could even point the *jednar*. If he even moved it, Umbro would kill him.

The result was paralysis of movement. Abrussi could not finish the draw and he could not drop the weapon. Like Mahomet's coffin, suspended halfway between Earth and Heaven, the *jednar* hung in the air.

Umbro also held his fire. Either party could deal death but neither could save himself. Gillian and Eck stepped apart so that Umbro's line of fire was clear to Abrussi.

Abrussi's guard had not even attempted to draw their weapons. The ship had landed so quickly that there had not been enough time.

Abrussi knew that the time had come to talk and to talk fast. Perhaps, if he could stall for a few minutes, the fools might relax their guard. "How—how did you find me?" he gasped.

"You made a mistake," Gillian answered. "You used your *jednar* once too often. No doubt you killed somebody. Who was it?"

"That—that's a lie!" Abrussi gasped.

"*Jednar* number 6 A 743 was used recently. Probably it is the one you have in your hand at this moment. If you will give it to me, I will show you the *Tejani* number on it." Gillian held out his hand for the weapon.

"No, you don't!" Abrussi answered. "The only way you can get this gun is to kill me. If you try that, I'll take you with me." The glare in his eyes was that of the trapped tiger.

"You will also die, Mr. Abrussi," Gillian said. His tone of voice was polite. Much too polite, Abrussi thought.

"Hunt finished," Umbro grunted.

"What do you mean—hunt?" Abrussi demanded.

"The *Tejani* have been hunting you for a long time," Gillian explained. "The use of a *jednar* sends out a strong radio impulse. Each *jednar* operates on its own individual frequency. When one is used anywhere, the *Tejani* know exactly which *jednar* was in action. They can pinpoint the spot where it was used with great accuracy. Each time you killed someone with the *jednar*, you left evidence behind you. Umbro has been hunting for you but up until now, you have always managed to slip away."

THE DARKNESS BEFORE TOMORROW

This thought shook Abrussi. Many times he must have been close to death without knowing it. Unless he could talk his way out of this situation, he was so close to it now that he could smell the mould on his graveyard clothes.

"What are you doing with these—*goats?*" he snarled at Gillian. "You're human. In a pinch, you've got to stick with your own kind."

Umbro caught the contempt in the words. "Hunt finished!" he repeated emphatically.

At the wave of Gillian's hand, Umbro was silent.

"So maybe I did shoot a Mexican," Abrussi said. "It was self-defense. He drew on me first."

"Did Washington Moses draw on you?" Gillian asked.

"He double-crossed me!"

"Did Samuel Ronson draw on you?" Gillian continued.

"He double-crossed me too!" Abrussi screamed. Spittle was beginning to form on his lips. "What are these goats doing here on Earth? This planet belongs to us!"

"These *goats*, as you call them, are the most advanced race in the Solar System," Gillian answered. "They're trying to help us save our planet, for our far-distant grandchildren."

"Grandchildren!" Abrussi answered. "If we aren't taken care of, there won't be any grandchildren!"

"Precisely," Gillian answered. "That's why we are going to take care of you."

Abrussi didn't like the tone of this but he liked even less the expression in Umbro's eyes. He began to edge an inch at a time to get Gillian between him and Umbro.

"In about five hundred years, the whole Solar System will collide with a dark star. To prevent this collision will take better brains in better bodies in greater numbers than exist today, not only on Earth, but all through the System. Here on this planet, the *Tejani* are forcing evolution to produce these better brains in better bodies. Unfortunately, this process is also producing a great many misfits, people who won't or can't adjust to the changing times, people who are actually throw-backs to the animal level of evolution. If the *Tejani*—and in the long run we here on Earth—permit this, these throw-backs can throw the whole vast plan out of gear, perhaps can defeat it altogether."

115

THE DARKNESS BEFORE TOMORROW

"Let the people who live five hundred years from now solve their own problems!" Abrussi answered. He edged another short step toward Gillian.

"Through such relay pendulums as the one you saw in the cavern, which take their energy from a central pendulum, they are bathing this planet in radiations which will produce, eventually, the desired result."

Gillian, fully aware that Abrussi was inching into a position that would place him in front of Umbro, was also aware that to the right, Eck was also moving inches at a time. He hadn't told Eck to do this, nor were such instructions necessary. Eck intuitively knew what to do. Gillian thought, with real pride, that he and Eck made a team. There was a third member of this team but she had been required to stay behind. It had taken the combined persuasive powers of both Gillian and Eck to accomplish this result.

"We need every man on Earth today," Gillian continued. "It doesn't matter who he is or what he is, if he is willing to learn, he can be of help." He wondered if Samuel Ronson would have used these words in this way, and decided that the scientist would have done so. Ronson had taken a broad view of evolution and had insisted that even animals had to progress too, in time. In part, he had died for this belief.

"Don't be giving me any of that missionary talk," Abrussi answered. "You're only trying to stall me until you can get my *jednar* away from me." One more quick step and he would have Gillian between him and Umbro.

"Am I?" Gillian asked.

"Yes. And it's not going to work!"

Taking the last necessary step, Abrussi brought the *jednar* down so that it covered Gillian. "Tell that goat behind you that if he tries to shoot me, you'll go first!"

"Use your *jednar!*" Gillian said.

"W—what?" Abrussi gasped.

"Pull the trigger." Gillian invited.

Abrussi stared at him. "Your *jednar* won't work," Gillian said. "I told you each *jednar* had its individual frequency, much as your bracelets each had its individual frequency. The *Tejani* have the serial numbers of all the weapons in your possession. They left them turned on, until now, because this was the only way to locate you. They wanted the *jednars* back to keep you from learning their secrets. But now that we have you located, every *jednar* in your possession, including the one in your hand, is so much worthless glass."

"That's another lie!" Abrussi answered. "My bracelets are handled through a central control. Where's the central control of the *jednars?*"

"There," Gillian answered, pointing up.

In spite of all he could do to prevent it, thinking all the time that it was only a trick, Abrussi turned his head to look up. There in the sky, dropping slowly lower and lower, was the vast master ship of the *Tejani*. It was longer than the longest ocean liner, bigger than the biggest aircraft carrier, but it slid through the sky with effortless ease.

Beneath it, moving in the majestic rhythm of a time that belonged to great space, was a vast pendulum. Although the pendulum that had existed in the cavern under Mad Mountain was gone, this greater pendulum was still in operation, striving with all the vast power in it to keep forward time for the planet under it.

It was to this ship that Umbro had taken Gillian, Sis, and Eck. Sis was in this ship now. Sis! Through her, and through millions of other young women like her, flowed the hopes that the *Tejani* had for the future of the teeming population on Earth.

To George Gillian, this ship was a mighty dream floating in the sky, the greatest, finest dream he had ever known. Deep in his heart he knew that Samuel Ronson had shared this same dream.

"There's the master pendulum," Gillian said. "In that ship is also the master control for all *jednars*. They do not generate their own power. They take it from the master control within the ship."

In Gillian's mind was another source of wonder. The Z generator which they had built in his laboratory, and which they had called the monster, in derision, had actually come close to duplicating the master generator within the *Tejani* ship itself. The Z generator had not been a failure. Learned *Tejani* scientists had listened in awe while he had described

THE DARKNESS BEFORE TOMORROW

it to them, then had pointed out that what he had thought was a failure, had actually been a colossal success. In the fact that a woman of Earth had provided the drawings for the Z generator, and men of Earth had built it, the *Tejani* had found indisputable proof that their great plan of building better brains in better bodies was succeeding! The Z generator proved this to them.

Abrussi pulled the trigger of the *jednar*.

Nothing happened.

Abrussi had to face the fact that Gillian had told him the truth. He also had to face what he was, inside, an ape that had gone among men and had pretended to be a man.

Abrussi could not face either fact. Dropping the *jednar*, his hand darted into his coat pocket where he kept the little weapon that he had used before he found a *jednar*. Even if the weapons of the *Tejani* would not work, a human pistol would.

As Abrussi's hand went into his pocket, Eck Randolph leaped at him. Eck caught the hand that was trying to draw the gun. Simultaneously, George Gillian struck from in front. Gillian's fist went home on the point of Abrussi's chin. A short snapping sound followed.

Eck let a lifeless body slide from his hands. So powerful had Gillian's blow been that it had broken Abrussi's neck.

Umbro leaned over the body to make sure. Looking up, his yellow eyes glinted. "Hunt ended," he said. Looking at George Gillian and Eck Randolph, his eyes began to glow. Perhaps, after all, there were some good humans!

Umbro signalled to his *Tejani* crew to collect the *jednars* from Abrussi's guard and to find the hidden ships.

George Gillian and Eck Randolph looked up at the ship. They knew they would soon return to it. It was lifting now, rising higher in the sky as it returned to its normal position on the night side of the planet. Dreams were rising in their hearts, dreams of many things that were to come. Each could feel Sis smiling at him from the ship. Each, in a quite different way and for quite different reasons, was happy in the knowledge of her smile.

THE LADDER IN THE SKY

by
KEITH WOODCOTT

ACE BOOKS, INC.
23 West 47th Street, New York 36, N.Y.

THE LADDER IN THE SKY

Copyright ©, 1962, by Ace Books, Inc.

All Rights Reserved

Also by Keith Woodcott:
I SPEAK FOR EARTH (D-497)

THE DARKNESS BEFORE TOMORROW
Copyright ©, 1962, by Ace Books, Inc.

Printed in U.S.A.

I

To the haughty, speeding by with their hands heavy with rings and their heavily made-up women at their sides, the Dyasthala was a barely noticed interlude between the spaceport and the high-built modern quarter climbing up the green-fledged hills. By day the beams of the harsh sun slanted down into it, picking at the crumbled walls, the heaps of refuse, the cracked and mud-smeared paving, like the fingers of an idiot scratching his sores. Then the boldest of them sometimes ventured down the broadest of the alleys, escorted by a pack of bullies and followed by yelling beggar-children, and then went home and washed away the clinging odor in a tub of perfumed water, so that they could boast about it later. But never at night. In the Berak tongue, Dyasthala meant "a place to walk warily"—and it was.

Kazan knew that. He had lived all his eighteen years in the Dyasthala, and even now, tonight, he was afraid against his will as he picked his way down alleys not far from the overpass carrying the highway. There was no moon to spy lurkers in shadow tonight, and the darkness was so thick it seemed to oppress his ears as well as his eyes, numbing them. He had eaten nothing since yesterday, but if he had had two coppers to rub together he would have spent them on a flaring, resinous torch even before the bowl of broth and the hunk of bread he kept imagining.

THE LADDER IN THE SKY

Cautious, keeping an even distance from the walls on either side, he moved almost as silently as a ghost. But not quite.

Later, he told himself that being hungry must have made him lightheaded, for otherwise he would never have gone walking alone at midnight. But for the first few instants after he was set upon, he thought nothing at all, because his attacker, whoever he was, went first for his throat, and with expert fingers strangled him to momentary unconsciousness.

Indeed, it was so cleverly done that it was like a showman's trick, like the lowering and raising of the curtain before a stage to hide the mechanics of an illusion. One moment he was automatically clawing at the hands about his throat, trying to force a cry past their choking grip; the next he knew, he was sprawled on the ground, gazing up into the yellow glare of a handlight, his hands cuffed and his ankles hobbled.

His throat hurt abominably. Anyway, he could think of nothing to say. He kept silent.

Standing over him, holding the handlight, was a stout man of middle age with a melancholy expression. He wore an old, but once very expensive robe, the hem soiled with mud. He studied Kazan thoughtfully for a long moment.

At last he said, "Get him on his feet."

Kazan felt himself seized by his collar and his belt, and hoisted to a vertical position as impersonally as a tent pole being set up. With his ankles hobbled as they were, he had to give up any idea of trying to run.

As he swung through the air, he caught a glimpse of the man who had actually attacked him. He was a brawny bully with a battered metal helmet on his shaven skull and a power-gun thrust in his belt. Kazan's heart gave a lurch. Whose hands had he fallen into, in the name of the wyrds? In the Dyasthala you didn't show a power-gun— not unless you were the law and there were ten of you marching together in broad daylight. A power-gun was a fortune you could hold in one hand, and nine out of ten of the people of the Dyasthala would kill you to take it away.

The stout man raised the handlight to the level of his shoulder and looked Kazan up and down. Kazan topped the

THE LADDER IN THE SKY

bully by half a head, but the bully matched Kazan in height and was much heavier. If you lived in the Dyasthala you stayed thin; in all his life Kazan had had so few square meals he could practically recall them individually. He was lean, like a predator in a country of little game; his eyes and teeth were sharp like a predator's, and his fair hair was chopped crudely short so that in a fight his adversary could not get a hold on it. His shirt he had stolen from a clothman on the other side of the overpass, but since to wear a new garment in the Dyasthala was to invite its theft he had smeared it with dust and torn one of the sleeves off. His jeans of supple leather had come from a man dying in a doorway. He also possessed a belt, hose and boots which he was wearing.

"What's your name?" the stout man said.

Kazan didn't answer. The bully slapped him on the side of the head—not too hard, just by way of encouragement. But the stout man scowled.

"Hego!" he snapped. "Let him make up his own mind!"

The bully chuckled as if at some unknown joke, but let his hand fall. Again the stout man put his question.

"Kazan," came the reluctant answer.

"Just Kazan? Son of—?"

"Just Kazan." His throat was very painful. He tried not to have to swallow, but he was shaking from head to foot with ill-defined terror, and sourness kept rising in his mouth.

"How old are you or don't you know?" the stout man went on.

"About eighteen, I guess," Kazan muttered. He had come to a tentative conclusion about the stout man's interest in him, and if he was right then co-operation would probably be worth a warm bed and a couple of square meals, and perhaps some cash afterwards. You didn't learn to be squeamish in the Dyasthala; you took what came along, or you died.

"All right, he'll do," the stout man said abruptly. "Hego, get him moving."

A jab in the small of the back which almost put him back on the ground sent Kazan stumbling down the alley in the wake of the yellow handlight.

THE LADDER IN THE SKY

The new lords of Berak had laid the overpass ruler-straight across the slums, a roadway resting on a twelve-foot wall. If houses got in the way, they knocked them down. On one side of this barrier things had become worse and worse, even in Kazan's lifetime. On the other side, the one closer to the spaceport, the spacecrew and tourist trade had brought a hesitant advance of prosperity.

By day there were guards at the four tunnels piercing the wall, and by night heavy steel grills were locked over the entrances, connected to noisy alarms. Someone like Kazan, with neither documents nor a job to guarantee him, could only reach the far side by scurrying illegally across the overpass and running the risk of being scythed down by the traffic. He had done that, of course. There was nothing in the Dyasthala worth stealing.

But the stout man had a key to one of the steel grills, and they passed under the road without challenge, hearing the transmitted vibration of the late-night vehicles echo eerily about them. Once they were through, Kazan concentrated on memorizing the route they were taking, in case he was abandoned on this side. The streets were still alley-broad, except where houses had collapsed and the ruins had been swept away instead of being repaired, but there was some lighting and the paving was in good repair.

They headed in the direction of the spaceport, meeting almost no one, although they passed several taverns from which singing and laughter could be heard. At last they turned off into a pitch-dark courtyard where the stout man had to use his handlight again, and halted before the door of a house whose windows showed no light at all.

The stout man knocked; the bully Hego closed one large hand on Kazan's upper arm as though suspecting he might miraculously break his hobble and flee.

Shortly the door creaked fractionally open, and a whisper came from the darkness inside.

"Yarco?"

"Are you expecting anyone else?" the stout man said humorously, also in a whisper.

"Fool!" the speaker at the door hissed. "Come in quickly!"

The door opened fully. There was a high step in front of

THE LADDER IN THE SKY

it; Kazan almost fell because his hobble prevented him from mounting it, but Hego steadied him and pushed him inside. The door shut.

Like most houses Kazan knew, the ground floor of this one was open from wall to wall. The ceiling was supported on square pillars, the bases of which were low, padded plinths serving as seats. On one of these plinths a man sat, dressed in black, with a small black skullcap above his very pale face. There was no one else present except the person who had opened the door to them. As he was pushed inside, Kazan had seen by Yarco's handlight that this person was wrapped in a ground-length cloak with a concealing hood.

"Sit him down," a sharp voice said.

A woman's voice? Kazan snapped his head round.

The cloak was gone, tossed aside; the unsexed whisper had given place to a rich voice with a ring of authority, and she was beautiful. She was between the stout man and Kazan in height and moved with the grace of a wild animal. Her hair was long and black, her face oval but slightly hollow-cheeked so that her cheekbones seemed to be underlining her bright, fierce-burning eyes. Her mouth was finely shaped and showed red even in the dimness. She wore a smock-dress such as any servant might wear, but she carried it like a princess's gown.

Kazan found himself gaping. But he had no chance to speak; he was thrust towards a seat and firmly settled on it by Hego, who took up a position beside him, watchful.

"Put the light on him, Yarco!" the woman said. "You—conjurer! Will he do?"

The man in black shrugged, studying Kazan. "Who is he?"

"He's named Kazan." The stout man answered off-handedly. "Aged eighteen or so. I picked him up in the Dyasthala."

"Does he yet know why?"

"What difference does it make?" the woman cut in. "In the Dyasthala there's no one but cutthroats and thieves."

"Still, perhaps he should be asked if he will accept his task," the man in black said.

"Ohhh!" For a moment Kazan thought she was going to

refuse point-blank; then, however, she turned to face him, lifting her hand to her breast.

"Do you know me?" she said.

Kazan shook his head.

"I'm the Lady Bryda. At least you've heard of me!"

That—yes! Kazan was taken aback, but he controlled his face. He gave a cautious nod. From her disgusted expression he thought that she had probably expected him to make some obeisance, but that was another thing people of the Dyasthala never learned.

Richly sarcastic, she went on, "And has it also come to your notice that this country of Berak is ruled by foreigners? That the rightful governor, Prince Luth, is held a captive?"

Kazan returned her gaze boldly. He said, "I have heard so, but in the Dyasthala it has made little difference. We are treated the same as before."

He thought for a moment she was going to hit him in the face, but the dry voice of the man in black cut in.

"He shows spirit," he said. "That's good."

Bryda relaxed a little, breathing hard. A look that might have been a sneer on a less noble countenance came and went. She said, "Well then, you've been brought here to aid the prince if it can be done. If you're willing, it will mean for you release from the Dyasthala and chances of advancement that you've never dreamed of."

"In the Dyasthala," Kazan said stonily, "you don't dream."

Bryda stamped her foot and turned away. "I thought it would be useless to speak to the blockhead," she said. "I'll have no more time wasted. Conjurer, get to it!"

The man in black shrugged and picked up something which had been leaning against the plinth beside him. A ring, Kazan saw, perhaps two feet wide. No, much wider or else in some cunning way made to expand, for when the man in black laid it down on the floor it was as large as he was tall.

He settled it flat and returned to his seat. "Darkness," he said in a bored tone.

Yarco put out the handlight. A curious noise came to Kazan's ears; after a moment he identified it as the chattering of Hego's teeth. He was distracted from his own strange plight for a moment by amusement at Hego's, so that he could not tell whether the conjurer had done anything or whether the thing had happened by itself.

But a bluish glow now emanated from the ring on the floor, revealing Bryda's face ghastly gray as she leaned forward, and Yarco's also, set and serious, and the conjurer's impassive.

And within the ring, where moments before there had been the bare planks of the floor, a shape that moved, and opened eyes glowing like coals, *spoke*.

II

HEGO'S SELF-CONTROL broke. He gave a low shuddering moan, and could be heard to shuffle his feet backwards on the floor. Only his intense determination not to show such weakness prevented Kazan from doing the same, but he had to clench his teeth together so tightly that his jaw muscles ached. The rigid cuffs linking his wrists prevented him clasping his hands. He could only drive his nails hard into his palms.

He had thought he knew darkness. But the thing which had appeared in the circle of blue light was *absolutely* black except for the ember glow of the eyes—if they were eyes; they had neither iris nor pupil, and only the way they turned this way and that suggested that the thing looked out of them. Kazan stared at them greedily. To look anywhere else on that black form was to feel that the soul within him was being sucked out by the totality of the darkness, like air pouring into the vacuum of space.

The voice that came from the blackness was vast and sighing with an overtone of agony, like a gale piping on mountains, a noise that made Kazan shiver and shiver and

THE LADDER IN THE SKY

shiver. At its sound, even Bryda flinched back, although the conjurer sat calm on his cushions.

"What world is this?" the awful voice inquired.

The conjurer, as though prepared for the question, reeled off something Kazan could not follow; he assumed it to be a charm and hoped it was a very strong one. He had never before seen a spirit evoked; although the Dyasthala was full of cheating witches and wizards who played on the superstition of wealthy customers, he knew most of their tricks were worked and took the rest to be trickery also. But not this.

He felt ice cold, and yet sweat was trickling into his eyes.

"And what do you want with me?" the thing said then.

The conjurer looked at Bryda and indicated that she should speak. Uncertain, she licked her lips. The first time she tried to address the thing, her voice was a whisper; she broke off, swallowed hard and swelled her shapely bosom with a deep breath.

"I am the Lady Bryda," she said. "Until four years ago my—lover—Prince Luth was ruler of this land of Berak. Foreigners in league with the traders from space had taken the land over piecemeal; at last they grew so bold they dethroned the prince and set up a usurping government. They did not dare to kill the prince outright, but they hold him captive."

Kazan was beginning to make sense, if not of the thing in the circle, at least of Bryda's motives. But where did he come into her plan? He did not want to think of that.

"If he could be freed," Bryda said, "the people would rise and restore him to power."

For all its inhuman quality, Kazan thought that the thing's voice matched well with its master's faintly bored expression when it spoke again. It said, "Did the people desire his return so strongly, they would have released him."

Kazan reflected that this business was of small interest to the people of the Dyasthala. Who governed them mattered little; what counted was that they were always governed, never governors. Hence they were opposed to Prince Luth, or anyone else, and would not lift a finger to aid him.

"Many attempts have been made," Bryda said in a sub-

THE LADDER IN THE SKY

dued tone. "But understand: he is held in a fortress in the middle of a mile-wide lake of sour water, where savage carnivorous monsters dwell. A small boat cannot cross the lake; its crew would be spilled into the water by these creatures, and devoured. We have no way of getting a great boat to the lake, and in any case there are two heavily armed boats that patrol the lake continually, as well as the armed ferry which links the fortress and the mainland. We have considered tunneling, but the lake is too deep; we have considered flying, but there is no place to set down. The fortress completely covers the rocky island on which it is built, and there are rocket stands on the roofs. Yet we can see him at the open window of his apartment, and signal to him."

"And you wish him to be released," the thing said.

"Yes," Bryda said.

"It can be done," the thing sent on, as though ignoring her. "It can be done at once."

Bryda did not relax. She looked at Yarco, who sat with his face shiny with sweat and his lips pressed close together. Not turning to the thing again, she said in a barely audible voice, "For what price?"

"There is only one price," the thing said. "Service for a year and a day."

What could that terrifying voice mean by *service?* What could a black thing with eyes like coals want of a human being? Kazan's blood thundered in his ears, and forgetful of his hobble he tried to get to his feet.

"He will serve you," he heard Bryda say, and knew she was pointing towards him. Somehow, though, he could see nothing. Except a swimming pattern of dots which seemed to be inside his eyes. He felt himself seized and held, most likely by Hego, because the hands that closed on his arms were slippery—wet with the sweat of pure fear.

"It's gone," Yarco said wonderingly.

Then the conjurer's voice, "I must pass the ring over him. Free him, you!"

For a moment the grip on his arms ended. Something cold touched his nape—metal. The ring! He tried frantically to duck underneath it and escape, but it was let fall. He

13

THE LADDER IN THE SKY

flung out his arms, but it was too wide to catch, and like the knell of doom he heard it clang as it struck the floor at his feet.

Then he fainted.

He was lying on his back, his mouth slackly open. A taste of something warm and sweet invited him to swallow, and he did. Passive, he let the fluid run down his throat.

Memory seemed to trickle back with it. When the flow ended he opened his eyes. He was on a padded couch against the wall of the same room. A wheeled trolley stood next to the couch, with a steaming tureen on it. Yarco was ladling the contents into a spouted jug. It was that spout which had come between his teeth, Kazan decided.

Yarco's hand was shaking so badly that the ladle clinked against the jug each time he lifted it, and his face was as shiny as it had been when the thing was present. But he went on methodically with what he was doing.

"I suppose the others were afraid," Kazan said. He licked his lips.

Startled, Yarco almost dropped both jug and ladle. He said, "I—yes, I guess they are."

"And you?"

"I don't believe in being afraid," Yarco said. "We are at the mercy of the stars. If I am to be killed by a man possessed of a devil, it's the decree of the wyrds and I can't change it. Meantime, possessed or not, you seemed to have fainted with hunger. Do you want more of this?"

Kazan sat up, wondering at the calmness in his mind. He took the full jug from Yarco and drained it. Yarco stood watching, his face relaxing from tension to puzzlement.

He said at last, "You're all right?"

Kazan nodded. He stretched his arms out and flexed them. "Did you take off my manacles?" he asked.

"I did. For the same reason. Moreover, the thing which was called up seemed powerful, and you were pledged to it, and it would be well to attend to your needs." He hesitated, and then put the question that had clearly been itching in his mind.

"Do I speak to Kazan, or to the *thing?*"

THE LADDER IN THE SKY

For a moment Kazan was startled. Then the words made sense, and he realized that he might have asked the same of himself.

"How can I answer?" he said. "I feel like Kazan, I think—no, I think I think like Kazan."

Abruptly he leaped from the couch. He took a pace away from it and planted his feet together on the floor. His face went pale as death, and he began to shake from head to foot.

"For the love of life!" he forced between his teeth. "What have you done to me? *What have you done to me?*"

Accusing, his eyes sought Yarco's. The stout man met his gaze unflinchingly, and after a moment gave a sorrowful shake of the head.

Behind Kazan there were footsteps on the stairs leading from the upper story. Not changing the direction of his gaze, Yarco said, "He has not harmed me. Nor will he. You may come here."

It was Bryda. Her face showed the ravages of tiredness when she moved into Kazan's field of view, but her eyes were keen and searched his face eagerly.

Under her breath she said, "To think that this—this ragged wretch will be his salvation and mine." And then more sharply to Yarco, "What's to be done? Have you learned yet?"

"Did the conjurer say nothing?" Yarco countered, sounding puzzled.

"No! He said that the—the devil, if it was a devil, had entered into *him* and would know what needed to be done." A flash of dark suspicion crossed her face. "If he should try to trick us—!"

"What will you do?" Yarco broke in. "He's powerful—not one of these rune-casters and gibberers. I have not seen a devil before," he added in a lower tone.

Bryda shot out her hand and swung the unresisting Kazan to face her. She said, "What's to be done? How do we rescue the prince?"

Eyes haunted, Kazan returned her gaze. The unnatural calm which he had felt on waking from his faint was gradually returning. Yet in a detached way he was still fright-

THE LADDER IN THE SKY

ened. To himself, the strange episode of the thing in the circle felt like a nightmare—unreal, and over now. But this was impossible, for here Yarco and the Lady Bryda were speaking of it as a reality.

"If you don't speak," Bryda spat at him, "I'll send for Hego and make him beat you till you do!"

"Hego won't come," Yarco said. "It will be days before he can recover his wits."

Bryda, a prince's mistress, waiting for his word. His! Kazan's. Who spoke of devils? Were a man to be filled with a devil, he would know it for sure! And here he was, himself, thinking like himself, talking like himself—Kazan, the waif of the Dyasthala, self-taught thief, hungry, despised. With the calm, a cunning thought was entering his mind. Why not, for a while at least, make the pretense? Why not make Bryda for all her rank and airs squirm on his hook? He turned the idea over, as it were to taste it, and it tasted as sweet as honey.

He gave a little crooked smile. He said, "Of course I know what must be done. But I'm a ragged wretch, Lady Bryda. I'm a starving wretch, too. You get nothing without paying for it, Lady Bryda, not unless you're a thief like me. You've tried it, and you've failed. You've got to pay. You don't like it, do you? But that's the risk you run if you take without asking."

He threw his hand out in front of him, palm up, not in the beggar's gesture, but as a merchant would wait for payment.

III

HATE HIM she might—*did*, Kazan corrected himself smugly —but pay him she must, until the day she found out how she was being fooled. And the payment he was taking was not small.

THE LADDER IN THE SKY

For the moment he was alone. He could let himself enjoy it. From sheer jubilation he jumped in the air and spun round through half a circle to land without a sound on the soft warm floor.

By the wyrds, though Bryda could complain of this house as a place of misery and squalor, for him it was luxury unimaginable. Space! Thirty feet on a side, the room, and the ceiling so high he could not touch it if he jumped straight up; light always on call—not as it was in the few houses in the Dyasthala where there was a supply, an unreliable glimmer, but a steady brilliant glow; warmth unceasing and color. Almost, the color mattered more than anything; the greenness of the walls, the rich tan of the floor, the sunlight-yellow above.

There was a bowl of fruit on a low table. He snatched some and crammed it in his mouth, and washed it down with a swig of iced wine from the cup beside the bowl. Licking his lips, he took stance before the man-high mirror on the wall and stared at himself.

Even now, a disbelieving expression came to his face. The black shirt with the silver piping and the plain black pants, the low shoes, were things he would never have dared to steal for himself—only if he were sure of selling them, perhaps to a spaceman who would leave the planet before questions could be asked. It wasn't only their rich appearance; it was their thermostatically controlled circuitry.

His hair had been barbered by a slight, quiet girl who attended to Bryda's and Yarco's hair as well, and was brilliant as new silver. The edge had not been taken off his leanness. Indeed, the strange battle of wits of the past twenty days seemed to have sharpened it. But the pure animal hunger was gone from his appearance.

Now the only question was: how long would it last?

Vaguely at the back of his mind, when he began this, there had been the idea of making Bryda submit to the ultimate humiliation and lie with him. That possibility had vanished. Already only a hairline separated her suspicion from the certainty that he was deceiving her and Yarco and the other, rather shadowy figures who came and went at this house, usually by night, on business probably connected

THE LADDER IN THE SKY

with the escape of Prince Luth. Now it had become a delicate problem of balance, of postponing the inevitable moment when he himself fled by teasing out her hope that he would work the promised miracle.

Twice now she had threatened a showdown. The second time had been only yesterday. An inspiration had saved him. He had insisted on being taken out to look at the fortress in the lake where Prince Luth was imprisoned. She could not turn down such a sensible request, but she hadn't like her bluff being called.

That lake . . . The self-approving grin disappeared from Kazan's face. They had taken him up in the late afternoon to a high hill overlooking it, a mile from its shore, and given him powerful glasses to study it and the fortress. They had pointed out the main window of Prince Luth's suite, and the sheer sixty-foot drop from it to the water. But he had not wasted much time looking at the fortress. Prince Luth, for all Kazan cared, could stay there till he rotted.

He'd stared at the lake instead.

He hadn't known that such things existed in Berak. All he had ever seen of Berak, after all, was the Dyasthala. He was vaguely aware of a world outside, but it never mattered to him. The trip out to the lake—a twenty-mile journey—was the farthest he had ever been from the spot where he was born. And he was uncomfortable when there were no buildings anywhere in view, as happened for part of the time. Even the fortress, though it was gray and forbidding, was comforting when he tore his hypnotized gaze away from the water.

There were things swarming there. Twice he caught sight of slime-dripping, ropy tentacles that cracked out across the mirror surface like vast whips; once he saw the back of a monstrous, glistening, brown creature rise into view and spit blood reeking to the sky before something still more huge and very hungry cut it in two with a beak like giants' scissors. After that there was blood on the water, like an oil slick.

And a horde of little creatures came to feed on that.

"There," Bryda had promised, throwing out her arm in a

THE LADDER IN THE SKY

regal gesture, "is where I shall have you thrown if you do not keep your promise."

If he had had the slightest hope that she was voicing an empty threat, Kazan would have reminded her that he had promised nothing, that the conjurer had made the promises, and that he, Kazan, was merely a victim snatched at random off the streets to meet the price that the devil demanded. And that, if she wanted satisfaction, she would do better to go in search of the conjurer again.

But she meant what she said. It couldn't be doubted.

Kazan frowned at himself in the mirror. *Was* that devil real? Was it a devil? Had it all been a superbly clever trick by the man in black to part Bryda from her money? He would have been well paid, that was sure.

Because it was the likeliest explanation, and because he felt no different from the way he remembered feeling before, Kazan had accepted it as the truth and tried not to question it further. Seeing the monsters in the lake yesterday, though, had put him vividly in mind of the thing in the blue-lit circle, and he wasn't certain any longer.

Abruptly the dangerous nature of the game he was playing hit him, full force. He stood for a moment, calming himself, but seeing the way his eyes widened and the tendons stood out on his neck.

That couldn't be faced alone. He had to go somewhere. He had to get out, maybe. He had to go back to the Dyasthala and lose himself. At the back of his mind was the faint, unformulated idea that perhaps when it came to claim its year and a day of service the devil would fail to find him.

In the grip of something like panic, he slammed out of the room and went clattering down the stairs.

Halfway, he stopped dead, grasping the baluster. He had believed himself alone in the house; even Hego, who was his constant guard by night and day, would be outside the only door in preference to staying under the same roof as a man possessed of a devil.

But there, sitting comfortably on the padded plinth of one of the square pillars, was Yarco. He had a jug of wine beside him, and he was turning the pages of a large book on his lap.

THE LADDER IN THE SKY

He glanced up, nodded to Kazan, and went back to his reading.

That was a piece of bad luck, Kazan thought. Yet provided Yarco was on his own, not irremediable. He slowly descended the rest of the stairs, as though he had left his room out of mere restlessness, and began to wander about, eying the pictures, the racked books and recording crystals, the slow changing lines of words on the news machine.

Passing the window set in the front wall, he caught a glimpse of Hego standing stolidly before the door. Some small boys were going by in a group; they seemed to be shouting at him, because he turned thunder-faced and shook his fist. But no sound from outside ever entered the house if the door was closed.

He wandered on. Rounding the pillar at whose base Yarco sat, he looked down at the book he was reading. Reading. Well, the guy seemed contented enough, and maybe when a man got to Yarco's state, podgily middle-aged, and the fire in his belly started to die down, it was a way of passing the time. He craned his neck. There was a picture at the top of the page on the left, and he couldn't quite get the angle right for the depth effect from where he was standing.

"Can you read, Kazan?" Yarco said.

Kazan started. He hadn't noticed Yarco turn his head. Now he'd got his attention, and it would take a while to lose it again. Cursing his thoughtlessness, he said, "Why—a bit. I can read street names, and names on stores, and like that."

"Not much call for more than that, I guess," Yarco nodded. "You write your name?"

Uncomfortable, Kazan shook his head.

"You should learn," Yarco said. He put his book aside and helped himself to wine from the jug. "You can't go back into the Dyasthala the way you are now, and you won't get by outside without it. When do you work your miracle, by the way?"

"Miracle?" Kazan said slowly, studying Yarco's bland face.

"Yes. You know!" Yarco waved a negligent hand. "Your vanishing act."

THE LADDER IN THE SKY

There was a moment of frozen silence. "I don't know what you mean," Kazan said at last.

"You know only too well," Yarco corrected him. He got up and replaced his book in the rack on the far wall. Swinging back towards Kazan, he could be seen to be smiling.

"Oh, don't worry," he said. "I'm not going to interfere. As I told you when we first met, I believe we're at the mercy of the stars. If the wyrds decreed that you should become possessed of a devil, what can a mere man like myself do about it? Or you, for that matter! Of course, that may not be your fate. Perhaps you're due to wind up in the sour lake, eaten by savage animals. Perhaps you're due to disappear into the Dyasthala, to be garroted for your fine new clothes and dumped in a sewer, to end as an anonymous corpse. I hope not. You're a very astute young man, and I'm sure you're going to go far. If you live, that is."

A cold chill walked down Kazan's spine like an animal with feet of ice. He said, "I—no! What's your loyalty to Bryda?"

A shadow crossed Yarco's face. He said shortly, "None."

"Then what are you doing in this?" Kazan snapped.

"All right, I'll tell you," Yarco said after a second of hesitation. "I was lost on a bet to the prince's father a month before I was born. I have been the property of the royal family all my fifty years of life. I have never been able to lift a hand to serve myself. That is, I never could until Prince Luth was kidnaped and made captive. So I'm in no great hurry myself to let him free. But my experience of a lifetime has convinced me—oh, foolishly perhaps, but thoroughly—that it's no good railing against one's fate."

"So in one sense at least, you too are possessed," Kazan said. He gave a harsh laugh.

"Too?" Yarco picked the word up like a hungry scavenger pouncing on a scrap of food. "Do you mean—?"

It was clear what he would have said, "Do you mean that you are truly possessed by that thing—whatever it was?" And to that Kazan still had no answer. For, after all, he had no information to guide him. What should a possessed man feel like?

But at that moment the entrance door was flung open,

THE LADDER IN THE SKY

Hego appearing momentarily beyond it and then stepping back to make way for Bryda at the head of a small procession of men in dark clothes and outdoor boots. The one directly following Bryda was known by sight to Kazan, but not by name; he had visited the house twice at night, and Kazan had been produced for his inspection.

It was the man behind, however, who strode into the center of the room on entering and stared Kazan up and down. Meantime, his companions formed a close group just inside the door, their expressions dour and threatening.

He carried a short cane with jeweled ends, which he tapped on the palm of his hand while he was scrutinizing Kazan. When he was through for the moment, he glanced at Bryda, poking Kazan in the chest with the cane.

"Him?" he said in a disgusted tone.

"Not him precisely," Bryda snapped. "The devil which possesses him."

"I've heard too much of this devil nonsense," the man growled. "I want to hear—now!—what he proposes to do to help us, and if it doesn't make sense, he goes quietly tonight into a lonely grave. And there'll be a reckoning later. Is that understood?" He glared at Bryda.

"And you?" he went on after a moment, prodding Kazan again. "Do you understand it? Do you want to save your skin?"

One moment before he uttered an unconvincing lie, Kazan hesitated. Something had occurred to him, something he had not expected. A good and sensible reason for having delayed.

He said, "If I'd talked about what was going to be done, how many people in Berak do you think would know about it by now? And what do you think would be stupider than to try a rescue on a night when there's a moon?"

A sardonic twist of the lip went with the words, as unexpected and as unfamiliar as they had been—and as effective. Uncertainly, his challenger drew back half a pace. He said after a moment, "I'll accept that. But what's to be done?"

Kazan didn't answer. He felt his mouth open a little. He stared unseeing and disbelieving past the man before him

22

and towards Yarco, on whose face a look of astonishment was dawning.

Because he knew. He did know after all. And he didn't see how it was possible.

IV

NIGHT LAY over the fortress and the lake. The sky was as clear as crystal, and every now and again Kazan found himself glancing up at it, noting that the stars were organized in groups, noting that they cycled slowly, diagonally towards the horizon, so that there were now different stars behind the fortress from those that had been showing when the sun set.

He had never seen a night like this. He had never looked at the stars except from beneath the constant haze of the city. Up on the hill, around the homes of the haughty, the sky might be as clear as it was here. But not over the Dyasthala, from which the fumes of a thousand coarse fires and the reek of decaying rubbish oozed forever upward, a miasma fit to foul even the stars.

He had not yet made up his mind whether he liked the sky to be so naked over the world. But it was a new thing, and very interesting.

Out there in the louring bulk of the fortress a few lights gleamed; one in particular, directly facing them, was the window of Prince Luth's apartment. Almost anything might be going on there. It was too far to hear, and too dark to see.

But the night was not silent by any means. Something fearful was hunting in the lake; you could track it by the succession of splashes and howls that marked its victims' deaths. And to the right and left of the fortress other beasts, perhaps mating, frequently uttered a rasping hoot that rose to an ear-splitting whistle before its end.

THE LADDER IN THE SKY

Kazan was aware of a curious detachment from himself, although when he had to act or give orders he did not feel that it was something else in him working through him. Rather, the sensation each time it happened was like being struck by a transparently obvious, but brilliant, notion. He thought now that he ought to be afraid of it, but it was too enjoyable.

He had never had such subtle thoughts about himself before. Now, reclining in comfort, overlooking the lake and waiting for the moment which was sure to come, he was able to recognize that if the problem had been put to him to consider as happening to somebody else, he would have expected to be scared and worried and looking for an escape. Instead, he was full of buoyant confidence. Maybe he'd caught some of Yarco's fatalism.

Apparently from nowhere, Yarco's voice came softly to him. The stout man was sitting just beyond arm's reach, shrouded in one of the light, portable radiation deflectors that concealed all the watchers round the lake from the suspicious fortress guards.

"How do you feel, Kazan?"

"Confused," Kazan said. "But otherwise well."

"I've noticed," Yarco said, and after a moment's pause went on. "You're enjoying yourself. You've tasted power for the first time. Don't get the habit."

Kazan turned the idea over. Yarco was probably right. Since the moment when the stout man had shown his exact understanding of what passed in Kazan's mind, Kazan had had the healthiest respect for him. Almost, he had begun to like him. After all, to have been pledged before birth to the whims of the royal family was in its way a fate like being born into the Dyasthala, with so little hope of ever climbing out.

"You puzzle me," Yarco said. "I know quite well that you have not the slightest idea of what you're doing, that Prince Luth is nothing to you, nor is Lady Bryda, that your world yesterday was the Dyasthala and today still is. And yet, something moves you. Like an invisible hand. Have you ever believed in devils, Kazan?"

There was a note of mockery in the voice. It wasn't quite

24

THE LADDER IN THE SKY

sincere, as though he were pretending to laugh at what he was speaking of for fear that he might otherwise scream.

Kazan said shortly, "All I've ever believed in is hunger. And cold. And disease. And the inevitability of death."

"Have you added to the list lately?" Yarco pressed him.

"I guess not," Kazan said stonily. He glanced down towards the lakeside, and stiffened, everything else forgotten. There went the first stage of his plan.

His?

He choked the thought back, concentrating on the details of what must be happening. Lately, they told him, Prince Luth's captors had decided that there was now small chance of his followers trying to rescue him, and reduced their guards somewhat, so that the lakeside patrol now consisted of a mere four men—or rather, twenty in all. But at any time only four were actually patrolling; the remainder were in four watch-houses. Four men would search their quarter of the shore, then relieve the men in the watch-house they came to and send them off in turn.

Then, Kazan had said, send four men down a few minutes before the patrol is expected. Let them go to the watch-house as though they were the patrol, overcome the men inside, and then overcome the real patrol when it arrived. Let them make any necessary report by phone to the next watch-house, and it would be an hour or so before suspicions were aroused.

He waited tensely. From here he should be able to catch any slight sounds of scuffling. Yes, and there was something which fell dry upon the ear—feet on solid earth, not the noise of a thing out in the lake.

"Hear that?" he whispered to Yarco.

"I hear nothing," Yarco returned curtly.

A few minutes later, the shadows slipped down the hillside to where he was waiting. One of them, he thought, was Bryda, but it was hard to tell, for they were all draped in the necessary radiation deflectors.

"It's done," a harsh whisper informed him. "Move now!"

Kazan chuckled and rose lazily to his feet. The cream of the jest, he thought, was that none of them knew what he was going to do. And the cream of the cream—which

THE LADDER IN THE SKY

Yarco, he thought, might suspect—was that he knew no more than they did. He was merely utterly confident that he would know.

He walked down to the edge of the water and looked about him. The pallid gray beach was partly mud, partly rock, partly sand; where he had come was sandy. A dozen paces distant something cast up out of the sluggish waves squirmed and writhed. Even in the darkness it seemed incomplete—a torn-off limb continuing to move blindly by itself.

The others who had come down clustered around him, impatient but not daring to cross Kazan. He savored the sensation for a moment. Then he went to the very edge of the water and bent down, feeling in the air. It did not seem that he was doing anything else.

At a level slightly higher, he did the same. And then a foot higher still.

He turned and walked back to the others, leaving nothing behind that could be seen. With ironical grace he bowed to the shape of darkness that he took to be Bryda.

"Will it please the Lady Bryda to come with me?" he said.

She hesitated. After a moment he put his hand out and seized hers, drawing her down after him to the same spot on the beach where he had been a moment ago.

"There!" he said. "There, in front of you! The window of Prince Luth's apartment! Are you not going to it?"

Alarmed that he spoke aloud, the others hurried forward. Just before they came up with him, he seemed to lose patience. Catching Bryda around the waist, he whirled her off her feet into mid-air.

And stood her there.

Time hesitated for a moment. A little murmer of disbelief welled from the people on the beach. As for Bryda, she swayed, standing on the air, and gave a soft moan. But in a few seconds she had recovered herself.

"Will it go so all the way?" she said. Her voice shook.

"Of course," Kazan said.

"It's a miracle," someone said flatly. "I don't like it at all."

THE LADDER IN THE SKY

"A serviceable miracle is better than nothing," someone else cut in. "I'll pray only that I keep my footing."

"None of you need go," Kazan said. "None but myself, and the lady here. One to guide the prince, one to be an earnest that this is no deceit."

"And I," another voice spoke up, "I, Yarco. The prince will expect me."

"I beg to differ," Kazan said. "He will expect no one."

"He will expect it *of* me, then," Yarco said, sounding unruffled. He picked his way to the edge of the water and felt about him for the invisible steps. For a moment he shook his head in wonderment. Then he climbed up beside Bryda and bounced up and down on the balls of his feet, wheezing a little.

"What is your causeway made of, Kazan?" he said.

"Air," Kazan said. He knew it was so, but only in the moment after Yarco had spoken. For an instant his confidence wavered. To walk on air, over this dreadful lake, when mouths snapped almost at their feet? And then, why not? He could do this, and he would do it.

He leaped on the first of his steps, the second, and the third, and began to build his arch of air out across the menacing water.

Once—they must have been over the point where the lake-bed shelved—a lashing tentacle swept up at them, passing so close that it sprayed them with the tacky slime it used to cling to its prey. Bryda cried out; Yarco said something brisk and reassuring, and Kazan built higher. After that, they were well beyond the reach of anything in the lake.

The sheer splendor of what he was doing then took possession of him. Who would think to look for three unprotected people, walking through the air towards the prince's window? They looked for aircraft; they looked for boats. Indeed, as he came nearer Kazan could see the two armed vessels which by day patrolled the lake, lying at a wharf alongside the fortress wall.

But this they would not look for.

He placed the last few steps carefully, at the right height

27

THE LADDER IN THE SKY

for a man to step on to when he climbed out of the window. As he worked, he could see into the room beyond. It was well lit, but apparently empty. The casement stood open, and hardly a sound could be heard.

For himself, Kazan thought, studying the luxurious fittings the other side of the window, he would be fairly happy in such captivity.

He stood aside and again made a mocking bow to Bryda, who stripped off her radiation deflector and tossed it at him so violently that he almost stepped back off the airy support on which they now all three were poised. But he said nothing, only left her to think for a moment of what she had done.

Then she turned to the window. For this great event she had put on her most gorgeous clothing, aglitter with color now in the light from the window and changing its hue with every movement. The skirt of the gown went from gold through green to purple as she put her legs over the sill of the window and clambered inside.

"Luth!" she said. "Luth!"

A door flung aside. In the opening a tall man stood, wearing a blue suit crusted with gold, his dark hair foppishly waved, a narrow dark moustache laid down over his rather sensual mouth. For a second he stared, not believing his eyes. Then Bryda had flung her arms about him and was babbling of what Kazan had done.

No; of what Bryda had done. As he might well have expected, Kazan reflected in annoyance. But the annoyance did not last. After all, it would become clear to the prince soon enough to whose credit his freedom must be placed. What mattered now was to bring him safe to shore and—

To whose credit?

Like a worm cankering a flower, the nagging doubt began to gnaw at Kazan's mind. Perhaps it was triggered by the look on Yarco's face, visible now by the light from the window, because he had pushed back the hood of his radiation deflector.

Kazan stared down between his feet. He stood on air. They had walked out on air to this window. Down there the evil life of the lake seethed and perhaps yearned up at

THE LADDER IN THE SKY

them. Who had the power to make a man walk safe on air? Not Bryda. Not Kazan, who was a thief from the Dyasthala. But a devil speaking in a voice like a bitter gale playing on a mountain for an organ pipe.

At the back of his mind he heard again the dreadful words: "There is only one price. Service for a year and a day."

He began to tremble. When the prince came out to join him on his invisible platform he scarcely noticed the fact. All he wanted was to place his feet again securely on the ground.

V

To walk on air was not to the prince's taste. It took him a long moment to decide that he could plant both feet together outside the window, another that he could safely let the window ledge go. Even then, in quick suspicious tones, he ordered Kazan to go ahead of him, and Bryda next. Meekly Yarco fell in behind. Kazan wondered dully whether the prince would trust even Yarco at his back, but seemingly he did.

He went quickly down the steps of air. He knew, in the same unaccountable way he had known how to make them, that they would dissolve in another few minutes. Part of his mind was occupied in trying to recall the trick of them; he had felt—felt? No, it was clearer than thinking, but it was not as clear as remembering. He had been aware of something about the movement of the individual particles of the air and how to organize it in a direction opposed to gravity. But the knowledge was fading. Too much of his mind was busy with his footing, and long before he was back on firm ground it had gone as a dream goes when you try to recall it among the distractions of the daytime.

THE LADDER IN THE SKY

There was no one on the shore now. Everyone else had faded back among the rocks and shrubs of the hillside beyond. But once they left the stretch of sand and started to hurry up the slope the night seemed to come softly alive with murmurs of congratulation.

Bryda, darting ahead, led the prince into a little sheltered hollow, the same one where Kazan had earlier issued his instructions. There for a minute or two she spoke with him under her breath; after that, dark-clad men came out of the night and spoke with him also. Only brief phrases were exchanged. Kazan was glad enough to hang back at the side of the hollow, trying not to think of what he had done. He caught some words here and there—names of cities elsewhere in Berak, mention of the transport waiting for the prince, the route to be taken, the hiding-places arranged while the news of his escape was being passed to the royalist underground.

None of this concerned him, Kazan felt. Prince Luth was rightful ruler of Berak, perhaps. But of the Dyasthala, no. If anyone ruled there, it was Death himself. Or the wyrds of whom Yarco spoke so often, the mystical controllers of human destiny.

Suddenly the night was riven by a shrieking blast overhead, and instinctively everyone ducked for cover. Then, turning their faces to the sky, they saw that it was not an alarm on the fortress which had started them, but a spaceship broaching atmosphere and braking hard as it swooped down on the port.

By tacit consent they waited till the racket died away; then they rose and scattered into the darkness again. "If you'll follow me," Kazan heard someone say deferentially to Prince Luth, and took it for an instruction for himself as well. He got to his feet.

He could just make out Bryda, laying her hand on the prince's arm and turning her pale face in his direction. Some words passed, too low for him to catch; then the prince gave a brusque answer.

"Wait there, fellow," he said, and turned to go.

An intuition of danger pierced Kazan's strange lethargy. He

THE LADDER IN THE SKY

took three paces forward to confront Bryda and the prince, and snapped at them.

"Wait here?" he said. "When but for me you'd be waiting yourself, in that prison of yours for a rescue that would never come?"

"Mind whom you talk to!" Bryda hissed. "And remember—you did not offer your service to the prince, as a loyal citizen of Berak should! You were haled off the streets, a thief and a wastrel and you cannot say you've not been paid for what you've done."

"You price the prince low," Kazan retorted. "Some clothing and meals for one man for one month. What says he to that valuation of him?"

"I say you're an insolent fool," the prince gritted between his teeth.

"This insolent fool"—delicately, out of the darkness, the voice of Yarco with an apologetic edge—"has nonetheless been the instrument of the prince's freedom."

"You also are a fool, Yarco," Bryda said, rounding on him. "Did you not see what he did? Did you not walk the steps he made of the air? He's sold to a devil, and we cannot keep him in the prince's company! A man with power like that? The service promised to us is over. Now the service promised to the devil begins. Therefore let the devil look to his own. Hego! Axam! Do it now!"

Something vastly heavy crashed between Kazan's shoulders. His arms were snatched up behind him and manacles were forced over his wrists. A gag so thick and tight it almost choked him was slapped over and into his mouth. He kicked out, but strong arms were clapped around his shins and pinned his legs together. The two bullies were experts at their work; he had already known this of Hego, but the other, Axam, seemed still more practiced and ruthless.

"Let your devil take care of you," Bryda said. It was plain that she meant the words to sound sneering. Somehow, though, she failed, and a tremolo of fear broke through them. For a long moment she hesitated, as though about to say more. Then she caught Prince Luth by the arm and vanished with him over the lip of the hollow, down the hillside to the transport awaiting them.

31

THE LADDER IN THE SKY

Like a layer of ice on the surface of a river beneath which the current still ran strong, a skin of calm overlaid the raging terror in Kazan's mind. Even as they walked him to the beach he was casting about for a chance of tricking them.

But none offered itself.

Each of the bullies had his power-gun in his hand, leveled unwavering at Kazan's back; although his feet were unhobbled it would be suicide to run. He had no wish to be cast as a corpse into the lake, food for the monsters. He had still less wish to be cast alive in the water, which seemed the intention. Yet he felt obscurely certain that to stay alive as long as he could must be his immediate purpose.

"Stop there," Axam said from behind him. Obediently Kazan halted, his feet sinking a little into the loose sand. "Hego! Find the steps he made!"

Out of the corner of his eye Kazan saw Hego take a hesitant pace forward, then change his mind. "It's devil's work," he said finally. "I will not."

"Oh, for—!" Axam said, exasperated. He walked forward to the edge of the water and felt about him for a moment; he found solidity and leaned on it. "All right," he said. "Get him down here."

As though to make up for his moment of reluctance, Hego gave Kazan such a blow in the small of the back that it almost knocked him flying. He barely managed to keep his balance as he stumbled forward.

Could he make more steps? How? Already the knowledge was leaking away! Already it was dreamlike and unreal. And in any case he had known how to shape the steps of air only by making certain movements with his hands, which were manacled behind him.

"*Get* up there!" Axam snarled, cuffing the side of his head. "Go on!"

How soon would they dissolve, these steps? Kazan felt a rubberiness under the first foot he placed above the water. Could he break into a run, running on nothing all the way to the fortress in the middle of the lake? Sweat was springing out all over his body now. He had expected that some

32

THE LADDER IN THE SKY

new knowledge would come to his mind and save him. He did not want to die!

"Up!" Axam ordered. "Up—quickly!"

Yes, what they proposed to do was clear. Wait until he had climbed well out over the lake, then fire one silent power-blast, and—an open mouth in the water below. No trace. No hope.

The blood seemed to be draining away from Kazan's head, leaving his mind giddy and empty of ideas. He began to climb numbly, his eyes fascinated by the way the black mirror of the water sometimes broke apart in ripples to reveal a hump-backed shape or a whipping tentacle. Someone had mentioned to him—Yarco, perhaps—that these creatures had lived in many places all over this world before the coming of man, and that this had once been the private hunting lake of the royal family.

Glancing back, he thought he saw one of the bullies raising his power-gun. Perhaps it was a flinching in anticipation of the impact that made him slip; perhaps the step on which he had placed his weight a second earlier was failing faster than the rest; the air sagged beneath him and struggled to be more than air and was only air and he was plummeting headlong to the hungry water, thirty feet below.

In the bright, warm room—sealed utterly from the outer world so that no whisper of sound or ray of light might attract a passer-by—Yarco shivered and shivered again. Now and then his teeth escaped his control and chattered aloud.

From his endless succession of consultations with visitors who came through the door with backward glances and scrutinized the prince carefully before making obeisance, as if suspecting deceit, Luth looked up in irritation.

"For the love of life, Yarco!" he snapped. "Will you keep your foolishness to yourself?"

These matters of how strong sentiment is in such a town, what weapons lie in secret armories . . . Yarco flinched and muttered something which did not carry. Proud beside Luth, Bryda tossed back her dark hair.

THE LADDER IN THE SKY

"What's the matter, you dodderer?" she said. "Speak up if you've anything to say!"

"I feel you have done something evil and dangerous," Yarco said. "The young Kazan—"

"Enough!" Bryda cut in. "Have you not heard before from Hego how he fell to his death, manacled and helpless among the beasts of the lake? What are you afraid of?"

"He made steps in the air," Yarco said.

"And could not make them to save himself," Bryda retorted. But in her fiery eyes Yarco thought he could detect a lurking, shame-faced fear as great as his own. To cover this, she gestured across the room to where Hego stood, his loose-lipped mouth working a little, his huge hands nervously locking and unlocking with each other.

"I keep thinking of a beak like a giant's scissors," Yarco said. "Strong enough to shear through a steel shackle. I keep thinking of a tentacle that could whip a man through the air like a ball batted in a children's game, to land him bruised and panting in soft mud, but alive. I keep thinking of the hate that a man could bear you for condemning him to such a death. And the power that a black devil could give him to wreak his vengeance."

"If there was that power," Prince Luth said, "the devil would have saved him directly, not by this chain of fantasy you've pictured." But his eyes were shadowed. "Go, he said after a pause. "Your mind is wandering."

Yarco pulled his plump body up from his seat. He gave a formal bow to Luth and started towards the door. On the point of leaving, he turned back.

"It will go badly with this plan," he said. "I can feel how the wyrds are working.

"Get out!" Luth roared, half-rising. The door slammed. He sank back in his place, adding with a sidewise glance at Hego, "And no nonsense from you, either. Hear? The man is dead, a worthless Dyasthala thief!"

He went back to his business of available vehicles, codes, signals for action and means of assembling troops. It was not until near morning that he needed Yarco to answer a question for him and sent Hego up the stairs.

So it was Hego who found the stout man, lying back on

the bed which Kazan had used during his stay in this house, a look of frozen terror on his face and a tiny vial of poison clasped with death's rigidity in his plump left hand.

VI

UNDER THE gray sky, the gray people stood passively in a line across the expanse of concrete. The line was meant to be straight, but it bowed a little here and there like a resting snake. Or like a parasitic worm, the intellectual lieutenant thought, because the segments of such a worm could separate and start anew when they found something to sink their hooks into, going over to an ecstasy of ovulation. And this wavering line was splitting, dividing at the head, going this way and that into the parallel sets of prefabricated huts erected along the high wire barriers with the one guarded gate—and even sometimes getting through the gate.

It was the weather, he thought. Coloring his mind the same dismal gray as the sky.

So backward! He had walked twice the whole length of the sullen line, fascinated against his will by the dirt and the raggedness. Some of them lacking *limbs,* for the love of life, when a five-day graft and a course of cell-stimulant was all it took to replace even a leg. And sores dressed with foul rags. And teeth missing. It was a miracle that any of them were allowed through the gate at all.

Still, for the mines on Vashti . . . And after all, they were only cargo to him.

He cast a longing glance backward over his shoulder to the ship resting in its cradle like a squat egg, the planetary insignia of his home world glowing luminous on its nearer side. For all the good he was doing here he could be comfortably in his cabin, playing over that tantalizing not-quite-erotic recording by that new anonymous composer, the one

THE LADDER IN THE SKY

for whom they had made such extravagant and justified claims. Was it a man or a woman who had—?

He sighed. Surely the job wouldn't take long now. But it was a long time since any of the prospective workers had emerged from the examination huts and turned towards the gate. Almost all of them for the last half-hour or so had gone despondently back towards the city, growing smaller like insects as they walked across the concrete with lowered heads.

Eight hundred, they needed. Surely out of all these thousands it wouldn't take long to find eight hundred—even if they were undernourished miserable wrecks.

"How's it going, Major?" a voice behind him said. He half-turned, seeing a large, prosperous man in a temperature suit of dull green and black, his fingers heavy with rings. By his accent, an upper class native of the area.

"Lieutenant, not Major," he corrected. And went on, "Slowly, I'm afraid."

"So I gather, so I gather," the large man said. "Name's Zethel, by the way. Yes, I believe you can only take eight hundred. We're giving you too many to choose from, isn't that it?" he chuckled.

Not wanting to be impolite to this man who might be locally important, the intellectual lieutenant feigned an interest in a subject that he didn't care the fission of a nucleus about.

"There certainly are a lot of applicants," he agreed. "I wouldn't have thought you'd allow so many of them to leave the planet. Not that we're going to complain. Our mines on Vashti won't be automatized for another ten years or so, and we'll need plenty of human labor till they are. But I'm puzzled."

"First time here?" Zethel said. "And only just arrived?"

"Yes to both. All I knew when we touched down was what we were told from home—that there was mercenary labor available in quantity. So we came at once, of course."

Zethel grunted. "Well, let's be honest—you're doing us a favor taking some of 'em off our hands. You aren't going to have an easy time with some of them, I guess. We had a spot of trouble here recently. Maybe you heard about that?"

36

THE LADDER IN THE SKY

The intellectual lieutenant remembered something vague he had caught on a news channel without really paying attention to. He said, frowning, "Some sort of popular revolt?"

"Not so popular," Zethel said. "The last heir of the old ruling house—this island has been an incredible backwater area clinging with crazy doggedness to out-of-date ideas—anyway, this Prince Luth called a revolt against the government, and caused some small disturbance. Nearly ten thousand people were killed and quite a lot of damage was done. We had to divert space traffic to other continents for a period of about a month. Forlorn hope, of course. He was killed by one of his own followers and the movement fell to pieces. There wasn't any real support for it—just a vague mystical aura that stuck to the prince's name. Why should there be? Nobody in his right mind wanted to go back to the days of autocratic monarchy, even here on Berak."

"And these are the followers of this prince?" the lieutenant hazarded. His voice showed some slight interest at last. It was quite like something out of a historical romance, after all. Hereditary titles—why, even on a backward world like this you'd never have expected it. And the mystical influence of royalty.

"Some of them," Zethel said, shrugging. "The healthy ones. The rest are out of the Dyasthala—that's our thieves' quarter."

King of the Beggars, yet. That was an ancient phrase which had once stuck in the lieutenant's mind. His interest brightened still further. He said, "I guess the mystic aura you mentioned would be strong among people like that."

"No, you'd be wrong," Zethel corrected him. "That's what was so curious. It had always been believed that people in the Dyasthala didn't give a damn about who was at the top of the heap, because they were invariably at the bottom. Nonetheless there was a rumor, far too strong to be ignored, that the prince's escape from the place he was held captive—which is a story in itself, I may say; it's acquired overtones of pure legend in a shorter time than you'd think possible—but as I was saying, there were these rumors that his escape

THE LADDER IN THE SKY

had been masterminded by someone from the Dyasthala. Not unreasonable, I suppose. A really skilled professional thief might well be able to steal away a man for once, instead of goods.

"So to teach them a lesson we had the Dyasthala cleared. It was an appalling slum, anyway, and a sink of disease and moral corruption of all kinds. Quite a number of people we managed to hang criminal charges on—theft, mainly, or receiving stolen goods, or debauching children under the age of discretion. Those we put to use ourselves. The rest are out there, mainly. Now that we've cleared the area they used to live in, they haven't anywhere to go, and we're anxious to stop them from sleeping in the streets."

"And did you catch this mysterious personage who—what did you call it?—masterminded the prince's escape?"

"Him? Oh, I doubt whether he really existed," Zethel said. "We had the same more-or-less garbled story from several of the prince's sympathizers, though. Rather puzzling. He's said to have sold himself to an evil being in return for the power to walk on air up to the window of the prince's prison and bring him down again. Then the demon, or devil, or whatever claimed him by throwing him into the lake below. It's colorful, at any rate, isn't it?"

The lieutenant nodded. He was just going to put another question—after all, this would make a story to tell on the trip to Vashti, and when he'd polished the native crudities off it, perhaps even at home during his next furlough—when an orderly came out of the nearest of the examination huts.

"Sergeant presents his compliments, sir," the man said. "Wants a decision from you on a borderline case."

The lieutenant sighed and excused himself. Zethel gave a mechanical smile and moved away.

A tall, lean young man, quite good-looking except for his wolfish expression and lackluster eyes, was standing passive in front of the last table in the examination hut, the one at which the results of all the tests were collated into a whole and the subject accepted or rejected. The lieutenant glanced at him before turning to the sergeant behind the table with

THE LADDER IN THE SKY

his stacks of documents and computing equipment before him.

"What's the problem?" he said.

"Literacy, sir," the sergeant answered. "He passed the physical—here's the assessment: slight traces of deficiency diseases, but nothing serious, and a patch on the lung which can be cured with a day's chemotherapy. Passed the nonverbal section of the intelligence test and checked out at just under the limit. Passed the manual skills tests, the reflex tests and the speed-of-learning tests all within the permitted margins. The tester says he'd show up even better if he'd been fed first. But he can't even write his own name."

"Give me the speed-of-learning results," the lieutenant said. Waiting for them to be handed up, he took another look at the subject. Dirty, of course; his hair probably wasn't that tarnished color when it was clean, if it ever had been clean. But well set up. On the other hand, he must be past his teens. It was hard to judge his age, because of the prematurely ancient dullness in his eyes. Provided he wasn't word-blind, though, he sounded like a good prospect for training.

He riffled through the pages of the speed-of-learning test. There was one test used for illiterates which involved the recognition of quasi-letter shapes. If he'd checked out well on that one—yes, here it was, and he had—then he was acceptable.

"Yes, check him through," he told the sergeant. "Thumbprint his contract on the signature block, and that'll do."

Kazan, not caring in the least what happened to him because he ought by rights to be dead and could not find in himself the desire to live, mechanically obeyed the orders given to him. He had come here in the first place because that was where most of the people from the Dyasthala happened to be going; they had heard of a chance to leave the planet, and because the Dyasthala was a heap of smoking ruins and they had to sleep on the streets they were assembling at the spaceport. He had gone through the tests because they were put to him and he was given orders. His existence was not up to Kazan any longer. Kazan was dead.

THE LADDER IN THE SKY

This was a body operated in his name. Nothing else could account for the fact that he was still—apparently—alive.

The machinelike efficiency with which the applicants were processed suited his frame of mind, moreover. It was good to be organized, directed, measured, weighed, tested, moved from here to there by someone else's decision. He had not had to wonder what to do for several hours, since he joined the line waiting to be examined.

Half a dozen other acceptees were sent out with him to the ship. The processing continued: bathing and delousing; medication; physical measurements; a meal, taken standing in a large cargo hold where every footstep or word spoken above a whisper brought booming metallic echoes; the issue of a kit in exchange for the rags he was wearing, which had once been splendid but which were crusted with mud and blood.

Finally he was being led by a uniformed sergeant down a long corridor into the bowels of the ship. The sergeant had a list in his hand; one by one he allotted members of the group which included Kazan to certain doors off the corridor. Each time a door was opened Kazan had a glimpse of racked bunks beyond, separated head from foot by lockers and side from side by narrow walkways. Each room seemed to have about a dozen bunks.

He was the last to be ordered through a door. The sergeant opened it for him and closed it behind him when he had sidled through with his new kit. Suddenly at a loss because he had no longer any guidance, Kazan looked around him dully. There were four or five others already here—women as well as men—and one of the men was rising slowly to his feet from the bunk on which he had been sitting.

It seemed to Kazan that he remembered this man out of a distant past. Out of a previous life, perhaps. He did not remember the look of sick terror which was now distorting the man's features.

"Kazan!" the man moaned. Kazan gave him a further incurious glance. He nodded and looked for an empty bunk on which to set his gear.

The man seemed to gulp an enormous mouthful of air. As if compelled by something outside himself, he took three rapid paces to close the gap between them and put his big hard hand briefly on Kazan's chest.

"But you can't be here," he said. His voice broke like a child's, and the words were followed by a whimper. Then he spun to face the others present, who were staring puzzled at his extraordinary actions.

"He's dead!" he choked out. "It's his devil that's brought him! He's dead and eaten in the lake by the fortress, and his devil has brought him back! Don't you understand me? That's Kazan, the man Bryda sold to the power of darkness, the man who walked on the air to rescue Prince Luth! He's a dead man walking, I tell you! Get out of here!"

He was barely in time to lead the rush from the door.

VII

CAPTAIN OGRIC halted abruptly in his tracks. From somewhere in the belly of the ship was coming such a clashing and banging one would have thought a herd of wild animals was coming aboard instead of a collection of raggedy, underfed migrant workers. He had been on his way to dine with the port commandant, a traditional act of courtesy the last night before a ship lifted for space.

But at the racket which he heard, he turned aside and began to stride down a corridor in the direction from which the cries and crashes came.

Rounding a corner, he went full tilt into his master-at-arms, who jumped back with a cry of dismay and threw up a smart salute. Captain Ogric, who was known as White Dwarf to his crew because of his small size and illimitable energy, fixed him with a glare.

"For the love of life, what's going on?" he demanded.

"Beginning of a riot in the workers' quarters, sir," the master-at-arms said. "We're penning it up as much as we

THE LADDER IN THE SKY

can, but there seems to be some superstitious reason at the bottom of it which they're more scared of than they are of my men. A small group of them turned out of the cabin allotted because they said they wouldn't share it with another man who was just sent aboard. Claim he's a zombie, or something—say he's a dead man walking. Some local cult, I guess.

"We took out the man who started the trouble, a big bully called Hego—white as a sheet, practically wetting himself with raw terror. You never saw anything like it, sir! I thought I'd avoid further trouble by transferring the so-called 'dead man' to another cabin, but the word got around, and half of them are saying they won't fly in the same ship as him. Want to break out of the ship and go back to the city."

"Ugly?" the captain rapped.

"Quiet at the moment. But rumbling. Like a volcano." The master-at-arms wiped sweat off his forehead. "I was just going to send down to the examination huts for Lieutenant Balden."

Ogric kept his face from showing his feelings, but he made a mental note to remind Lieutenant Balden privately that when he was put in charge of getting a batch of workers aboard, that didn't mean lounging at the barrier gate and eyeing the women among them. But he wasted only a moment on that. In the forefront of his mind was what the port commandant had told him when he first landed and went to present his compliments.

"I wish you joy of them," the port commandant had said. "But I'll tell you what your advertising is going to bring in—the dirtiest bunch of thieves and cutthroats who ever disgraced this continent. They'll come out of the Dyasthala, the thieves' slum in the city which they cleared the other day about half a century after the job fell due. I guess your only advantage is that none of them will trust any of the others out of sight, so you won't have the danger of them organizing mutiny. But you'd best make the trip a fast one to Vashti—or I wouldn't put it past them to conceive the idea of taking over your ship and setting up as pirates."

THE LADDER IN THE SKY

Was it starting before they'd lifted for space?

Ogric wished profoundly that he could simply turn the lot of them back on the ground and go somewhere else for his workers. But he was in government service, and under orders to supply willing labor for the Vashti mines, so he'd have to make the best of it.

"All right!" he said, making up his mind. "Hold the rest of the intake in the hold where they're being fed. Close off all the corridors leading out of the workers' quarters. Get Lieutenant Balden to sort out the zombie, the man who started it, and anyone else he thinks, or you think, might put us in the picture, and have them up in my cabin in half an hour. And get the workers calmed down. And send a man to the port commandant with my compliments and tell him I'll be late for dinner. Got that?"

"Aye, sir," the master-at-arms said, and doubled away.

"He's a what?" the intellectual lieutenant said, sounding rather bored, when the master-at-arms came panting with the message.

"Sold to a devil, they say. And they're so scared of him they'd rather go back to starvation than ship to Vashti with him even with their contracts worth twenty thousand."

A horrifying memory clicked in the lieutenant's mind. He straightened up as though he had been kicked at the base of the spine and stared wildly around for Zethel. But there was no sign of the big man.

Sold to a devil? And supposed to be dead? It couldn't really be the original of the story. But if even the government authorities of Berak had taken the notion seriously enough to clear out the thieves' quarter and thus risk spreading some thousands of the criminal class all over their city, then who could say what the illiterate superstitious might not make of it? He had to swallow hard before he could trust his voice; then he barked at the master-at-arms to come with him back to the ship and show him where the trouble was.

The corridors in the workers' quarters were lined with anxious faces peering out of the doors. Some of the bolder ones had emerged despite the threat of men armed with gas-

THE LADDER IN THE SKY

guns at every intersection, and were warily eying each other as though none of them was sure who the "dead man" really was.

Lieutenant Balden halted nervously, looking down the corridor where the trouble had begun. In a low voice he spoke to the master-at-arms.

"Tell them I'm coming to put this thing right," he said. "Promise them there'll be no trouble."

The master-at-arms shouted the message ringingly down the corridor. It had no visible effect, except that some of the men and women in the passage drew back into nearby rooms. A dry feeling in his throat, the lieutenant allowed the master-at-arms to lead him forward.

Before the last door in the corridor they pasued. "I think he's still in here," the master-at-arms said, leaning on the panel and sliding it aside. "Yes. That's him."

"Him?" the lieutenant echoed in surprise. He stepped forward involuntarily. Yes, it was definitely the pale-haired, old-young man he had seen at the examination hut. And come to think of it, there had been a dead look in his eyes.

He choked the idea off firmly. Glancing around the cabin, he saw gear belonging to about four or five other people scattered on the bunks. And one other person besides the pale-haired young man—a girl, about the same age, with plain untidy brown hair cut irregularly short, her freshly scrubbed face rather attractive and heavily freckled across the nose and cheekbones, her mouth full and almost pouting. She was taking garments out of the bag in which they had been issued to her and stowing them in a locker, as calm as could be.

The pale-haired young man, on the other hand, was doing nothing at all but staring into space.

"You!" Balden said. "Are you the cause of all this trouble? Are you the man that everyone's saying is possessed of a devil?"

The lackluster eyes turned to look at him. The head gave a forward dip that might have been a stillborn nod.

"The name's Kazan," the master-at-arms supplied. "Anonymous orphan; that's his whole name."

THE LADDER IN THE SKY

"Kazan!" Balden said. "What's it all about? What started this nonsense about you being back from the dead?"

"I am," Kazan said in a rustling voice, and went on staring into space.

Helpless, Balden hesitated a moment and then switched his attention to the girl. "You there!" he said. "What's your name?"

"Clary," she answered. "That's my whole name, too."

"Were you here when this began?"

"Yes."

"Why didn't you run with the rest of them, then?"

She raised burning eyes to him. They were a little sunken in her face, as though she had been undernourished for a long time. She said with a touch of scorn, "The man who started it was a lumbering fool called Hego, with much more muscle than brain and less guts. I'm from the Dyasthala. I don't believe in devils. And anyone with an eye in his head could see that *he* isn't any more dead than I am. Feel him—he's warm. He's got a pulse. Hego must be insane."

The master-at-arms said puzzledly, "If he is crazy, sir, how come he got through the examinations?"

It crossed Balden's mind wildly that a parallel question might be, "If Kazan is dead, how did *he* get past?" But he pulled himself together before he voiced the words. He said, "All right, both of you. Come with me. We'll take you up to the captain and get it straightened out."

His impatience mounting visibly, like a needle on a dial ascending towards the red danger mark, Ogric listened to Hego, then to Balden's gloss on the story, quoted from Zethel, then to the master-at-arms, Clary, and four other workers who said they also knew the story, chosen from at least a hundred.

Halfway through the fourth confirmatory recitation, Ogric slammed his open palm on the arm of his chair with a sound like a firecracker and bounced to his feet.

"Enough!" he barked. "I never heard anything like it! A walking corpse! Devils! Miracles! Lunacy, all of it—half comet-dust and half nightmares! You there sitting like a booby in the corner—what's your name, Kazan! You've

45

THE LADDER IN THE SKY

listened to this garbage about your coming back from the dead. What have you got to say about it?"

Kazan shrugged. He didn't seem very interested. He said, "You heard what Hego said. It's quite true. They threw me in the lake with my hands manacled."

"Then how by the blaze of Sirius did you get out alive?" Ogric demanded.

A curious look crossed Kazan's face. He said, "I—I think something bit through the manacles. And something took hold of me, and another creature attacked it, and I found myself in the mud on the beach."

From Hego, standing by the door with his face sheet-white, a groan like a dying man's. He could not tear his fascinated gaze from Kazan, not even to blink.

"Quiet, you!" Ogric ordered. He drove fist into palm. "Well, the answer's simple enough. We'll put him back on the ground, since most of these idiots won't ship with him, and we can better afford to lose one man than hundreds."

"Did he sign the same contract I signed?" Clary said. Her small face seemed to have set like stone, and her eyes burned more fiercely than ever.

"What?" Ogric snapped.

"I can read," Clary said. "The contract I signed was solid as rock. Bound you, as well as me. I have my eye on cash at the time when I think about marrying. Did you ask *him* whether he wants to dissolve the contract? Or do I go back down with the rest of the workers and tell them the contracts they've signed are so much wrapping paper?"

Ogric lowered himself into his chair again, staring at her. He said, "What's your interest in this, young woman?"

"None, specially." She shrugged. "Except I don't like fools" —she shot a contemptuous glance at Hego—"and I don't like seeing people made fools of."

Balden cleared his throat. He said, "If I could make a suggestion, Captain—"

Ogric spun his chair to face the lieutenant. In a frosty voice suggesting he didn't think the suggestion would be worth hearing, he said, "Yes?"

"I saw this man's test results. He'd be worth keeping anyway as valuable material to train for a responsible job. We've got one worker here—this girl Clary—who scoffs at the superstitious nature of the others. We can probably find enough to fill, or partly fill, one of the cabins. Then we can persuade the rest by playing on their greed or by shaming them that they're being foolish. The Vashti pull isn't too long from here."

"Any pull with this situation stewing aboard the ship would be too long," Ogric growled. "But the proposal seems sensible enough. Come to think of it, if anyone might well be put on the ground again, it's this shivering idiot Hego. But no doubt you, young woman"—he gave an ironical half-bow to Clary—"would have something to say about that as well."

Clary returned his gaze evenly. "You wouldn't be making a fool of him," she said. "He's been one since birth, looks like."

Ogric couldn't help it. He chuckled. "You've a head on your shoulders," he said approvingly. "Let's see if there's something in it. You're going to see if you can find ten more like yourself among these silly workers, who'll have the sense you've shown—and if you do it, there's a bonus for you on top of your contract pay."

VIII

No one could have said whether it was the struggle between superstitious fear and simple greed, or merely Dyasthala cunning, which in the end compelled Ogric to promise a contract bonus to those workers who agreed to share quarters with Kazan as well as to Clary herself for finding them. There were going to be some pointed questions asked when he presented the accounts for this trip; still, he'd got off lighter than if he'd been obliged to honor the forfeiture clause in one of the contracts, or if he'd lost half the workers

THE LADDER IN THE SKY

already signed up and had to hold back his departure while he hunted down some replacements.

In fact, it had not occurred to Clary to suggest to those she approached the idea of holding out for a bonus like hers. It wasn't in the frame of reference of Dyasthala thinking. The reason she had sprung to Kazan's aid in the captain's cabin was because she and he both were opposed to authority—it wasn't out of sympathy. The offer of the bonus, certainly, had worked in her case very well; without it she would never have argued so persuasively with the reluctant workers.

And it was clear that she wasn't completely successful. That could be seen from the way the new occupants of the cabin hesitated when they came through the door for the first time, looking about them, seeing Kazan, being only slightly reassured on finding Clary calmly sitting on the next bunk to his. And it went on as it had begun. None of the others spent any more time than they had to in Kazan's company, and often during the sleep period a light would go on, and one of the people in the cabin would lean over the side of the bunk and stare down at Kazan as though to make sure he was genuinely asleep and not dead.

At first Clary had viewed these goings-on with real scorn. In her mind she classed Hego with the foolish but wealthy people who had sometimes sent into the Dyasthala to consult the so-called witches and wizards there. Everyone in the thieves' quarter knew that their trances and oracles, their illusions and their speaking with tongues, were just another way of parting rich folk from their money, rating somewhere on the criminal scale between confidence trickery and the disguising of stolen goods for resale.

Then it gradually dawned on her, first, that many of what she regarded as her own people seemed to have caught the contagious fear of Kazan; second, that Kazan himself—aside from confirming Hego's story in the captain's presence, which could be discounted—had never said anything one way or the other.

This was alarming.

Kazan, indeed, appeared not to be in the least involved in what went on around—and often because of—him. It seemed to make no difference that for the duration of the voyage

THE LADDER IN THE SKY

he was the key person aboard the ship. When he was not required for some duty or other, or to collect his thrice-daily rations in the workers' canteen, he lay on his bunk, staring at the underside of the bunk above. It occurred to Clary at last that he might as well have been really dead. He was dead in his mind.

She'd seen cases like that in the Dyasthala. They were everywhere. But at first she could not associate the pale, calm, rather handsome Kazan with the slack-lipped and filthy idiots who could be found in the old days playing with the gutter mud of the thieves' quarters, sometimes seizing a bright coin tossed to them with a little chuckle of pleasure at such a gaudy plaything—and usually losing it again to a child of normal intelligence who knew how to trade it for some worthless but glittering scrap of colored glass.

Long experience in handling random-gathered groups of migrant workers had developed a system in the fleet of ships serving the Vashti mines. Though Ogric had spoken dismally of any voyage as being too long with a problem like Kazan aboard, in fact the tension was kept under control by fairly simple means. Keep the minds of the workers occupied, was the prime rule.

Hence during every arbitrary day there was a training class in the canteen, to teach some administrative job, or to put a shine on the reading ability of those who possessed it. There were also many entertainments—by the standard of the crew's home world, very crude, but to the children of the Dyasthala and in fact to most of the other workers new and interesting. As a result, Kazan was often left by himself in the cabin, staring at nothing.

That gave Clary her chance.

She slid back the door-panel almost silently and stepped through as though afraid of being heard, then closed it with equal care. No one was present except Kazan, who lay as usual flat on his back, his vacant eyes on the bunk over him. There were folding seats clipped to the walls. Clary took one of these gently from its place and opened it as she walked to the side of Kazan's bunk.

Then she slammed it down on the floor with a crash that

THE LADDER IN THE SKY

made the metal of the cabin ring angrily, and sat on it. Even that barely disturbed the mirror surface of Kazan's calm.

"All right," she said when he had rolled his head incuriously to look at her. "Out with it, Kazan. Who are you?"

As simply as that, it began.

For that question was the key to the nightmare haunting him—a darkness populated with hungry monsters, in which his mouth, open to scream, filled with sour water and the taste of the beasts around, in which his ears were deafened first by a rasping hoot rising towards a whistle, then by a rush of water. A struggle against cruel steel shackles holding his wrists, so that he could not even strike out against the huge threatening creatures that shared the darkness with him.

That was the beginning. What followed was that the darkness took a shape—a vague, formless, ill-defined shape with ember eyes. He seemed to be outside it and inside it at the same time, for he could look at it and still be engulfed by it.

The remorseless argument that went with the macabre images fell too readily into words. Kazan had gone to his death. Kazan manacled and helpless who had forgotten the trick of making steps of air had plunged into the lake and been swallowed up.

But Kazan had also been sold to a devil by human devils who had not asked his leave, and the devil had taken him out of the clutch of death to serve for a year and a day. Kazan accordingly was dead. Let the devil move the corpse as he would, Kazan could have no part in it.

Yet, he was still aware. He could remember things, foggily, as he had remembered that he knew Hego. He had no sense of discontinuity except the break between the moment when he was seized by the thing in the black water, and the moment he realized he had been flung on to a patch of soft mud beside the lake, and aside from his bruises and the sickness the foul water had brought on him was unhurt. He could even remember the click which he had felt rather than heard when the vast cruel beak made its first stab at him and severed the steel cuffs linking his wrists. He could even remember that the end of the beak was rough, and had

50

THE LADDER IN THE SKY

rasped the skin of his back, and torn a hole in his fine black shirt with the silver piping, so that afterwards the thermostatic circuitry did not work.

Or perhaps the water had put it out of action.

Was he Kazan, saved by a combination of miracles? Or was he the puppet of a black being with eyes like coals?

"Who are you, Kazan?"

That fresh-faced girl insisting that he answer—he could hate her for voicing the question, he could pound her to a sack of bones in blue-bruised skin because he had wished to do that to Bryda and her sneering lover, the prince. He had come from the shore of the lake driven by only that lasting hatred out of all the many desires which once had motivated him as Kazan. He had been cheated, as they informed him much later.

Some of that part was blurred, too. Could the break have come there? No, for when he set his mind to it and concentrated he knew there was, in fact, no break.

Only his mind flinched away from some of the happenings at that time. The memories blended and ran into each other, like wet colors laid too closely side by side. The burning of the Dyasthala, the laying low of the buildings with crackling violence, and the people swarming out like insects from a disturbed nest—was it then that he had suffered the beating? Or was that when he went hunting for Bryda and Luth, and they took him for a madman and wanted to put him in a hospital, misled by his fine clothes into thinking he was one of the haughty? Then, the quality of what he wore showed despite the soaking in the filthy lake. Later he was dressed as he had been for most of his life—in rags. And a stink of himself.

Part of that picture ran off in its turn into a vision of the fine big room, and himself in front of the mirror, admiring garments he had demanded as the price of doing—what? No one could believe that he, Kazan, had carved steps out of the air and brought Prince Luth down them from prison. Not even Kazan could believe that. The devil did it. Using the body named Kazan. The vision of the mirror and himself so smartly clothed ran into a blurred picture of his rags and dirt, sometimes before his encounter with Bryda and the

THE LADDER IN THE SKY

conjurer, sometimes after, at the time when he went with the rest to join the gray line on the gray concrete under the gray sky because in some obscure manner he had understood that this was a means of escape.

And last of all the vision of himself changed to a black, ill-defined shape which gazed into the mirror with eyes like dying coals.

That was the point where he started to scream.

Unnerved by the suddenness of his tortured cry, Clary leapt back from his side, upsetting the stool on which she had been sitting. Her face going pale, she listened and watched for as long as she could endure it. Some of the things that poured out made her mouth work and forced her to close her eyes for long seconds together.

Then, when she could stand no more, she hurled herself at the door and clawed it open. She fled incontinently down the corridor.

At the barrier between the crew's quarters and those of the worker-cargo, she hammered till a spaceman came in answer. Seeing her, he immediately made to slam the barrier into place again; a worker had no business bothering the crew. He just had time to regret so doing.

Panting, Clary stood over his unconscious form. She hoped she hadn't hit him too hard. A blow to the vocal cords was dangerous, and could easily kill. But it was his own fault, for not realizing that a weak-looking girl in the Dyasthala could not possibly have been weak, or she would never have survived her teens.

She had no idea which way to go now she was in the crew's area of the ship. She could see only more corridors. The ship was riddled with them, like a piece of old and worm-infested wood. Things were rather more luxurious here, but to a Dyasthala thief gradations like that were of small importance. At random she decided which way to go, and broke into a stumbling run.

By a chance which later she looked back on as a small miracle, the first crewman she encountered since the misguided man who had tried to slam the barrier in her face was the only officer she had seen before except the captain. Catching sight of him fifty paces distant down a corridor that she crossed, she shouted at him and he turned. He recognized her at once. After a glance behind him, seeming nervous, he began to walk towards her.

"What is it?" he said. "And what are you doing in this part of the ship, anyway?"

"Have you got a doctor in this—this flying mantrap?" she flung at him.

Balden blinked. Again he glanced behind him, as though hoping someone would come to his aid. He said, "Ah—yes, we do have doctors aboard."

"Then you'd better get one of them down to Kazan quick," Clary said. "He's sick in the head. That's what's been the trouble all along. What difference does it make whether his devil was real or not, if he thinks it was real? And"—her face twisted suddenly with remembered disgust—"he thinks it was real. By the wyrds, he thinks it was real!"

IX

WHEN THE white-coated young doctor brought Kazan back to the boundary of the crew's and workers' quarters two ships' days later, Clary was waiting for him. He seemed to be in a daze, but it could be seen at once that something had happened to change him. He walked as though he meant it, was the way Clary summed it up to herself, instead of going with a kind of indefinable reluctance.

The doctor nodded to her. "You must be Clary," he said. "Well, here he is. All yours."

"How is he?" Clary demanded. "What was wrong with him?"

"Interesting case," the doctor said with a trace of professional warmth. "I'm not absolutely sure what happened to him, of course. There hasn't been very much time, but what I think is that this narrow escape from death he had sent

THE LADDER IN THE SKY

him into a sort of fugue. The lack of affect was typical, and he had incomplete amnesia—rejection of unpleasant memories. I see this doesn't mean very much to you, though. Get him to talk to you about it himself, then. He has all his memory back now, and it's up to him to make his own kind of sense out of it. You're his girl?"

"Not that I've noticed," Clary said.

The doctor looked her up and down in a way that was not at all professional. A glint of humor showed in his eyes. He said, "He must have been in a worse way than I thought. Well, he'll get another check before we hit Vashti, and I'll have a word with the base doctor—show him my records. But he ought to be okay from now on."

He raised his hand and stepped back while the barrier was pushed into place again. Clary found herself thinking that he was rather nice.

She turned away and found Kazan studying her as though seeing her for the first time. His eyes had come alive in his face now, as if his mind had been brought out from under a cloud. He said, "I feel a lot different. Thank you."

The moment she heard his voice she too had a feeling that this was a first meeting. Unaccountable embarrassment made her glance down at the floor; she saw herself make a childlike movement with one foot, as she might have dug her toe into the ground a long way away in the Dyasthala. She muttered, "Well, I didn't do anything."

"Thanks anyway," he countered.

She hesitated. Then the urgent need to know what had come of this startling change in him caught hold of her. She gestured down the corridor. "Everyone is at the class in the canteen," she said. "Come and tell me what they did to you, and what really caused your trouble."

A few moments later they were sitting facing each other in the empty cabin and Kazan was leaning back and looking with a puzzled expression at a spot on the far wall.

"What they did to me," he said. "That—well, I'm not sure. The doctor tried to tell me, but I didn't get most of it." A frustrated note crept into his voice. "He said something about selective stimulation of the brain. They put something over my head, and I went through all the things that were

THE LADDER IN THE SKY

bothering me in a sort of slow motion so I had the chance to pick out what was real and what wasn't. It didn't hurt, but some of the things made me *sweat*."

"But you know why you were in the mess you'd got into?" Clary pressed him.

"That, yes." Kazan rubbed his hands together thoughtfully. "Do I have to tell you about the lake, and the rest of that?"

Clary shook her head quickly. She said, "I heard that just —just before I went to get the doctor to you. It was horrible."

"That's so. But—well, see it like this. I came to on the mudbank by the lake, and just about all I could feel was that I was full of hate. To my ears I was full of it. I didn't care about that dustbrain Hego, or the other one who helped to put me in the lake, Axam. It was Bryda I was after, and her sneering Prince Luth. I was going after them. I was going to sell out Luth's proposed revolt, first of all. But that was too remote to satisfy me. Short of throwing him and Bryda in the lake where they'd thrown me, I wanted to see them die some other way. A good, ugly way."

Clary tried not to shudder, and failed. There was still acid venom in Kazan's voice when he spoke of Bryda and Luth.

"Well, it would take too long to tell you everything that got in my way. The thing that finished it was simple. Luth had this man Yarco serving him—a good guy, that I might have liked if I hadn't met him the way I did. Yarco had been lost on a bet before he was born to the prince's father, and he'd spent fifty years of life pledged to the royal family, never free to lift a finger for himself. And the night I was put in the lake Yarco killed himself. Word got around. It was held to be a bad omen. So when the prince's revolt started to go wrong, someone close to him decided to cut his losses and poisoned him. I don't know what happened to Bryda. Maybe the same.

"You see, the only thing which had been driving me since I got up off the mud by the lake was my need to get even with Luth. I lost the chance. I got the idea into my head

THE LADDER IN THE SKY

that I should have been dead anyway. So I acted as dead as I could, I guess."

"How did they get you out of it?" Clary said.

Kazan shrugged. "Just made me see I was being a fool. I don't know about that devil yet—and what seems crazy, I know for sure now that I didn't dream about making the steps in the air. I really did that, and not even what the doctor put me through made me remember how I worked the trick. It doesn't worry the doctor; he just said it was a quasi-real memory, whatever that means, and would take a long time to set right, but it wouldn't worry me badly any more. Because he made me see the important thing."

"Which is—?"

"That it was me, and not any devil, that got me out of the lake alive. He said some of it was sheer luck, but the rest was myself. He explained how sometimes under stress your mind will go into overdrive, and you'll do things that will get you out of trouble without having to waste time on figuring them through beforehand. He made me see that the way my manacles were bitten through was the result of my desperately trying to get away from the monster's beak. And the way I got thrown on shore was a result of the monster trying to get a tasty morsel—me—out of reach of a competitor."

"You're not satisfied with that, are you?" Clary said in an even voice.

There was a long silence. Kazan stared at her, a haunted look coming and going behind his eyes. He said at last, "No. How could you tell?"

"You sound as though you're trying to convince yourself," she answered.

He got to his feet and began to pace back and forth in the narrow limits of the walkway between the bunks. "The doctor did warn me," he said after three turns. "But he said what counted was that now I've started to think that I can do something about it again, instead of just refusing to face it because it was too big for me."

"You've certainly made a start on that," Clary said, wanting to reassure him. "But something is still worrying you."

"Yes, this devil, that's all. Because if the devil was a clever conjuring trick to delude Bryda, then I didn't make the steps in the air. I couldn't have. But Hego was there and saw me do it. Many people saw me. And if the devil was real—"

He broke off and sat down, his face going pale.

"What?" she prompted.

"Then I'm pledged to it for a year and a day," Kazan said in a dull voice.

She rose from her place opposite him and sat down beside him, putting her arm round his shoulders in a comforting gesture. She said, "Kazan, why don't you just think it out? Do you feel that this—this devil is doing anything to you? Haven't you been shown that your own actions can account for what's happened? Surely if you can't find any difference in yourself then that's the same as there being no difference."

"I guess so," he said wearily, putting his palms up to rub at his eyes in a quick tired gesture.

"What did the doctor say about that?"

"Pretty much what you've said. Tell you the trouble, though. There's one man I'd have liked to ask about it, and I can't, because he's dead. That was Yarco. He used to sort of hint at the way he felt, never having been his own master. He used to talk about the decree of the wyrds, and about our being at the mercy of the stars. It seemed to make sense to him. It explained his life for him. But I never took the opportunity of talking about it with him, and now I never can."

Clary was silent for a moment, frowning. She felt frustrated. Her mind wasn't used to coping with such abstract problems as these—the nature of possession if there was such a thing, of human destiny, of free will and bondage. She could get an intuitive grasp of the way Kazan must be suffering, but she could not hold on to the concepts long enough to show in words that she understood. But there was something frightening about his predicament, she could tell that, and she was moved to do the only thing she could, which was to show her sympathy.

She said awkwardly, "It seems to me you could think yourself into his place. It doesn't seem all that different from

THE LADDER IN THE SKY

having been born in the Dyasthala, to me. That was a weight, too. I made up my mind when I was just a kid that I was going to get out of the Dyasthala, and I worked at it. Learned to read. Learned to count. Took whatever I could whenever I could that looked as if it might come in useful to get me out of there. I'd looked at all the people who didn't make it. I didn't want to end like them. Know what I mean?"

Kazan turned his head and after a moment's pause nodded.

"But I guess I wouldn't ever have made it," she went on in a lower voice. "Not if they hadn't cleared the whole quarter and made us get out. There were always too many problems. There was always the one you couldn't figure out before you ran into it, because it wasn't part of the Dyasthala's world. And those were the problems you didn't get the chance to tackle a second time, so it wasn't any good learning from your first mistake."

"I do know what you mean," Kazan said. He leaned his elbows on his knees. "Is that why you signed on to work on Vashti?"

"Well—somewhat. But there was the man I was living with, too—the man who taught me to read. He thought he was going to live off me, and I didn't."

Kazan nodded. He didn't need details.

"And you?" Clary said.

"Why did I join the line to sign on, you mean? Oh, mostly I went because that was where people from the Dyasthala were going. I had this crazy notion out of fear. I was going back into the Dyasthala because people have always gone there to hide, and I guess I hoped in the back of my mind that the devil couldn't trace me there. Same reason took me out to the spaceport with the rest. Maybe the devil couldn't follow me off the planet. But that was a crazy hope, of course."

Something in his tone alerted Clary. She said sharply, "What do you mean?"

"When the conjurer called up the devil inside his ring," Kazan said slowly, "the first thing the devil said was, 'What world is this?' And the conjurer said something in reply. I

THE LADDER IN THE SKY

thought it was a charm to control the devil. But I heard it pretty clearly, it turned out, and the doctor was able to make me remember it even though I didn't understand it. He recorded it and played it to me, and said that it was a set of stellar co-ordinates. Like an address, he said. The conjurer was actually telling the devil what world he had come to and where it lay in the galaxy."

He shivered; she felt it all up the arm she had laid across his shoulders.

"If you want to look at it that way," she said, "it's a pretty poor devil that has to be told where it's come to. I think you're right in hoping that it can't follow you to Vashti. How's it to know where you've gone?"

He shook his head. "No, you don't understand," he said in a hopeless voice. "I was pledged for a year and a day, and only a couple of months have gone by. The problem isn't: how would it know where I've gone? It's how am *I* to know what it meant by service, and how do I know that I'm not already serving it by going to Vashti? Maybe it wanted me on Vashti!"

When Clary could offer no answer, he got to his feet. A crooked smile lit his face, which reassured her a little. He said, "Of course, I know the only thing to do is to wait and see. And a year and a day isn't long anyway. Whatever the doctor did for me, he at least seems to have given me the guts to sweat it out. And you're helping me too, you know."

Clary met his eyes steadily. After a moment she said, "I'm very glad. I really am very glad indeed."

X

FOR KAZAN, that was to be born—into this curious self-contained traveling world which was the ship, the thing by definition going somewhere and yet as it vibrated through the dark spaces carrying ignorance within itself, in the skulls of the travelers. The ship was enclosed. It was still, so far as anyone aboard could tell; even the engineers who controlled it never directly perceived its motion, but read dials emotionlessly. To Kazan this was a parable of himself. A journey undertaken in a womb, like a mother bearing her foetus unknowing, beginning at the familiar Berak spaceport and ending soon on Vashti.

A word. A label without an object. A scrap of tacky paper clinging to the fingers against attempts to throw it away.

Here, there had to be the start of an understanding of himself. To accept was not enough if he had to wrestle with the central problem: is Kazan Kazan or is he a black devil? They had said, "He is highly intelligent." He began now to realize what the word meant, because it applied itself to his worries. It wasn't the Dyasthala comment: "He's sharp." That was a business of assessing risk, of knowing how best to organize a pattern of action centered on a clothman's store, or a drunken spaceman, so that it ended with safety and anonymity and a handful of cash instead of the impersonal retribution of the law.

In the Dyasthala, Kazan's world: hunger yesterday, fullness today, randomly. The belly had no chance to build its own clock. Time was different. The wakening into the world of the ship, so arbitrary—like being *inside* a clock, because the passage of time was totally controlled—was another difference to add to others. Emergent, the new Kazan chose this fact for a centerpole of personality, thinking of Yarco and his sighing resignation to the decree of the wyrds. He would still have liked to talk to Yarco about his situation, but not to learn more of Yarco's way of adapting; now, to try and make him see that it was not universally applicable.

The Kazan of the Dyasthala (curious, that Clary should have seen the same parallel as he, between Yarco's state of bondage and the invisible bonds tying down inhabitants of the Dyasthala!) had been tempted by Yarco's philosophy. The Kazan of the ship was not. It was clear to him from looking around that men could organize the events they ex-

THE LADDER IN THE SKY

perienced. What he had to do was make himself believe that he was the organizer, and that was difficult.

A creature hatched from an egg, he thought, would be in his condition. In the egg it was certainly—for at least a little while—living and aware. It could be heard to move for a time before it cracked or tore open the shell or tough integument about it. Already it was in a sense independent, before it came out. He also. Not as a womb-born child. For him this would come later, perhaps, after landing on Vashti, with the opening of the ship, which would be soon.

Meantime he had to wrestle in his mind, and fanatical urgency stemming from the shortness of the time till the shell opened on Vashti created for him the exact reverse of the dull apathy he had shown when he came aboard. He had to know. He had to know his past as much as his present.

The Dyasthala: the cracked walls and the tilted flagstones of the streets, the smells and sights and sounds. List them, and they were not pretty. They were smells of rotting garbage, which was not garbage in the Dyasthala so long as anyone could conceive any use at all for it, and of the people who found such uses and descended to them. They were sights of children in gutters and parents in rags. They were sounds of screams, from pain or from hate.

The heritage Kazan carried with him into his new existence was compounded of that, and his need to be himself. He had to work hardest of all at being himself, because he was so frightened of being a black devil instead.

Who was anybody? He took to staring curiously at the other workers, sometimes without their noticing for long minutes together as they attended to some small task or relaxed, eyes closed, wondering: what is in that person which makes him, or her, *not me?* There would be a clue to himself there, perhaps. And again he had to spend time feverishly working over the Dyasthala memories, the memories of the period of parturition, the memories of the new and vivid self, which seemed to be lit from within by a powerful lamp.

Merely to be able to categorize his existence in that way —as a sentient egg-born creature might categorize his into intra-ovular preconscious, intra-ovular conscious, and extra-

THE LADDER IN THE SKY

ovular—led him to views of being which he could not before have found the mental strength to handle.

Still he lacked words for much of what occurred to him; among his fellow workers were some whose education had gone beyond an elementary level and he cornered these and sweated out for them a set of verbal parameters defining the thing he wanted to name and had no word for, while they cowered back and flinched and shot glances from side to side, seeking a way of escape. Often they gave him words; often they could not. He made the best of what they offered. Fixation. Conditioning. Instinctual. Subconscious. Logic. Intellectual. Whether he attached the handles to precisely the right concepts didn't matter. At least he had something to take hold of in his mind.

The effect of this on the workers was to create dismay. Just when they had shamed themselves into seeing that the object of their superstitious fear was an apathetic and harmless being who hardly offered a word even when spoken to, and never any violent act, he turned to this baffling dynamic person who did not seem able to find time even for sleep, but must always be demanding knowledge of themselves, how they thought, why they thought as they did, what they thought about life and awareness, problems that few of them had ever considered and none of them could discuss.

His whole world had opened out again, like a shell being cracked. It was as it had been when Bryda had him taken to the shore of the sour-water lake, and he had known discomfort because he was out of sight of buildings. His perspectives had broadened in a day—from the Dyasthala to the whole of Berak then, and knowledge that human affairs could transcend such business as he had learned in the Dyasthala; from that hesitant halfway stage now, to a burgeoning concept of the stars. It was painful in a way, but it was necessary and sometimes it was also exciting.

He was intelligent, they had told him. This was what it meant to be intelligent: not to close in the universe around oneself for comfort and reassurance, but to have the itch in the brain which demanded return again and again to insoluble problems. Who? What? Why? How? The archetypal simplicity of basic questions astonished him. It had never

THE LADDER IN THE SKY

struck him before that the simpler a question the more general it is, and hence the more complete the answer it demands. All this from wondering how he could tell whether he was Kazan or a black devil acting in Kazan's name!

Like firecrackers spitting tiny red sparks in darkness, a succession of memories crackled in his head. Bryda, throwing back her dark hair scornfully—she had been very beautiful, no denying—and being afraid of what she had brought about, afraid of the gutter-born thief on whose shoulders she had shifted a burden she dared not carry herself, and who mocked her by displaying a power that could have been hers had she not lacked courage. That was clear at once. She had wished Luth free not for any love she bore him—because gratitude then would have made her repay him, Kazan—but for the hope of regaining some lost power and position in the state. In Kazan she had seen a rival with good cause to hate her. So she had ordered him disposed of. He could almost pity her now.

And back beyond Bryda and everything that she had stabbed into the flesh of his life like a bright dagger were the people of the Dyasthala that he had known, not in friendship—for hunger was the eternal enemy who could split the fondest allies—but objectively, as those parts of his environment who were characterized by the ability to move and communicate. A certain woman with a scrofulous head who had kept a dirty bakery; a youth who, when Kazan was ten or twelve years old, had made himself the joyous subject of all the Dyasthala gossip by getting himself enrolled on someone else's birth record into the law force, so that by day he was the guardian of the city, and by night plundered it. He had had the first power-gun Kazan ever saw.

He had killed himself with it the day his confidence overreached itself and he was discovered for what he was.

These pawns of circumstance! These people who *must* have shared with his new self the power to ask questons and organize events, but to whom simple material problems were the equal of the bonds holding Yarco! Clary had said that but for the clearing of the Dyasthala and the compulsion to find somewhere else to go, she who had dreamed all her adolescent life of getting out, and had taken

THE LADDER IN THE SKY

the dream seriously enough to sell her body in exchange for being taught to read and count, would never have actually gone.

True. Why?

Once he went to the barrier at the entry to the crew's quarters, and there hammered till he was answered, and asked to talk with the doctor who had treated him. He was allowed that much, and out of curiosity Lieutenant Balden also came to the doctor's office, and for the better part of an hour he fumbled through some of the ideas obsessing him.

But Balden grew bored quickly, and gave patronizing answers as to an ape with a rudimentary gift of speech, and after a short while the doctor—who up till then had been much more friendly—decided that he wanted to give Kazan another set of tests, and became so eager that he started to interrupt every few moments.

Eventually Balden left the office, and Kazan sighed and consented to take the tests, the doctor baiting the hook with the offer of advice and help when they were over. He dashed through them all; they were similar to the ones he had taken without interest in the examination hut at the spaceport in Berak. He waited, itching with impatience, while the doctor looked over what he had done, and finally demanded the advice and help he had been promised.

The doctor looked up with a wan smile. Then he rose from his chair and slid back a panel in the wall, revealing shelf upon shelf of tiny oblong boxes not much larger than Kazan's thumb. He indicated the lowest of the shelves.

"Those are microfilms," he said. "These boxes—there are a hundred and sixty-five of them—form one single set. I've owned them since I was a student, eight years ago, and I guess I've actually worked through less than a tenth of the total wordage in them. The title of the set goes like this: *Human Philosophy, Ethics and Religious Beliefs, a Five-Thousand-Year Survey*. The only advice I can possibly give you, Kazan, is this. Teach yourself to read, make yourself a fortune, pay for a century of geriatric treatment—and go and live by yourself out of reach of anyone else till you've read that book. If you don't go away by yourself, someone

THE LADDER IN THE SKY

else will have invented a new philosophy before you've more than begun."

Kazan looked first blank, then angry. The doctor shrugged.

"I'm sorry," he said. "The simple fact is that there are that many answers to the kind of questions you're asking, and none of them is definitive."

When he left the office Kazan was fuming. By the time he was back in the workers' quarters, though, he had realized how sensible the doctor's suggestion was. He slid back the door of his cabin and found Clary there alone. She was often there alone now—not because she was a person to shun company, but because by imperceptible stages she had come to see what was happening to Kazan and had been fascinated by it. There had obviously been instructions to the crew to treat Kazan as a special case and allow him to do what he liked so long as he did not interfere with the other workers, and no attempt was made to force him or Clary to the daily classes or the entertainments. Far from objecting to this special treatment, the others seemed to find it a relief that they could be away from Kazan for most of the day.

At his slamming entrance Clary looked up, startled. She said, "Kazan, you look angry! What is it?" She put aside a book she had been leafing through. Kazan seized it and thrust it towards her again.

"Can you teach me to read?" he demanded.

A hint of a smile came to her mouth, and she cocked one eyebrow at him. "I've been wondering when you were going to ask that," she said composedly. "I'll try, if you like. Sit down."

Instead of obeying immediately, Kazan hesitated. He said after a pause, "How did you know?"

"I've been watching you," she answered. "Sit down!"

He obeyed slowly, not taking his eyes off her. Suddenly he burst out laughing. Then, still laughing, he threw his arms round her.

THE LADDER IN THE SKY

XI

THERE WAS nothing much on Vashti except the mining settlement, a city of oblong apartment blocks faced with the dusty reddish color of the iron-rich rocks so common in the equatorial zone and so pregnant with metal that the saving in refinement time more than outweighed the expense of shipping bulk cargoes off a planetary surface. The native vegetation had been cleared off about eighteen thousand square miles of rolling land—some of it was poisonous to human beings—and over the area it had occupied the mining machinery and the processing equipment had spread like another kind of plant, like vigorous weeds driving out competitors. As well as iron there was rutile; there were brine-beds left from a vanished sea which were an economic source of magnesium; there was some tungsten, a lot of antimony, there was gallium in such quantity that the eventual plans included factories for semiconductors and solid-state circuitry on the spot.

But that was about it, and Ogric sometimes had the feeling that the bleakness of the environment had left its stamp on Snutch, the general manager of the entire mining complex.

He was a much bigger man than Ogric, but he had the same kind of explosive manner, suggestive in his case of overcompensation for some real or imagined inferiority. He was a superb organizer, that was known; he could hold every last detail of the program for his mines in his head, and under his management production had expanded eight-fold in six years. But Ogric found him the kind of person about whom it was reassuring to tell oneself, "Well, you don't *have* to like him."

He came out to the ship directly after it landed, to take formal charge of his new employees, and sat in the captain's office sending snapping glances all around him.

Hoping to get his business over quickly, Ogric went straight to the point.

"Eight hundred for you this trip," he said. "Usual contracts—five-year, wide range of work listed, twenty thousand cash payment at end of term, and home world repatriation if required or another thousand in lieu."

"Gutter-sweepings," Snutch grunted. "I checked up on the place where you were getting 'em from. Have any trouble on the way?"

Ogric frowned. He'd hoped Snutch might forget to ask—but still, there it was. He bent sideways in his chair so that his voice would be caught by the hear-this microphone and called for the doctor who had attended Kazan. While waiting for him to arrive, he ran over the bald facts of the affair.

Snutch stared at him. When he had heard the story to its end, he threw up his hands.

"Not just gutter-sweepings!" he said. "But lunatics! How do I account to the government for production lost when they start worshiping the big excavators, or refuse to work a night shift because of the ghosts?"

"It's not like that at all," Ogric said stiffly. "After the first day or so we had no trouble. The only two you'll have to watch out for are this man Hego, who's as strong as they come and passed very high on the manual skills tests—he'll probably make an excavator driver—but who's not very bright, and Kazan himself. Ah, doctor; come in. We were just talking about the Kazan problem."

The doctor nodded to Snutch and took a chair. He laid a file of documents on his knees. He said, "It seems to be working itself out satisfactorily. You know I gave him a course of treatment for this hysterical state he was in?"

Ogric nodded. Snutch looked coldly attentive.

"I have the results of another set of tests I gave him afterwards," the doctor said. He took a sheet of paper from his file and handed it to Ogric. "Just glance down that. And note the times marked against the individual results."

Ogric obeyed, frowning. After reading the page carefully twice he passed it to Snutch and stared at the doctor.

"What have you got there?" he said. "A freak of nature?"

"It looks like it, doesn't it?" the doctor said with a smile. "I'd dearly like to take him home with us and run a full-scale investigation of him. His genetic make-up ought to be something out of the galaxy."

THE LADDER IN THE SKY

Snutch snapped one finger against the paper he was holding, making a noise like a rubber band breaking. He said, "These results must be faked."

"I promise you they aren't," the doctor said. "I gave him the tests personally. You can check up for yourself, if you like. When we lifted, he couldn't read—except very haltingly, and about three or four words at a time. Names of streets and stores—that was his limit. And he couldn't sign his name. About halfway through the trip I advised him to learn. He got himself some lessons from a girl who'd taken an interest in him. She reads slowly, with a lot of subvocalization, but fairly well. He took two days to memorize the letters and a basic syllabary by the shape-technique. I checked him out of curiosity just before we broached atmosphere. Know what his reading speed is?"

"Whatever it is, he was faking before," Snutch snapped.

"It's eleven hundred and sixty a minute," the doctor said imperturbably. "I've been reading since I was five years old, and my speed has never topped nine hundred. And his retention is nearly eidetic. I'd dearly like to buy him out of his contract, I must say, and see where he's going to go from here."

Snutch's eyes narrowed barely perceptibly. He said, with an effort to hide his reluctance, "Well, I guess I'll have to take your word. According to what you're telling me, he's a magnitude one genius, is that right?"

"And going up," the doctor said, nodding.

"Well, we can do with some intelligence around here," Snutch said after a pause. He got to his feet. "I'll go and take my first look at what you've lumbered me with."

When he had gone, Ogric exchanged a wry glance with the doctor. He said, "You *didn't* fake those results, I suppose?"

"For the love of life, no!" The doctor stared at him. "Why do you think for a moment that I did?"

"Because I never saw anything like them before," Ogric growled. He tapped his fingers on the arm of his chair. "Let me see them again." He reached for the sheet of paper.

"And you're not likely to again," the doctor said with unusual solemnity. "If he hadn't spent his life in the slums

68

THE LADDER IN THE SKY

of Berak, if he'd had a proper education, that boy would be famous by now. I didn't mention it to Snutch, because I felt he might think I was overdoing it, but at the same time as I ran the reading test I gave him the literacy section of the intelligence tests, which I couldn't do previously, of course."

"And?" Ogric said, as though not eager for the answer.

"How do you measure the man who goes through the highest grade of test you have in four minutes under the theoretical limit?" said the doctor. On the last phrase his voice shook.

There was a pause. "Vocabulary?" Ogric said in a tone to suggest clutching at straws.

"I think he was getting at the words he didn't know by sheer logic—deducing the sense from the context or from resemblance to other words. When he came aboard I'd say his vocabulary was what you might expect—six to seven thousand. It's well over twenty now and probably rising continually." He hesitated. "You know something, Captain?" he said at last.

Ogric cocked an eyebrow.

"Next time we pass Vashti—maybe not until the time when we pick up the repatriates five years from now, but probably a lot sooner—I think you're going to find Kazan either running this place instead of Snutch, or dead."

"If you mean what I think you mean," Ogric began. The doctor cut the sentence short.

"Then you'd better not take me seriously," he said.

When he lined up to come aboard, nothing had suited Kazan's mood better than the mechanical business of processing the applicants. Now, during the disembarkation, he chafed and fretted. They were being handled by room-groups; consequently he and Clary moved up the line together.

"This is stupidly inefficient," he muttered to her when they had been out of the ship for twenty minutes. "What would it have cost them to signal ahead full details of everyone aboard? If they'd done it yesterday, people could have been ready now to split us up, jobs allotted." His voice trailed away as he frowned at the officious supervisors attending to

THE LADDER IN THE SKY

the third or fourth group of workers. Trucks stood waiting on the edge of the landing-ground; there were ore tubs in the background, ugly squat ships whose only permanent feature was a drive-unit, the rest of the hull being manufactured crudely on the spot out of Vashti metal and broken up on arrival.

In five more minutes, under Clary's gaze—which when it was turned on him was becoming by marked degrees more adoring and worshipful every time—he had worked out in his mind a foolproof system for getting any number of new workers off a ship and into their jobs within fifteen minutes of landing. Since the idea had no practical application at the moment, he was about to dismiss it as a mere mental exercise.

Then he checked himself. There was something new about it for him. And yet something familiar. He sought about in his memory as an animal might snuff for the source of a tantalizing odor, and was startled to realize what he was reminded of: the early part of the day when he rescued Prince Luth, the time he had spent giving instructions as to how to dispose the forces available. At the time he hadn't given it a second thought—it was not so far removed from planning a gang raid on a store, which was part of his life in the Dyasthala.

Now it felt different. It had a different texture. Call it the idea of organizing people. Or events. Systematization. It would probably be easier with machines than people, naturally.

It was something he could do that he hadn't known about. That was the crucial point.

It gave him food for thought right up till the moment when the group to which he and Clary belonged was called down to the line of trucks, almost half of which had now filled up and moved off. There were men and women with lists here, most of them wearing drab, serviceable uniforms of a reddish-brown which matched the general tone of the landscape, noting and ticking off the individual workers and sending them to various trucks, presumably to different areas of the settlement near their allotted jobs.

As the first names were being called and checked, Clary

THE LADDER IN THE SKY

suddenly squeezed his hand. She said, "What are we going to do if they split us up?"

"Argue," Kazan said shortly. His eyes were on the one man in the cluster of supervisors who was not dressed in the red-brown uniform, but in a black temperature suit. He was big, and carried himself well, but showed a definite nervousness in his expression and his restless hands.

"Clary, no other name, female," the bored voice of the checkman said. "Truck six, administrative and supervisory. Kazan, no other name, male, illiterate—"

"Literate," growled the big man in black. He looked Kazan up and down. "So you're the phenomenon!" he went on. "They tell me, that is."

Clary hesitated. For a moment the checkman was distracted by the big man's words and did not hurry her along. He said, "Uh—Manager Snutch!"

"What are we going to do with you?" the big man contined, ignoring the interruption. "From all acounts, you're too good for any jobs we have here. That right?"

As though the man's thoughts had been laid bare for him by some psychic scalpel, Kazan found he could see why Snutch was so heavily sarcastic, and why he was afraid. He had no wish to touch a raw spot in him. The checkman had called him manager, and he was clearly in authority, but it was plain that his personality was as sensitive as a broody bird's breast.

He said, "I'll do what I'm set to do, Manager."

Snutch seemed to turn the reply over as though looking for a cause of offence in it. Failing, he grunted something which sounded like, "I hope so!" He made to turn away.

"Manager Snutch!" the checkman said again. "He's down as illiterate—allotted to repair and maintenance training, truck twenty. Did you say that was wrong?"

There was a mutter of dismay from Clary. She moved back to Kazan's side and took his hand again. Snutch watched the movement, scowling, and then studied her from head to foot.

He said, "Where's the woman down for?"

The checkman told him.

THE LADDER IN THE SKY

"I see," Snutch said heavily. "*I* see." And was going to turn away again, but paused.

"He's down for repair and maintenance," he said. "He goes to repair and maintenance, and we sort him out later if we have to."

Clary's fingers pressed Kazan's sharply. He cleared his throat. "Uh—Manager! I can read now, you know. I—"

"You just said you'd do what you were set to do," Snutch broke in. "Get to it."

"This isn't a jail, you know," one of the supervisors added reassuringly. "Okay, move it along there! Move it along!"

"Right!" Snutch said. "But it isn't paradise either, and it isn't a vacation resort. It's a place for getting things done. Move it along. You heard the order!"

Huddled together against the lonely strangeness of this wide-open world and its arching roof of sky, the other workers waiting to be allotted to their jobs listened and grew restive.

"We want to be together," Clary said obstinately. The supervisor who had spoken before, sighed and exchanged a glance with the checkman.

"Look!" he said. "This is what there is on Vashti—what you can see and damned little else!" He waved at the landscape around them. "Tomorrow you file an application with the accommodation bureau and we'll fix you up, right? Now you move and stop being in other people's way."

Kazan hesitated. He too shared Clary's automatic, Dyasthala-bred distrust of people in authority. But he could sense that this was a different kind of authority from that which he had known before. He said, "Go on, Clary. We'd better do as they say."

Snutch took a huge stride forward and confronted Kazan less than an arm's length distant. He said, "Better do as we say? Better than what? Now you get this through your head at once! You do what you're told or you break your contract and you go back in the gutter you came from, understood?"

Kazan gave him a level stare and said nothing. After a moment in which Snutch's face grew redder and redder a jolting fist came up and took him under the jaw. He reeled back, recovered his balance, and still said nothing. Out of the corner of his eye he saw that the checkman had caught Clary's arm to prevent her from going for Snutch.

He shrugged, rubbed his chin, and walked towards the truck.

XII

NOT A JAIL . . .

This was such a transparently obvious fact that Kazan could not understand why so many of the people working here felt otherwise. There were about six thousand personnel altogether: a couple of hundred forming a permanent administrative core, mostly career government servants from the parent world of Marduk, the rest labor recruited on a contract basis from a number of planets, ranging from highly skilled metallurgists and personnel experts to the least educated, least skilled of the workers who had come in with Ogric's ship. Merely to come into contact with people from so many different backgrounds was fascinating to Kazan, but there was something infinitely more significant still.

Not a jail, for him, in any least sense of the word. An incredible liberation.

He could see a very pale reflection of his own feelings in some of the other workers from Berak, especially among the people of the Dyasthala. It didn't apply so much to those who had come to Vashti because they had supported Luth's abortive revolt and wanted to escape the consequences. As nearly as he could put it into words, it was release from the naked problem of staying alive, warm and fed.

Most of the people of the Dyasthala had never worked regularly or been fed and clothed without having to beg or steal. Those who had been passed by the selectors at the Berak spaceport were those who innately disliked such an

THE LADDER IN THE SKY

existence. It would obviously have been foolish to choose recruits who had a real psychological need for theft and violence.

Now they found themselves at a complete loss. Once, living had been a clock-round business for them, extending not only to the question of where the next meal was coming from, but as often as not to the question of where they could safely sleep the night. Free from the perennial preoccupations which had faced them, they were now fed, clothed, housed and entertained in return for undemanding work. It was said that in ten years' time the Vashti mines would be fully automatized and would require only a token corps of engineers and surveyors to run them. Already the process had gone so far that the crying need was for labor to undertake the simple tasks which machines would take over completely in the first stage of automation. That was why Ogric had gone to Berak; unskilled labor was growing steadily rarer.

Not a jail, for the love of life!

Already aboard ship Kazan had begun to realize how much of his thinking had formerly been wasted on problems of survival. Already he had cast around for other things to apply himself to, and had fetched up with a crash against the blank wall of the ultimate simplicities which the greatest human thinkers of many worlds had tackled, and failed to answer. But new horizons were opening before him all the time, and it did not really seem to matter what he concerned himself with because so many things were offered.

First there was the work he was assigned to, doing repair and maintenance under the supervision of a tubby, pleasant man with a shiny bald head named Rureth. His life in the Dyasthala had brought him no nearer to contact with machinery in general than an occasional theft of a vehicle for a job. And that was an incidental, an accessory, which did not involve his interest.

Confronted with the machines they worked with here, he was jerked again into a new view of the universe in which he existed. They assigned a large number of illiterates and slow readers to the repair shops, because the tough, reliable equipment seldom needed more than cleaning, servicing and changing of parts which could be done by following colored diagrams. Most of the other workers were content with that. Kazan could not stop there. He wanted to know more; he had to discover the system behind the effects. This was an excavator which shifted and piled overburden at the rate of a ton a minute. What went on in the magnet-cased fusion chamber to produce so much power? This was a separator, which sorted streams of finely ground mineral dust according to its composition, into forty vertical storage tubes. How could it tell one kind of dust from another?

At first Rureth was irritated by Kazan's insistent questioning. Then he began to understand the reason behind it, and to think that he ought not to try and stop Kazan from improving himself. He sent him to the library.

The library, with its stock of microfilms and recordings, was a revelation to Kazan. When he had been spending almost every free moment there for a month, Rureth decided that something ought to be done about this young man so hungry for knowledge.

Not a jail, Clary thought dully. That was a joke, if you liked. It was all very well not to have to worry any more about where the next meal was coming from, where you were going to sleep tonight, but with that much taken out of her pattern of existence, what could she put in its place? She felt empty, and bored, and frustrated.

And as for Kazan, who seemed not to be worried, she was disgusted with him.

Her work was of no particular interest to her. It was simple clerking and maintenance of records. She could already read and write fairly well; she was taught to use a keyboard computer input, to select the appropriate program from the limited range required to administer the small settlement, and to interpret results. Mostly she had to handle dietary and leisure-time programming. The department was also responsible for accommodation, but that was a subject she would rather not think about now.

True enough, she wasn't deliberately kept away from Kazan. Although the mining area sprawled over large distances, the accommodations were concentrated for conven-

THE LADDER IN THE SKY

ience together with the canteens, the leisure facilities and such ancillary establishments as the hospital and library. There was not even a need for internal transport in the dwelling area—everywhere was in easy walking distance, and helibuses were only necessary to transport workers to their jobs.

But she was separated from Kazan in another way, and a far more effective one.

They had allotted him to a room in the block where repair and maintenance staff lived, her to a room in the administrative staff's block. Remembering what the supervisor had said when they arrived, she inquired and found it was permissible to apply for shared accommodation; a lot of the staff formed more or less permanent arrangements together, because they were mostly here on two- or five-year contracts. Provided you showed up in time for the transport to work, she was told, no one would mind.

But her carefully worded application came back vetoed by Snutch.

In charge of records and programming, and therefore of her department, was a middle-aged woman called Lecia. She was well liked by her subordinates, though she was merciless with their shortcomings. Clary demanded of her why the application had been turned down. There was vacant accommodation available, she knew from the department's charts.

But Lecia merely said that she could not override a decision by Manager Snutch, and gave no further explanation.

According to the results of her examination on Berak, and the brief training course she had been through, Clary should have been a good and reliable worker. Her attention seemed to move somewhere away from her work after that. Lecia tried half a dozen times to shake her out of her apathy, but after a month she decided something was going to have to be done about the root problem.

This was not the separation which divided Clary from Kazan, though. It was worse than physical. It was as though since coming to Vashti Kazan had become another person as different again from what he had been on arrival as he then had been from the way he was when he left Berak.

THE LADDER IN THE SKY

"Why did you let him hit you like that?" she demanded of him, thinking of Snutch's suddenly reddened face and unreasoning violence.

Kazan frowned. "I felt sorry for him," he said after a pause.

"What?"

"Yes, sorry for him. Don't you see that the only reason he could have for doing such a thing would be because he's not completely responsible? I've asked some people who've been here for a long time, and they tell me they think he's bitter about having come from Marduk to run things here. He feels that if he had stayed at home he might have got further ahead in life; he thinks he's traded his chance of fulfilling his main ambitions for a second-best job where he can rise no further."

"That's his fault, then!" Clary snapped. "I suppose he's vetoed the application for shared accommodation for the same reason!"

Kazan shrugged. He said, "I guess so."

"Don't you care?" Clary pleaded. "Don't you want to do something, even if it's only to complain about it? There isn't any regulation or anything to stop us being together—only Snutch's decision. And—and—wouldn't you like us to be together, Kazan?"

"But we can be," Kazan said, and she realized with a sinking heart that he had missed her point. "And you know as well as I do that if Snutch vetoed the application for some emotional reason he won't change his mind. Also I think he knows he made himself look foolish in front of his staff when he hit me for no good cause, and the way a twisted mind like that works, it seems to him that it was my fault he looked foolish. It's inconceivable that he would change his mind simply because I asked him to."

"You know a hell of a lot about what goes on in Snutch's mind," Clary said sharply. "But you don't know a thing about what does on in mine, do you? Or do you just not care?"

She left him there before he could answer, hoping against hope that he would come after her. But he did not, and the next time they met it was like meeting a stranger, who

THE LADDER IN THE SKY

could seemingly talk only about stellar processes and numbers and facts of the physical universe. But of these he talked with the excitement of a man who has made a miraculous discovery.

By instinct rather than conscious understanding, she saw then that Kazan as he had been for so short a time was lost to her. It was not his fault, and for all her reflex bitterness she could not make herself think that it was. She knew too well that he was being driven now by his own nature, and until the impetus was exhausted she could not hope to follow him. She could only wait until he was over the violence of this new enthusiasm for pure knowledge, and then—perhaps—he would remember that he had been grateful to her and had even liked her very much.

But the waiting was going to be intolerable, and there was no certainty that it was worthwhile.

XIII

THERE HAD been a fight between two of the workers in the repair shops over some contemptuous reference to the Dyasthala background of one of them; it took Rureth to Snutch's office to get the matter straightened out, and afterwards he used the opportunity to broach the other subject concerning him.

"One of that new batch of workers," he said thoughtfully, staring out of the big window which gave Snutch a general view of his nearer empire. He had heard the stories about what happened the day Ogric landed this batch; he was not at all surprised to see Snutch lift his head like a hunting animal snuffing a scent on the wind.

"Yes?" the manager said sharply.

Rureth settled his tubby body deep in his chair. He said, "Kazan. Know him?"

THE LADDER IN THE SKY

Snutch gave a wary nod. "What about him?"

"You're wasting him on me," Rureth said. "What I needed was dumb oxen who could be taught to turn a wrench or weld a seam—not high-calibre engineers."

"He isn't one," Snutch said. "He's a slum-bred thief."

"But he is," Rureth corrected gently. "Who do you think is in charge of the shops while I'm over here with you?"

Snutch stared at him for a long moment. Then he slammed his open palm down on his desk. He said, "You have no business doing that, Rureth! Putting an unqualified novice in a position of responsibility—it's insane! Do you want an adverse entry on your service report?"

"I'm *telling* you," Rureth said patiently. "It's been a bit more than a month since I took him on. The library records show that he's requisitioned most of the texts on engineering and physical science that are available, and I can say from my own knowledge that he's learned them. It doesn't make sense to keep a man with learning ability of that order in the repair shops. Also I was told he was illiterate, and he's not. As you may have gathered."

"So what do you want me to do?" Snutch demanded. "Anyone would think that you'd be pleased. From what you say, you could sit back till the end of your contract and leave your work to him to handle!"

"I probably could," Rureth agreed. "But it wouldn't suit me, and I doubt if it would suit him. The suggestion I was going to make was that you transfer him around the settlement to as many different jobs as you can, for short periods, and then let him wind up on the planning staff. Maybe I'm being optimistic, because the only signs of original thinking he's shown so far have been in petty matters. But I prefer to back my hunch that he'd be a valuable planner, and he'd probably find ways of cutting the ten-year period to full automation."

"You said you'd had him for—how long?" Snutch commented sarcastically.

"Long enough to know when I'm on to a good thing," Rureth answered. "Another point: the rest of the workers from Berak regard him with almost superstitious awe. I doubt if it's rooted in sense, but it works all right. You ought

THE LADDER IN THE SKY

to come out and see him handle them some time. It's hard to define, but he's got a sort of impatience with anything that's less than perfect, and what's more he can make it catching. Even to me.

"He'll gather round the four or five workers responsible for a particular job—say, replacing the magnet windings on an excavator's power unit—and spend ten or twenty minutes going over the diagrams with them. At the end of that time he'll have got the idea of what they're doing through their heads. Then they throw the diagrams away and they do the job. You see what I'm getting at? For years I've been plagued with knob-headed wrench-pushers dim enough to follow the diagrams by rote, which is all right but calls for unceasing supervision. When Kazan gets them working, they aren't just going through the motions—they know the reasons for the motions. And the difference is fantastic."

"Make your mind up!" Snutch rapped. "Either you want the job done like that, or you want dumb oxen. You've asked for both."

"I managed without him before he got here," Rureth said imperturbably. "I can manage again. But if he can do this in a repair shop he can probably do it for the mines as a whole, in which case he ought to be given the chance."

"Nonsense!" Snutch said with finality.

"You're the manager," Rureth shrugged. "Mark you, I guess I'm wasting my time anyway, because he's going to make his own chances. It'll just take him longer. In a year or two you're going to find him involved in planning anyway. It's his natural habitat. He'll make for it whether he knows about it or not."

"That's as may be," Snutch said. "But you keep your views to yourself."

"No," Rureth said. "Not without a good reason." The change that had come over his normally rather sleepy, casual voice was astonishing in that instant. It rang now like a beaten anvil. "And it's got to be better than the reason which people ascribe to you right now."

"What do you mean?" Snutch said slowly.

"It's good sense to make exceptional arrangements for an exceptional person," Rureth said. "Kazan is exceptional. But

THE LADDER IN THE SKY

I was talking to Lecia yesterday evening, and I understand from her that for Kazan you won't even make ordinary arrangements."

"What was the idiot woman talking about?"

"That isn't fair to Lecia," Rureth said. "But let it pass. Kazan had a woman—Clary is the name—and she applied according to regulations for shared accommodation with him. You vetoed it. Any good reason?"

"That pair were troublemakers!" Snutch barked. "Didn't you hear what happened aboard Ogric's ship on the way here? A near-riot to start with, and tension from then on. This Clary threatened to make the workers welsh on their contracts, and blackmailed Ogric into giving her a bonus for not doing it, and as for Kazan—well, it was over him that the riot brewed!"

"I haven't had any trouble with Kazan," Rureth said. "And he's only been working directly under me. With others from Berak, yes, like that one who got involved in the fight this morning. If you want trouble from Kazan, you're going about it the right way."

Snutch leaped on that like a hungry animal on a scrap of meat. "You think he's contemplating trouble?" he said.

Rureth sighed and got to his feet. "No, but you are," he said. "You only have to wait until the rest of the workers from Berak start to feel the same way about Kazan as the ones in the repair shops already do. Like I said, they have this superstitious awe of him. But it's turning into a kind of reflected pride. They're thinking, 'This guy is from Berak, and he's hell with jets!'"

"If he tries whipping up a personality cult for himself among the workers, that can be dealt with," Snutch said, and compressed his lips whitely together.

"Listen!" Rureth said, leaning on both palms on the front of Snutch's desk. "You'd better hear this from me rather than someone else. Everybody knows—but *everybody*—you're ashamed of yourself for hitting him the way you did. It made you look like a fool, no denying. Pretty soon everybody will know about Kazan's talent. If you don't want the word to go around that you're scared of him, you'd better do something. Fast."

THE LADDER IN THE SKY

"Get out before I throw you out," Snutch said between his teeth.

Snutch had not seen Kazan since the day of his arrival. In some strange way he was surprised when an ordinary enough young man entered his office, wearing the standard reddish-brown work uniform. What had he been expecting—superman? He wondered for a moment, then checked himself and wished he had not thought of the question. An instant later he caught himself looking for traces of a bruise under Kazan's chin.

He waved him to a seat.

"I've been hearing things about you," he said, leaving the phrase deliberately vague and pausing after it. Kazan showed no sign of preconception; he merely nodded.

"I understand," Snutch went on, "that you've been trying to create disaffection among the workers."

Kazan cocked his head. He said, "How's that, Manager?"

"You've been going around starting arguments between your people from Berak and the staff from Marduk and other places, about conditions of work, about living conditions—"

Kazan started to laugh. Snutch broke off, his face reddening. "What are you laughing at?" he barked.

"I'm ahead of you, Manager," Kazan said. "I guess all I can say is that whoever told you wasn't listening."

Snutch hesitated. There was an uncomfortable confidence in Kazan's voice, which reminded him of the younger man's expression that moment before he was so incredibly foolish as to hit him. He drew a deep breath.

"All right. Give me your version," he said.

"I'm not sure I can make it clear to you—"

"Are you hinting that I'm stupid?" Snutch cracked out, and instantly regretted it. What in the wyrds' name made him so sensitive to this calm young man? He recovered himself. "Go on."

"It's a question of background," Kazan said, ignoring the other's outburst. "It's like this. I come out of the Dyasthala in Berak. To me that's like being let out into fresh air, being here. I feel I'm awake for the first time. What I used to think of as impossible luxuries are commonplace here. And I'm getting to learn things I didn't know existed. It's like being

82

THE LADDER IN THE SKY

born all over again. But there are people here—the people from Marduk especially—who think they're hard done by when they have to make do with what I call luxuries. They think they're trapped and enclosed here because they have a contract to work out on Vashti, when it's a liberation for me. I feel like"—he hesitated, hunting a comparison—"someone who's been in a cage all his life. Now I'm out of it. I want to know about outside life. That's all."

Snutch studied him with narrowed eyes. It sounded convincing. It made sense, if it was true that he was a frustrated genius out of the slums. And it implied that there wasn't much to fear from Kazan, if he was actively grateful to be on Vashti instead of in the Dyasthala.

Cautiously he said, "You like it here?"

"Better than the Dyasthala."

"Your work?"

"Fine. I don't have to spend too much time at it any more. Supervisor Rureth tells me I don't need any more training than I have already. So I have a surplus of leisure."

Without changing his expression, Snutch came to the alert. That was a problem he hadn't foreseen. To leave this fellow, about whom Rureth made such astonishing predictions, with time on his hands—that was probably what Rureth had meant about heading for trouble. Let someone intelligent and restive get bored, and the consequences might be dangerous.

He felt calm, and pleased that he had exorcised the irrational specter haunting him from their first encounter. He debated with himself for a moment. It looked as though he'd better do two things: arrange to keep Kazan occupied by making him undergo several more training courses, as Rureth had suggested, meantime watching him closely, and secondly try and eradicate any source of a grudge Kazan might bear against him, Snutch. Provided what he had said proved to be the truth, there wouldn't be any need to worry.

"Your girl put in for shared accommodation with you," Snutch said after he had made his decision. "I hear she's been miserable because I held over my approval. I wanted to make up my mind about you first. I'd heard you were talented. Supervisor Rureth's confirmed that now. So I have

THE LADDER IN THE SKY

some plans for your future here. You can take your girl a couple of presents."

He had to avoid Kazan's emotionless gaze. He fumbled up an authorization pad from a drawer in his desk.

"I'll authorize your shared accommodation," he said, writing rapidly. "And I'll get you out of the repair shop. If you know all there is to know, you must be bored, hey?" He tried a friendly grin, and it failed. But Kazan smiled back, politely and mechanically.

"Shift you to the refinery," Snutch said, after a moment's thought: where is he likely to find the going toughest? Refinery work called for a keen understanding of chemistry; not even Kazan would hurry through his training there. "Give you something to chew on. Here you are."

He held out the two authorizations: the accommodation and the work-transfer. Kazan took them and stood up.

"Thanks very much," he said. "Is there anything else?"

It hadn't worked. The devil wasn't chained. "No," Snutch muttered. "No, that's all."

And as the door closed he knew grayly that small bribes and favors were so utterly useless that even big ones probably would fail as well.

He felt trapped.

XIV

HE FOUND Clary that evening in the leisure hall, the huge domed structure on the edge of the dwelling area where most of the staff passed part of their free time. Its mechanism allowed it to serve many purposes; tonight it was a place of pale blue and red mists, with half-glimpsed panoramas of landscapes on other worlds showing occasionally in its walls and small temporary rooms set off at random on its vast floor for music, dancing, drinking and conversation.

THE LADDER IN THE SKY

Some time, Kazan thought, he must find out about the way it worked.

The mists were intangible—tricks played with light—and upset perspective in curious ways. Some of the young workers were playing hide-and-go-seek with screams of laughter, taking advantage of the visual effects which could make another person seem at one moment close at hand, the next infinitely far away.

Clary sat by herself, despondent, in a place where the mist was so strongly distorting that even people sitting next to one another, if they relied on their eyes, felt that they were swinging through vast unrelated orbits. Kazan loomed up to her; she caught sight of his face, saw it change as with recognition, and in the next instant had to wonder whether she had imagined it, for he seemed unreachably distant. Out of wisps of pale blue mist his hand shot up to touch her, its speed and trajectory magnified past possibility by the same wrong-end-of-telescope effect which made him appear remote.

Then he was standing before her, and with the additional information from the arm his hand was touching she knew he was really there. In a dull voice she greeted him.

"Here!" he said smiling, his head receding, his legs becoming treetop-tall, and all being twisted at once as he made to turn and sit beside her while taking a piece of paper from his front pocket. When he held the paper out to her the words twisted and writhed unreadably.

"What do you think of that?" he said after a pause.

"I can't read it," she said.

"Try again."

She frowned and forced her eyes to follow the wavering of the words; then she caught a clear glimpse of what it said, all the way down to the signature of Snutch at the bottom, and felt her heart turn over.

"Glad?" Kazan said. She considered that for a moment, and finally sighed and shrugged.

She said, "You're very clever indeed, Kazan. I'm sorry."

"For what?" Looming, his face showed puzzlement.

"For thinking you didn't want that, I guess. I might have known that if you did you'd fix it when the time was right."

THE LADDER IN THE SKY

She found it an effort to speak to him; it was easier if she shut her eyes and abolished the swinging cycle of looming up and receding which dizzied her. The piece of paper was lifted gently from between her fingers, and she felt his hand brush her skin.

Convulsively, the instant following, she clasped at his wrist and held it tight, feeling by chance the pulse under her fingertips. She said, "Kazan, it's—well, it seems like a long time. I keep wanting to ask you as though you'd been off on a long trip—how are you, what's happened to you?"

She opened her eyes briefly, but he seemed terribly far away.

"I know," he said.

"Are you frightened any more?" That wasn't how she had meant to say it, but it was the thing she needed most to know.

After a small eternity he answered, "Yes. More than ever. But I don't think I would tell anyone else."

"The same thing?"

"The same thing? Oh, yes."

She turned to look at him, trying to fix him steady with her gaze by a sheer act of will. "But why, Kazan? I keep hearing that everything is wonderful for you, whatever you do turns to gold. Isn't that true?"

"I guess. But that's half the trouble, you see." He had his own eyes focused somewhere beyond her, looking at space. "Do you remember in the Dyasthala how if the day was gray and misty the ugliest things were veiled? Then, when the sun came out, and everything was harshly lit, you couldn't pretend any more. All the dirt showed for what it was. All the sick and twisted people could be seen. In my mind the sun has come out, Clary. I can't hide things from myself any more."

"What could you need to hide?" she demanded.

"I was thinking—and hoping—that I would come to terms with my memory. I hoped that as I learned more about myself and the way the mind works I would find that what troubled me was an illusion. Instead, it's become clearer, more solid, like a black rock. I did rescue Luth. Something that was not Kazan gave Kazan miraculous

THE LADDER IN THE SKY

powers for a few short hours, and then—well, it named its price."

"But what has it cost you?" Clary cried. "When everyone's talking about how they envy you! Is there any single drawback from it—if it's true?"

"It makes me suffer," Kazan said after a pause.

"How, for the love of life?"

"This way." Kazan deliberated for a moment, as though lining up his words precisely. "The Kazan that was could have disregarded it. He could have fooled himself into thinking it really was an illusion, and if he could not have forgotten it he could at least have learned to live with it."

There was something almost eerie about the way he spoke of his former self in the third person, as though about someone altogether different. Clary shivered.

"But the Kazan that is," he went on, "can't fool himself. As my insight into my thinking grows clearer, I realize more and more that I'm not as I used to be. There is something in me which is different. True enough, I've learned how to absorb facts spongewise; my mind is keener—but for that very same reason the pain of knowing I am not *I* is keener too."

He broke off. While she was still hunting for a way to answer him, a change came over him. He gave a quick bitter laugh and shook his head.

"Still, I won't be past hope till the year and a day is up. A Vashti year? A Berak year? Or the year of some other unimaginable planet where the black thing comes from? I wonder. And at least Snutch has done me a great favor."

"That?" She gestured hopefully at the paper in his hand, and her own arm seemed to her to be swinging through an arc of many miles as the distorting mirage effect took hold of it.

"So long as I can find new things to distract me," Kazan said, not appearing to notice, "it won't be unendurable. He's moving me to refinery work; I guess after that he can be persuaded to shift me again, and again, so I hope I won't have time to think too much. I haven't told anyone else about this, Clary. I'm too exposed."

"I don't understand," she said in a dead voice.

THE LADDER IN THE SKY

"I can't help myself now, I must do everything as well as I possibly can, and too many things I find I can do so well I terrify myself. So far I've been lucky. People have taken a reflected pride in it. But I could make one wrong step, and they'd be jealous. Some of them might remember what Hego said on the ship. And I could be destroyed."

"Nonsense," she said automatically.

"You know it's not. If I frighten myself, how can I keep from frightening others?"

"You don't frighten me," Clary said. "I think you must be going through hell."

"I know that," Kazan replied. "I—you know something? I never thought I'd be so grateful just to have someone who was not afraid of me. I don't like it! I *hate* it! And that's another way I've changed—Kazan that was knew that Bryda was afraid of him, Hego was afraid of him, perhaps in the end even Yarco and Luth as well, and that made him proud. But now, to see the fear in Snutch's eyes—that's horrible."

"Snutch?" she said.

At that moment there was a twisting of the mist and a sudden clear patch appeared. In the middle of it, only an arm's reach away from where they were sitting, they saw two of the young people who were playing their seeking game among the mirages—a husky youth with a laughing face and a tawny-skinned girl with eyes like a startled deer. He had just caught her by the arm and was swinging her round to kiss her when the mist lifted. Together they turned, startled, on seeing Clary and Kazan, and were about to speak when a sort of intangible tunnel gathered about them and without moving they were whisked away into distant isolation.

"Yes," Kazan said.

At first she thought it couldn't be like that; then she began to learn how true Kazan's gloomy analysis had been. As he was shifted like a chess piece across the board of the mining settlement, she saw the aura of disturbance follow him. This man—it equated to in words—this man is a strange phenomenon. Unpredictable. Dangerous.

The settlement was not small enough to be a microcosm of

THE LADDER IN THE SKY

frictions, and it was organized on a highly efficient basis. But that organization depended on predictability; Kazan was a wild factor now. Not all his immediate superiors reacted to him as Rureth had done. Some shared Snutch's emotional response, and tried to pin him down, but that was like trying to dam a river with spadefuls of soil; behind the obstacle the water still flowed, and sooner or later dug itself another channel.

Aside from Clary herself, there were very few people in the settlement who were at all close to Kazan. Rureth was one; he took a diffuse paternal interest in Kazan's progress because he had been the first to diagnose his probable development. Another was Jeldine, the rather gloomy, withdrawn woman who acted as educational supervisor for the workers and incidentally as librarian; a spark caught from Kazan's blazing need for knowledge started a fitful glare in her mind also, and she helped him in several small ways.

But it was on Clary that the burden mainly fell. She had not foreseen that it was going to be a burden; when she made the discovery, it was too late to do anything about it. Helpless, she was trailed along behind Kazan, fascinated by the firework sparkle of his mind, the paradoxical contrast between his much-envied gifts and the torturing pain of the self-knowledge they had brought him.

For days or weeks together he could lose himself, either in new work or a new problem of a philosophical kind; then the darkness would close again, and he would question her fiercely—sometimes all through one night—about the way she remembered her own past, about her reactions and attitudes which he needed to compare with his own.

It became still worse as the year and a day period which he so greatly feared drew to its close. Then the black devil in his past seemed to become more and more real to him; once he spent many hours trying to recreate from memory the face of the half-noticed conjurer, the black-clad man with the black skullcap who had been hired by Bryda. Also the various kinds of work to which he was successively transferred seemed to involve him less and less. His need to know narrowed down to a single focus, and when he was not consulting all the available literature he was sitting in

THE LADDER IN THE SKY

isolated corners away from interruption, his eyes closed and sometimes with sweat on his face, as he struggled to bring up from memory the one thing from the short but crucial period of his life when he was involved with Bryda which remained unclear to him: the way in which he had molded air into solidity with a few passes of his hands.

"If I could only do it again, I'd know!" he would say to Clary.

To which she could only reply, "But since you can't, why doesn't that prove the contrary?"

He would shake his head.

"If it would make me do something extraordinary! So that I knew I was 'serving' it! But I can't tell if I'm serving it, or if I'm being myself; I only know I've changed, and the uncertainly is intolerable!"

It was torment. Clary knew that merely from seeing the haunted expression in his eyes. But it was of such unimaginable subtlety that she could not reach out to him, there where it hurt him, and give him comfort. She wondered how long she could endure this, and what would happen to Kazan when the time finally ran out.

Wondering about what would happen to him was the worst of all.

XV

THE EQUABLE climatic curve of Vashti's long year dipped by degrees towards its winter. The morning of the day when Kazan was transferred yet again—to the outward shipping complex—was gray and overcast, with occasional spitting rain and a cool fitful wind. He was to work under Rureth again; the former manager of the shipping complex had worked out his contract, and Rureth had been transferred and upgraded about two months before.

THE LADDER IN THE SKY

Kazan walked slowly in the direction of his office. There was always a slight smell of sulfur in the air hereabouts, and the peculiar baked tang of red-hot metal cooling. This was the key point of all the mining settlement's industry, lying between the refining complex and the spaceship landing ground. On one side metal came in, some piped as white-hot liquid, but mostly as a suspension of fine particles in a wet flurry, or dancing on a stream of air. The metal was sintered, or cast and stamped, and from it were formed the ribs and plates of the squat ships nicknamed ore tubs. The assembly line for these was the biggest single unit of the complex.

The normal output was a ship every four to six days, depending on whether it was to carry a cargo of crude metal, in which case it needed only to be approximately hull-tight and strong enough to stand the strain of lifting to orbit on its own, prefabricated power unit—or whether it was to carry semiconductor material, in which case it required somewhat more elaborate preparation. There were huge parabolic-roofed loading bays beyond the assembly shops, down which the ovoid bulk of the hull slid on rails; finally, complete with cargo and preprogramed electronic controls, it emerged into the open and was fired to space.

After that it ceased to concern the staff of the mining settlement; masterships came from Marduk, gathered together anything up to eight of the crude ore tubs, and flew them back to the parent world. While orbiting, the power units of the tubs stored solar energy; consequently the cost of shipment was comparatively small. It was a very ingenious system, and Kazan had made all the inquiries about it that he wanted to some time ago.

Because the slightest hitch in the shipping complex could make the operation of the entire mining settlement uneconomic, it was here that automation had progressed furthest. Kazan paused at a point from which he could look right down the loading bays into the assembly shop beyond, to watch for a moment as the current ship rode up the electric monopole rails for final inspection.

On rotating quadrants sonar probes and low-intensity radiation sources scanned the hull for flaws; when one was

91

THE LADDER IN THE SKY

found, as now happened, a gentle alarm bell rang and a splash of paint was applied automatically to the weak seam. From galleries under the arching roof men rode down on jointed pillars; each was strapped to a chairlike cradle and wore an airmask and goggles of dark pressure-glass. With deft movements they touched their welders to the flaws and pressurized liquid metal sealed them up.

Looking carefully to one side of the brilliant beads of light from the welders, Kazan went forward. One of the men nearest him glanced up, blind for a moment because of his goggles, and then pushed the goggles aside.

It was a few seconds before Kazan recognized the upper part of the face so exposed, with the air mask still hiding the nose and mouth. It was Hego.

He had not seen Hego for a long time except from a distance; he did not know if this was because Hego still kept his superstitious fear of him, or whether he merely felt that he had made himself ridiculous by his behavior aboard the ship which had brought them. He would have thought the second the more likely—except that Hego hardly seemed intelligent enough to worry about fine points of embarrassment. Because he knew that among the other workers from Berak there was little trace remaining of their original fear. The passage of months, combined with the comparative security and freedom from worry which they now enjoyed, had dimmed their first startled reaction; moreover they had come into contact with people from other worlds whose skepticism about devils and men back from the dead had proved contagious.

Kazan gave a wary nod and would have passed by, but Hego, after a brief hesitation, jerked the controls of his cradle and swung through the air on the jointed pillar bearing it. He brought himself to a point directly in front of Kazan, and poised in the air where he could look down on him. With a jerky movement he dropped his air mask on his chest, then hung his welder on its hook beside the cradle he sat in.

"Where do you think you're going?" he said thickly.

"I work here," Kazan said. "As of today."

"So we heard," Hego agreed. "And we decided we didn't want you. Do you understand me?"

THE LADDER IN THE SKY

"I'll take my instructions from Supervisor Rureth," Kazan returned peaceably. "Not from you."

"You talk big," Hego said. He *was* afraid; it showed in the way he could not quite make his eyes stay still when he looked at Kazan. "I been wanting for a long time to find out if you really can't be killed—understand me? So have a lot of others here in this shop. Maybe you want to find it out too. Okay! Come right in! You'll get your chance—or you'll turn around smart and go beg Snutch to shift you somewhere else."

Beside them now the other workers were pulling back on their jointed pillars, and the hull was beginning to slide towards the loading bay. From up near the arching roof a voice boomed, immensely amplified.

"Hego! What are you playing at?"

They glanced up together and saw the tubby figure of Rureth on the under-roof gallery, a microphone on an extension arm held to his face. Hego spat sidelong.

"Come to give you your instructions!" he said. "Or to take some from you, maybe. We heard how you move in wherever you go and start pretending to run things. Well, we don't want it here, get me? You sold out to a devil—it's bad enough having you on the same planet, but by the wyrds we won't have you under the same roof!"

"Oh, for the love of life!" Kazan said wearily, and made to walk by. With a quick twitch on the controls of his cradle, Hego was in front of him again. He put one hand to his welder and made to lift it from its hook.

"The devil pulled you out of the lake of monsters," he said. "Want to see if he can pull you out from under me?"

He snatched the welder up and jammed the power-switch to maximum, slapping his goggles back over his eyes. Kazan had to cry out with the shock as the full power glare of the tool—almost as bright as the naked sun—seared into his eyes.

For a moment he thought Hego had gone totally insane, and was going to spear him with the welder's arc; he could see nothing beyond the dazzling afterimage. Then he realized that it was only the afterimage now—the welder had been shut off—and out of the side of his eyes he could see what

THE LADDER IN THE SKY

had saved him. Rureth had clambered into a vacant cradle and swung down from the gallery, just in time to break Hego's power supply by opening the main switch mounted behind him where the welder lead was attached to the cradle.

The fire of fury in Rureth's eyes was nearly as bright as the extinguished arc as he confronted Hego. His voice crackled with the same blistering anger.

"Maniac!" he barked. "Moron! Blockhead, clubfooted, ham-handed, blubber-lipped, superstitious *imbecile!* I've had enough of your lunatic gabble about devils! You'd have killed Kazan if I hadn't cut the power in the nick of time—and that's the finish as far as you're concerned. I'm sick of you, and everyone on Vashti is sick of you. How are you, Kazan?" he added from the side of his mouth, not moving his eyes.

"Eyes are a bit sore," Kazan said, breathing heavily. "I guess I have you to thank that I still have eyes at all."

By now the completed hull had slid all the way into the loading bays, and beyond the inspection shop the ribs of the next in line could be seen waiting for the automatic transporters to fit the hull-plates. Some of the other workers who had swung down from the gallery at the same time as Hego had returned there, but two or three of them had seen Rureth come down and had waited to find out if there was trouble.

To them, Rureth now turned. Strapped in his cradle and with the power turned off where he could not get at it, Hego could only fume and snarl.

"Get this savage up on the gallery!" Rureth ordered. "Manager Snutch is due here in a few minutes' time. I'm going to have him put Hego in for psychiatric reorientation. If I hadn't managed to cut his power he'd have burned this guy alive with his welder. Did you see it, you?"

He flung his arm out commandingly at the nearest of the other workers. Out of memory Kazan conjured the fact that he had seen this man before aboard Ogric's ship. He had been one of the previous occupants of the cabin where Kazan was assigned, and had been among the first to join the rush to get out.

The man exchanged glances with his companions, and

THE LADDER IN THE SKY

then shot a hating glare at Kazan. It lasted only a second; then he was smiling easily.

"Why, no, supervisor!" he said. "I didn't see a thing. Nor did either of these others—*did you?*" he finished.

Together they shook their heads. For a moment Rureth was taken aback.

"Now see here, Dorsek!" he began.

The worker cut him short with a gesture of phony meekness. He said, "We had our dark goggles down, Supervisor!"

Rureth drew a deep breath, held it, let it out under control to calm himself. In a disgusted tone he said, "I get. *I* get. But you can see well enough now, and I'm ordering you to get Hego back on the gallery. Ride him up there with your own cradles, and anyone who turns the power back on for him goes under managerial detention and forfeits his contract. Is that clear?"

"Quite clear," Dorsek said with irony, and waved to his companions to close in on Hego and pull his cradle back up to the gallery. The dead power-joints of the pillar on which it rode hissed and sucked complainingly.

"Climb on the back of my cradle," Rureth said to Kazan when he was sure Dorsek was obeying him. "I'll lift you up the top. Did Hego start it? I guess I'd better settle that before Snutch hears the facts."

Awkwardly, having to move more by touch than by sight, Kazan clambered on the flat footrests behind Rureth's cradle. He said, "He just told me that they—whoever that might be—didn't want me under the same roof. Does he give you much trouble?"

"Pretty often," Rureth said, activating his controls. The floor of the inspection shop fled dizzily away beneath them. "He's so stupid he can barely count; welding is the most complicated job you can trust him with, and that's three-quarters automatic. All he needs to know is which button to press on his welder, and the rest is done for him. There's a sort of gang of them, though, with him and Dorsek at the head—guys from Berak who got the thin end of this prince's revolution which I gather you were tied up in somehow."

95

"Is that what's behind it?" Kazan said. "Or do they believe what Hego says about devils?"

The cradle rocked and hovered as Rureth brought it tidily up to the edge of the gallery.

"Is anybody that stupid, to really believe in devils?" Rureth said.

There was a short pause. Then, sounding as though he was a long, long way away, Kazan said, "I guess some people must be. I have to."

As he scrambled out of his seat, Rureth stared at Kazan.

"Are you as crazy as he is?" he demanded.

"Could be," Kazan said. "The year and a day runs out on me any time now, so I'm just about due to find out."

"What?"

"Nothing," Kazan said. "Give me a hand onto the gallery, will you? I can still barely see."

When Rureth seized him by the arm to guide him over the narrow gap between the cradle and the gallery, he was astonished to find that he was shaking violently.

XVI

When Snutch arrived he was looking harassed. He had come up through the shops and spoken to one or two of the foremen on the floor, and his first remarks to Rureth were brusque.

"What's going on?" he demanded. "You have three men pulled out of the inspection team, and that's no joke at this of all times. There's a big demand for magnesium at home right now and they want an eight-ship load for the master that's coming in next week, and the stuff is piling up in the loading bay stores!"

Rureth told him, crisply and with emphasis, while Hego, Dorsek and one of the other workers stood by in the back-

THE LADDER IN THE SKY

ground with tolerant expressions. Kazan listened passively. He wished Rureth hadn't put that question about devils to him.

His eyes hurt, and there was a blur in the middle of his field of vision which had replaced the long-lasting afterimage.

When Rureth had finished, Snutch turned to Kazan, scowling. He said, "Is that true? Did he try to kill you with his welder?"

"I can't say what was in his mind," Kazan said wearily. "I know he said he didn't want me under the same roof."

"Hego?" Snutch said, turning.

"He's sold to a devil," Hego said. "He's bad. You can feel he's bad, just by being close to him. If you want work to go on in this shop, you'll get rid of him."

"Devils!" Snutch said. "Comet-gas! I'm not going to pay you the compliment of taking that garbage seriously! Rureth, put 'em back on the floor. There's work to be done."

"Not Hego," Rureth said.

There was a frozen silence. Snutch's face went red. He said, at last, "Are you presuming to question what I say?"

"Where Hego is concerned, yes," Rureth snapped. "I saw him attack Kazan with a welder. He came within an inch of murder. Men I'll work with. Wild animals I will not. Hego belongs in the psychiatric ward of the hospital, undergoing massive personality repair. I won't have him under my responsibility one day longer. The rest is up to you. But I tell you this! If he does kill somebody, I'll see to it that you're paid for disregarding my warning."

"You two, get back to work," Snutch said in a low voice, pointing at Dorsek and his companion. They obeyed; the moment the door had closed behind them, he went on, "I'll go along with you this far, Rureth; I'll get a doctor's report on Hego. If it confirms what you say, all right. Otherwise I'll break you. Two can make threats, and I'm better able to see them fulfilled—clear?"

Rureth returned his gaze steadily, but said nothing.

"As for you, Kazan!" Snutch barked, rounding on him. "I feel just about as sick of you as Rureth says he is of Hego! You can't be in here two minutes without trouble brewing and men are being dragged off the production line!"

THE LADDER IN THE SKY

Kazan also said nothing. It was sheer self-defense that was driving Snutch to try and shift the blame for Rureth out-facing him. You couldn't do anything about that.

Snutch stormed to the communicator on Rureth's desk and made the promised call to the hospital. The threat of psychiatric examination seemed to have cowed Hego for the moment; he raised no objection when Snutch ordered him to report to the doctor.

"Think you can keep things under control now, Rureth?" Snutch demanded sarcastically.

"With Hego out of the way, no problems," Rureth answered.

"Glad to hear it," Snutch retorted. "If you'd been on top of your job, you'd have known this was likely to happen and you'd have taken some action in advance." He jerked his head in Kazan's direction. "He's all yours—make the best of him. I remember it was you who first told me was supposed to be an all-around genius. Let's see you get matching results."

He marched out. After a long pause, Kazan stirred on his chair.

"I'm sorry," he said. "I'm a source of continual headaches and it isn't only Snutch who gets them."

"Him!" Rureth said violently. "He's scared of you, for the love of life, and for no saner reason than Hego is! I wish I could figure out what goes on inside his head."

He dropped into his chair and studied Kazan across his desk.

"Not that you've made an auspicious start in this place," he went on. "Snutch is damned right. I should have known what Hego's reaction was apt to be, crazy or not." An idea seemed to strike him. "And speaking of crazy!" he said. "What was that you were saying as you got up on the gallery, about you believing in devils? Or was my hearing playing me tricks?"

Kazan shrugged and forced a smile. Rureth didn't press him, being glad to let the matter slip. He said when he had waited for, and not had, a reply, "But what the hell I'm to do with you, I just don't know. I was going to give you the straight training course, condensed to fit you. But that means

THE LADDER IN THE SKY

you go to work on manual jobs first. The wyrds know what would happen if I set you alongside Dorsek, for example—and it'd be still worse if you ever tried to give him orders."

The communicator signaled on his desk. He answered it, listened for a moment, and said crisply, "On my way!"

He got to his feet. "Trouble everywhere today!" he said. "Now there's a hitch in hull-plate supply. There's a die broken on number four press. Well, I guess that solves one problem, though. That's where you go to work."

It had never been like this, Kazan thought. He felt as if he had been beaten steadily from head to foot all day with clubs; the sheer nervous tension had exhausted him and dulled his mind.

It would be good if he could stop. It would be good to find peace.

With the clangor of the shift-end bell in his ears, he walked moodily out of the shipping complex in a direction opposite from that of most of the other workers, who were headed for the point at which the helibuses waited to return them to the dwelling area. It was more than two miles across reddish dusty ground if you went on foot, but Kazan thought he would rather walk. Half an hour's silent reflection would be a comfort.

Instead of following the ordinary route, therefore, he went out past the exterior of the loading bays and for a short distance along the edge of the spaceport. There wasn't much to the port; only a cluster of half a dozen ship cradles and the rails on which the ore tubs slid after loading to wait their turn to be fired into space, and a group of reddish, low-built blockhouses with narrow-beam antennae on their roofs, which sufficed for the control staff. The concrete of the field was dusty too. The spitting rain of this morning had ended by noon, and a steady wind had dried up behind it.

Often there were two or sometimes as many as four ore tubs lined up, when the shipping complex somehow got slightly ahead of schedule—perhaps if an exceptionally pure vein of ore was struck and refinery time was reduced. This evening there was only one, the ship which had been completed and inspected this morning.

THE LADDER IN THE SKY

Ugly things, Kazan thought. Nothing but a roughly finished ovoid, made of stamped plates over coarse strong ribs, and full of dust. There was nothing about them not dictated by absolute necessity; they were simply a means of getting a bulk of metal out of Vashti's atmosphere. You could hardly even call them ships, because the only thing that made them more than inert metal lumps was the power unit which socketed home in a tunnel down the long axis of the ellipsoid, and that was strictly detachable; before the master ship collected its cargo and departed that power unit would be removed and returned by itself to crash in the desert a few miles away. Then it would serve to hoist another lump of metal into space.

Like insects, a small group of the control staff swarmed over the ore tub on its rails. There was clearly going to be a firing shortly. It occurred to Kazan that he had picked a bad time to walk in the open—a firing was noisy, and there was always a good deal of stray energy owing to the virtually pure metal structure of the ore tubs, which sometimes caused lightning although they usually sprayed the hull with water from fog-nozzles to carry away the greater part of the charge as the power unit warmed up.

Yes; they were moving away from the hull now, and the monopole motor on which the ship rode was driving it forward into the nearest ship's cradle. Kazan cursed. He had been looking forward to a slow stroll home, and time to think. Now, if he wanted to live, he would have to start running, or risk yet more dislike from the control staff this time. They would have to hold back the firing till he was off the field.

He was not absolutely certain, he found, that he did want to live. But if he stayed here, they would send out transport and carry him away.

He compromised by walking fast. By the time the wail of the firing siren reached him, he knew he was well past the danger zone. Another five minutes, and he would be in the dwelling area. He paused and turned to watch the ore tub go up.

A sudden demand for magnesium, Snutch had said. This

THE LADDER IN THE SKY

would be a light lift, then, taking only a few minutes, compared to one containing the more usual heavier metals.

Faintly he could hear the complaints of the cradle's plungers as they pushed the blunt nose of the ore tub up towards the correct angle of ascent; the thrust from the power unit on the centerline was strictly longitudinal. There were no minor adjustments after firing, when the trajectory became purely ballistic.

A second blast from the siren. Twilight was closing in, but when they turned on the water-fog it could be clearly seen how the spray veiled the cradle and the hull resting on it. A few random sparks struck, but Kazan was too far away for them to be dazzling.

Just as well, he thought. His retinas had had enough punishment for one day.

There followed the usual pause while they scanned the area over which the ore tub would travel, making sure there were no obstructions such as unscheduled helibuses, and more sparks struck through the water-fog. And the final, prolonged siren howl announced the actual firing.

Afterwards Kazan could remember what happened in his mind during the next half-minute or so. But at the time he was consciously aware only of external things.

First, the awkward, wobbling rise of the ore tub from the cradle. The moment it came clear of the water-fog it was alive with ungrounded energies, and some of them converted into visible frequencies, making the hull glow faintly blue.

Then the noise, of course, like a lunatic drummer hammering his instrument as though trying to drive the sticks through the heads. It was always like that when an ore tub took off. There were a dozen resonances in the best of them, and this was not one of the best.

Then the calamity.

Something seemed to give at the nose of the hull. A brilliant, white-hot glare appeared. The acceleration of the whole which had previously been steady seemed to be divided—part of the glowing object at the nose, and a much smaller part to the remainder. The hull twisted. By now it was a thousand feet up. The twist became a spin. The forces act-

THE LADDER IN THE SKY

ing on the hull seemed to go insane, and drove it sidewise and still, for a short distance, upwards. But the sidewise component mattered.

It was arcing towards Kazan, towards the dwelling area where the workers from the outlying areas were now returning for the night; the power unit had broken through the nose; there was a continuous spark between the power unit and the hull hot enough to have fired the powdered cargo.

Like a firework built by a lunatic giant, the ore tub nosed down on the settlement of six thousand people, showering burning liquid magnesium over an area of ten square miles, a fountain of dazzling death.

It was then that Kazan knew two things: first, that it was his fault, for he had interrupted Hego as he was about to close a flaw in that same hull which was breaking apart above him, and second, that he did not really want to die.

A chunk of solid white magnesium oxide struck the concrete a yard from him and splashed; it was still fiercely hot, and specks stung his exposed hands and face. As though the momentary pain had been a trigger, Kazan remembered how to solidify air.

And the ore tub, and the thousands of tons of incandescent magnesium pouring from its riven sides, fell on a hard invisible nothing a hundred feet above the settlement and roofed it over with a sky of fire.

He had been slow. He had not stopped it all from falling in the dwelling area—only most of it. There were screams. There were fires starting in the leisure hall and on some of the dwelling blocks. But at least when it exploded it would—

It exploded, and the world went black around him.

THE LADDER IN THE SKY

XVII

IT WAS NIGHTMARE made flesh from that moment on. For a long time the sea of fire overhead glared down so brilliantly eyes could barely be kept open; those who fought to rescue victims trapped in the leisure hall and the worst hit of the apartment blocks had to improvise antiglare filters from loose-mesh cloth, or use one eye only and squint narrowly between two fingers, keeping the other eye closed.

The heat was terrible. It was as though the whole sky had suddenly been filled with suns.

Wherever the incandescent magnesium had fallen, there was appalling destruction. Some of the first spurts from the ore tub as it broke apart had created liquid drops of the metal fully twenty pounds in weight, and wherever they fell on steel girders—mostly on the roof of the leisure hall—they melted them through. The girders bowed, caved, broke, spilling the roof on the ground below.

Aside from the leisure hall, the buildings worst affected were food storage warehouses set a short distance back from the dwelling area, and the shipping complex. A veritable river of liquid magnesium poured off the incredible barrier in the air and flooded over the loading bay where yet more magnesium was in store. There were explosions which sent gouts of white death soaring for miles across the countryside.

After the heat, as after a nuclear explosion, the rain that had been poised ready to fall in the air came gushing down.

A crust of white insoluble magnesium oxide formed over the settlement and darkness followed, almost less bearable than the hideous glare which had gone before. Most of the power was out, and people had to work in the ruins by handlights. There was effectively no disease among the workers on Vashti—the land was sterile for many miles around—and the resources of the medical staff were only designed to cope with the occasional injury and with the known allergies which sometimes resulted from contact with native vegetation.

Where fats remained in the food warehouses they were

THE LADDER IN THE SKY

pillaged to provide emergency burn dressings; the deaths were amazingly few, but the casualties numbered more than half the total population, from sprains and scratches to third-degree burns and broken limbs.

Through an inferno of collapsing walls and moaning victims Kazan walked like an unseeing ghost. He kept thinking of the fear which was to him a certainty—that when Hego turned aside from his work, he had left unrepaired a flaw in the hull of the ore tub, and no one had remembered the fact in the confusion following his attack on Kazan.

True enough. "He's bad. You can feel he's bad just by being close to him." True enough. This happens; without intention, simply by Kazan being Kazan.

Was this the purpose of the devil that possessed him? A devil was said to hail from a place of torment; this was a place of torment now. He was too dazed to wonder why—if pain and destruction were intended—he had suddenly regained the power to make air solid, and so saved the settlement from total obliteration.

All he could think of was that this happened because he was here.

He came to what he recognized as his own apartment block; a small fire burned at one end, allowed to remain alight so that rescue workers could see to carry casualties to the emergency hospital set up in front of the building, but carefully watched by grim-faced men with hoses ready to damp it down when there was no more need for it. Squatting or lying hopeless on blankets were more than a hundred injured people, some with terrible burns. He walked between them, scarcely seeing.

"Kazan!" a shrill voice called to him. "Kazan!"

He turned slowly, and saw Clary rising from beside one of the casualties, a roll of bandage in her hand. She was dusty from head to foot and her shirt was ripped jaggedly from the left shoulder down, but she moved smoothly as she hurried towards him. He did not move when she flung her arms around him.

"Kazan, you're safe!" she sobbed. "I was afraid—!"

"Of course I'm safe," Kazan said in a gravelly voice. "It was my doing. What do you expect?"

THE LADDER IN THE SKY

"What did you say?" Disbelieving, she drew back from him. A pace or two distant two men who had paused to rest and wipe their faces after carrying a casualty to join the rest exchanged glances and moved closer. Clary read menace in their faces and tried to pull Kazan away, but he was like a wooden dummy.

"What happened?" the nearer of the men said. "I still don't know what happened."

"Did you see it?" his companion demanded of Kazan.

"I saw it," Kazan said. "The ore tub. The power unit broke loose. It spilled its cargo of magnesium over the settlement."

"Everyone knows that by now!" Clary said, still trying to make Kazan move away.

"Yeah!" the first speaker said. "What held it up? That's what I want to know!" He gestured at the opaque roof closing in the settlement. "It's up there! Hot as blazes—like the sun falling down!"

"Don't worry what caused it—just be glad!" his companion contradicted. "Aren't things bad enough? Look at these poor devils half-roasted on the ground here! Look at the buildings! Look at the whole place. It's a shambles!"

Another man, husky, dirty, moving tiredly, helped a limping woman to a place on the roadway where a doctor was at work, and turned to go. He caught sight of Kazan and the two men interrogating him, and came suddenly alert. He strode over.

"Kazan!" he said. "I'd hoped something fell on you! We could spare you well enough, but I'll lay you aren't even scratched!"

Dorsek, Kazan realized dully. He said, "I—I don't know. I guess I'm okay. But by the wyrds I wish something had fallen on me."

"Do you now?" Dorsek said softly. "I wonder why that is."

And in the same moment came Clary's despairing cry, "Kazan! Don't listen to him—he's suffering from shock!"

"You keep quiet!" Dorsek snapped, round on her. "I want to hear this. Go on, Kazan—bring it up!"

"Hego," Kazan said thickly. "The seam he was going to

105

THE LADDER IN THE SKY

plug when I came this morning. He didn't do it, and nobody realized."

Dorsek's face twisted into an ugly mask of rage. He said, "Why, you miserable sniveling insect! Aren't you satisfied yet with what you've done to Hego? You aren't going to get away with this! You aren't going to unload the blame that easily! It happened because you're here, and we knew it was going to happen and we tried to stop it. If you'd kept your contagious nose out of that inspection shop then from what you just said it would never have happened and—"

"Stop him!" Clary shrieked, and the two puzzled men standing by made to grab Dorsek as he lunged forward, but they were too slow. Kazan made no attempt to avoid the blow. The fist took him full in the face, and he toppled and slid to the ground, the last sound in his ears being the voice of Clary crying his name.

Eyes red-rimmed, Snutch looked around the assembled remnants of his senior staff. Some of them were wearing surgical dressings, and all of them were dirty and weary. The only light came from a hand lamp on the table in the middle of the room, which gave each of them a vast shadow like a carrion-eating bird poised with folded wings on the wall behind.

"What in the name of the wyrds *is* it?" he said.

They all knew what he meant, and exchanged worried glances. For lack of the chief scientist—unconscious for the past several hours—Rureth spoke up.

"A force field, I guess," he said. "I know force fields are supposed to be impossible. But that's one. There's an invisible dome over the settlement. We mapped it." He took a rolled paper from his front pocket and threw it down on the table; several people craned to stare at the circular red line inscribed on the outline of the settlement.

"Far as we can tell, there isn't anything there but air," Rureth went on, bowing his head to rub his eyes and then shaking back his thin fringe of hair. "It's fairly elastic, but if you hit it with a heavy hammer it transmits force instead of absorbing it. It's coated on the outside with a layer of magnesium oxide which in places is feet in thickness. I've

THE LADDER IN THE SKY

got a couple of dozen men working on the thin areas. We've managed to crack loose a few sheets of the crust and we won't have to worry about ventilation because air diffuses through the field. Or whatever you like to call it."

"What shape is it?" Snutch demanded.

"Roughly spherical, but since it's elastic there's a dip in the middle where the remains of the ore tub are lying. We figure there's about three to six hundred tons poised up there. If whatever's sustaining the field gives out, it'll come crashing down on our heads. Has anyone any theories about it?"

He looked dispiritedly along the table as though expecting no reply. His expectation was fulfilled. He went on, "I guess to be on the safe side we'd better evacuate the spot directly under the wreck of the ore tub. But if the field collapses we're going to be buried under chunks of magnesium oxide anyway, so I don't think the odds are good."

"Anybody left outside?" Snutch said.

"The control staff at the landing field," someone said. "I hear they're all right."

"Any chance of our getting out?"

"Right now, I'd say none whatsoever."

"And nothing can get in," Snutch muttered. "And until the master ship comes to collect the ore tubs, no way of getting a signal out because we haven't the power to reach Marduk with surviving equipment, and even at maximum drive it'll take weeks to get supplies here and they'll have to be— Rureth! How about a tunnel?"

"We thought of that," Rureth said. "But the trouble's this. The whole area where the force field meets the ground is concreted, except for a small stretch where it's been so hammered by the impact of the ore tub that it's practically fused together. Inside the field, where we can get to, there isn't enough equipment to break through concrete and make a tunnel. I signaled the landing control staff to see if they could find some equipment out by the mines themselves, but there's been subsidence and a lot of the underground machinery is buried. When the ore tub hit, it must have been equivalent to a small earthquake. Shook all the tunnels down."

Snutch's hands were shaking where they lay on the table.

THE LADDER IN THE SKY

He noticed them and clasped them hastily together. With much effort he said, "Casualties—oh, what's the *use*? We're done for."

All eyes switched to him. Someone said, "While there's life—"

Snutch thumped the table and leaped to his feet. He said hysterically, "Hope? Where's the hope? When's somebody going to show me hope? All you do is drone on about disaster and how we're imprisoned and—"

Inconspicuously Rureth exchanged glances with the chief of the medical staff, on whom Snutch had been about to call for his casualty report. The doctor nodded; he made some motion or other beneath the table, and suddenly clapped his hand against Snutch's thigh.

The manager's eyes rolled upwards and he began to sag at the knees. Rising unhurriedly, the doctor helped him to fall back accurately into his chair.

"Shock," he said to the others. "He'll be out for about three minutes. I gave him a palm-injector load of anti-tension specifics. I'd pass them round, but my supplies are short."

"All supplies are short," someone said pessimistically.

"Yes," the doctor said thoughtfully. He looked at Rureth. "By the way, some of your men aren't helping any. Last night, we had enough casualties from the main disaster without having to waste material on men beating each other up."

"My men?" Rureth said.

"Yes. The one who started it seemed to have been unstabled by shock, and claimed that the guy he was beating up was responsible for the crash. Dorsek was the name. The other was a youngster." He snapped his fingers. "Someone did tell me who he was; he couldn't talk for himself. He had a concussion and his face was badly bruised."

"Kazan?" Rureth said.

"That's right. Young fellow. Fair-haired."

"Dorsek's fault, then," Rureth said after a pause. He debated with himself: should he inquire how Kazan was, do anything about him? He found he hadn't got the spare energy. He said, "Dorsek has a case of the same thing as that moron Hego I sent over to you yesterday. What did you make of him?"

The doctor shrugged. "I didn't get very far. Ran some tests. But when the disaster hit, I figured a strong man was going to be useful in rescue work. So I turned him loose. I guess we can pick the threads up later. After all, he can't run away."

XVIII

You COULD feel the terror, Clary thought. As though the fantastic enclosure of the settlement were a bowl, filling slowly, trapping the people inside with a rising wave which in the end was sure to drown them.

How long they were going to be safe, she dared not guess. This was the safest place she had been able to find, and by the same token it was the least safe of all, because it was precisely under the sag in the—whatever it was—force field, someone had said; they were theoretically impossible according to someone else but that was what it seemed to be. Anyway, the orders had been to abandon this building, which was half devastated by fire but still had many habitable rooms, in case the field gave way and dropped the remains of the ore tub to the ground.

She stared out cautiously over the settlement. There were some lights on now, like little miracles in the overpowering gloom. At a few points the domed crust had been smashed away, and gray sky could be glimpsed, but there was almost no light from overhead.

There was some sort of rescue work still going on. She felt guilty to be hiding here when she was uninjured, but there was no knowing how the poison of suspicion was working on the minds of the terrified workers.

A moan came from behind her. She darted back from the

THE LADDER IN THE SKY

gap in the wall through which she had been peering, and dropped to her knees beside Kazan. She could just make out that his eyes were open in the mask of regenerative ointment the doctor had smeared on him so angrily the night before.

"What—happened?" he said thickly.

She laid her finger on her lips. "They're looking for you," she said. "I've had to hide you. Dorsek tried to beat you up. Do you remember that?"

"I remember." He forced himself into a sitting position, grunting with the effort. "And I remember that I was too dazed to talk to the doctor, isn't that right?"

Clary felt a heart-lift of relief. She said, "That's right!"

"And you—you helped me away, and then somebody shouted for Hego. I remember that." She could see his frown as a kind of blurring of his forehead. "Someone came after us. And then a wall fell down, I think."

"It saved our lives," Clary said. "I'm sure of that. A piece out of the side of a building fell in front of them." She hesitated. "Kazan, what were they angry with you for?"

He made to bury his head in his hands, but she stopped him with a quick movement. She told him about the ointment on his bruised face. He shrugged, nodded, and folded his hands.

Then he told her about the seam that Hego hadn't plugged.

"And they think the disaster is your fault?" Clary said incredulously. "When it's Hego's?"

"Is it?" Kazan said. He coughed; there was a lot of dust in the air. Then he wiped the back of his hand across his mouth. "Or does it go back a lot further? It's Bryda's fault, maybe. Or the conjurer's—whoever he was. But they aren't here. I am. And—Clary, why is it so dark?"

"There's something over the settlement. Nobody knows what it is. It stopped the ship from exploding right in the middle of the settlement and killing everyone. But nobody can get through it to the outside."

"So that's what I did," Kazan said.

"Kazan!" She seized his hand. "You've got to stop blaming yourself for all this!"

"No, I'm serious." He sounded calm now, as though his

THE LADDER IN THE SKY

faculties were coming back. "I remember quite clearly. I made the air solid. I've done it before, and I forgot how I did it because, of course, it wasn't me that did it at all." He gave a hysterical chuckle. "It was the black thing that did it. Well, at least I know beyond doubt now."

She stared at his vague gray outline, uncertain whether she was really seeing his face or only remembering it. She said, "Can you undo it again?"

There was a silence between them. At last, in a voice like dead leaves, he said, "No. No, I've forgotten again."

He cocked his head, listening. "What's that?" he said, his tone changing completely.

Clary lingered for a moment and then she too strained to hear a kind of rasping sound, coming from one of the inner walls, or rather from beyond it. Footsteps, cautiously feeling for secure support among powdered debris.

"Don't move!" Clary hissed, and soundlessly rose from beside him. Casting about for something to serve as a weapon, she saw where a chunk of the room's ceiling had fallen, and for want of anything else caught it up clubwise in her hand. She took three light steps towards the door.

The door ground back and a hand light transfixed her with its beam.

Instantly it was extinguished; there was a scuffle and the door closed rapidly.

"It's Rureth!" a voice said. "For the love of life don't beat my skull in, you fool!"

"Clary! Stop it!" Kazan said, rising on one knee and feeling himself too weak to go any further. "Rureth, what are you doing here?"

"Finding you ahead of Hego and Dorsek," Rureth said. He moved shadowy across the floor, his feet crunching slightly in the powdery droppings from the damaged ceiling. "I should have come looking for you earlier, but I was so exhausted. I got myself a meal and some pickup drugs from the doctor and then I started to make sense of what was happening around me. You know that Hego and Dorsek have more or less taken charge of the Berak workers and made them up into teams to find you and murder you?"

Clary drew in her breath with a little moaning sound.

THE LADDER IN THE SKY

"And you!" Rureth said, half-turning to her. "Damned lucky I got here first. I gave you credit for thinking that the area we kicked them out of with such dire warnings would be the area they'd be most reluctant to look for you in. So far that's held good. I can't say how long it will last."

He pulled some dark lumpy objects from his pockets and held them out to Kazan and Clary. "Stole some provisions for you," he added gruffly. "Thought you'd need them by now."

They accepted the food silently and began to eat. Kazan's jaw was so stiff after Dorsek's attack on him that he could barely chew.

"I gather you decided to take the blame for what happened," Rureth said after a brief pause. "Better set me straight on the facts."

Kazan did so. When he came to the end of his recital, he heard Rureth give a low whistle of astonishment.

"I never took any of these tales about you seriously," he said. "I thought they were just so much superstitious garbage, but come to think of it, you told me yesterday that you had to believe in devils. Now I've seen that force field holding up the wreck of the ore tub, I'll accept anything. You can destroy it again? Hold it—even if you can, that means the wreck, and all the tonnage of magnesium oxide it's supporting, will come down round our ears!"

"Anyway, I don't know how I did it," Kazan said shortly.

"We'll fix that," Rureth countered. "Get the doctor to work on your memory, and the scientific staff. But we'll have to start by getting you out of reach of Hego and Dorsek, and that won't be easy. Better get you to Snutch's office, or his quarters. No, his office would be better. People don't break into the manager's office so readily. Not that Snutch will be exactly pleased to see you."

"I can imagine," Kazan said.

Rureth pondered for a moment. He said finally, "I guess it must be the fact that I know if I don't do something I'm going to die right here. Otherwise I'd never take this business of you creating a force field seriously, let alone, the part of it involving devils. I'll go make certain the coast is clear;

112

THE LADDER IN THE SKY

then you'll have to run like blazes straight to Snutch's office and we'll take it from there."

Luck was on their side. They saw several people on their way, but no one who recognized Kazan with the mask of ointment on his face or who knew Clary as his companion. And Rureth, of course, was hardly a suspicious character. But there was no doubt about the terror reigning beneath the impossible roof.

No one was in any of the administrative offices they had to pass through to reach Snutch's; no pretense could be made of keeping up normal work, and anyway power was too precious to be squandered on office equipment. There was a smell of dust in the rooms. It seemed appropriate.

Their entrance into the actual office was spectacular. With Snutch were Lecia and the medical chief; they could be heard through the door discussing something in raised voices. Rureth wasted no time on politeness and opened the door abruptly with no warning. All three of the room's occupants turned, exclamations rising to their lips.

But it was Snutch who made himself heard. His face went death-pale and he rose slowly from his chair, pointing a shaking arm at Rureth and looking at Kazan as if hypnotized.

"Are you insane?" he said in a shrill voice. "What do you mean by bringing him here? They want to kill him, and they'll kill us too if you don't take him away!"

Rureth hesitated, taken aback, and glanced at the doctor, who shook his head barely perceptibly.

"What good do they think killing Kazan will do?" Rureth barked. "Is that going to get us out of here? I don't pretend to understand how he did it, but it seems pretty certain it was Kazan who stopped the ore tub falling right in the settlement and killing the lot of us!"

"He's going to make up for it by coming here!" Snutch broke in. "Take him away!"

"Shut up," Rureth said coldly. "Sit down. You don't have to prove that you're overwrought—just keep quiet." He turned to the doctor and briefly outlined what Kazan had told him.

"What it needs, obviously," he finished, "is to bring back

113

THE LADDER IN THE SKY

the conscious knowledge of how it was done. I don't know if you have any drugs or anything which you can use, but it seems our only chance. We can't wait for outside help. We'll die of thirst even if we don't starve first."

The doctor put his hands to his head. "It makes as much sense as anything else that's happened," he said. "I don't know about drugs I can use. What I had, I had to use as make-do analgesics or euphorics. But I guess I could try hypnotic regression."

"It's up to you," Rureth nodded. "We'd better call together as many of the scientific staff as we can, to see if they can make sense of whatever physical principle is involved."

The doctor was going through his pockets; he laid half a dozen palm-injectors on the desk. "Those may help," he said. "Random assortment, but the best we have." He looked at Kazan speculatively. "So Dorsek wasn't so crazy when he tried to beat you up," he added.

"I guess not," Kazan said listelssly.

Snutch, who had been staring wildly from one to another of the people in the office, burst out, "Don't *any* of you understand? If they find he's here—"

"Go cut your throat," Rureth snapped.

And there was a sound of heavy footsteps in the anteroom.

They all froze, wondering who it might be, except Snutch. He paused for only an instant, his mouth working, and lunged forward past his desk, avoiding Rureth's startled attempt to catch hold of him, and flung open the door. As the others started to rise, appalled, they saw the blank and astonished face of Hego over Snutch's shoulder. The bully was covered in dust, and there was dried blood on his forehead. Behind him were two more of the Berak workers, each carrying a length of metal rod as an improvised club.

"He's in there!" Snutch babbled. "You can have him! Take him! Get him away from me!"

"Who?" Hego said in a thick, uncertain voice, frowning at the manager's peculiar behavior.

Rureth caught the doctor's attention and gestured at the palm-injectors on the desk. The doctor's eyes widened. Nodding, he snatched up two of the little sac-and-needle devices and thrust one at Rureth while palming the other himself. They rushed after Snutch.

Perhaps mistaking their appearance for the launching of some unaccountable attack, Hego's two companions blanched and beat a hasty retreat. Rureth caught Snutch on the nape with his injector; the doctor sank his into the flesh of Hego's bare forearm. In a moment they were slumping unconscious.

"That gets rid of two of our problems," the doctor said without emotion. "Call up the rest of the scientific staff, Rureth. I'll try and get some drugs here before the word reaches Dorsek. Hego is merely a fool, but from the way he's been behaving since the disaster, I'm inclined to think Dorsek is insane."

XIX

"SUMMARY OF human existence," the doctor said with a twisted smile, looking round the office.

"What?" Rureth said, glancing up, eerie in the fading glow of an over-used hand light.

"Look around you," the doctor said. "I feel there's something—I don't know—epic? That's not the word." He snapped his fingers. "Archetypal is what I mean. About situations like this. The contrast."

"Don't understand you," Rureth said curtly. He wiped his face. It was getting stuffy.

The offices were in a state of siege. They had called up on the surviving communicator channels all the personnel who could be spared from such essential duties as power maintenance or nursing, and there were now fifty-odd people in the office and the anterooms. Most of them were the uninjured members of the Marduk staff. Hego and Snutch, who would be unconscious for some time yet, were roughly piled on the floor in the corner.

THE LADDER IN THE SKY

The doctor said, "I'm a romantic, I guess. But hasn't it generally been like this in history? A permanent crisis between ignorance and fear on one hand, and desperate attempts to get at the facts on the other?"

"Could be," Rureth said, not seeming very interested.

"I'd like to talk with you, Kazan," the doctor said, turning. "If we get out of here alive, that is. Those workers out there, from Berak, who seem to have decided that you're purely a bad influence and they'd solve everything by getting rid of you. I can understand their situation, I think. It's got precedents. Primitive history is full of them. Like—what were the great prespace empires?"

Kazan, sitting passively beside Clary at the side of the room, seemed to spark alert. He said, "I didn't think of it like that. The—the Romans, I read about."

"That's right," the doctor said. He picked up some surgical cleansing cloths from a pile on Snutch's desk and wiped his exposed skin. "They came, and they built their surprisingly advanced houses with underfloor hot-air heating systems, and their metaled roads that lasted for centuries, and the serfs all around kept on grubbing in the dirt and worshipping their nature spirits. And later on, when the Age of Technology got started, some people were traveling in airliners and rockets and enjoying quite an advanced standard of living, while a lot more people were still at the nature-spirit and manual agriculture stage. And, as I picture it, the situation where you come from was similar again. Your home world was colonized, and because it was hospitable the population increased rapidly, and then because it did increase so fast and there wasn't a solid foundation of production to feed and clothe and house so many people you got this unlikely return to basics—staying alive and fed. And political divisions, and contrast between wealthier and poorer areas on the same planet. Isn't that the picture?"

"I guess so," Kazan said. It felt strange to be making this academic analysis in the shadow of death, but it also felt calming, because it was exercising his rational faculties, and he needed to be reminded that he possessed some. "I don't know the whole story. But as I piece it together, when the main wave of expansion caught up with the trail-blazers and

THE LADDER IN THE SKY

the pioneers, Berak was an isolated backwater. When I was a kid—Luth's father was the ruler then—there wasn't a spaceport on the continent. Luth had one built, but it wasn't until he was kicked out that much use was made of it. And even then it didn't make much difference to most people."

"Right." The doctor eyed him speculatively. "But your background is the same as that of most of those howling idiots out there, and you've managed to escape your circumstances. I want to find out how. Afterwards."

One of the young men from Marduk who had been keeping watch outside thrust his head through the half-open door of the office. He said, "Group of Berak workers coming this way. Some sort of trouble—I couldn't see what."

"Any sign of those supplies they were supposed to be bringing up from the hospital?" the doctor rapped.

"That seems to be what the trouble's about. There's one of your staff with them, being frog-marched along."

There was a clanging hammering noise from outside. The doctor looked at Rureth.

"Any use reasoning with them?" Rureth said hopelessly.

"Probably not," the doctor said. "But we'll have to try."

Gloom lay over the settlement like a pall. It was like being inside a tomb to emerge into what should have been open air and instead was the hollow semidarkness over which the impossible roof arched. There were perhaps forty or fifty people approaching in purposeful silence, with Dorsek at their head.

Seeing that someone had come out to meet them, Dorsek gave a brusque command to his companions and walked forward the last few paces alone.

"You got him in there?" he said.

Rureth stared at him stonily. "Do you mean Kazan?" he said.

"You know who I mean. The man who condemned us to death like this."

"I wouldn't know about that," Rureth snapped. "Kazan is there. And that man you're holding captive"—he pointed at the medical aide who had gone to fetch the necessary drugs from the half-ruined hospital—"has drugs which the doctor wants."

"Kazan's in need of no drugs," Dorsek said. "He wasn't even scratched till I got my hands on him. And I was pulled off before I'd done more than bruise him."

"I need them to get at facts he can't remember," the doctor said. "To learn how to get us out of here."

Dorsek drew his lips back from his teeth. He said, "He's got you fooled too, hasn't he? But he doesn't fool us. He caused this. He's got to be punished for it."

There was a grumble of agreement from those behind him.

"What are you expecting to happen if you get your hands on him?" Rureth demanded. "You expect to kill him and find the dome, whatever it is, vanish? So you can get out?"

"We'll make him let us out," Dorsek said.

"You're out of your mind!" Rureth said after a moment of astonished hesitation. "You can't—"

"Hold it," the doctor cut in quietly. "Explain, Dorsek."

"What is there to explain?" Dorsek countered stubbornly. "He put us here, he gets us out, or we square accounts with him before we all die."

"Where is he?" someone shouted from behind. "Get him out to us!"

"You heard that," Dorsek said. "Send him out. Unless you want us to smoke you all out."

"You want to suffocate yourselves?" the doctor said evenly. "You're not such a damned fool that you can't smell how thick the air is getting, even though we managed to knock away some of the crust overhead. Smoke us out? You'd stifle first."

Dorsek hesitated. The doctor seized the opening.

"I want twelve hours," he said. "If he can undo the—well, whatever it was that made the force field over us—if he can, it'll have to be done in that time."

Dorsek shook his head. "Twelve hours is too long," he snapped.

"I want to get out of here as much as you do," the doctor retorted. "More, apparently!" He raised his voice to make sure his words would carry to Dorsek's companions. "You're talking about smoking him out, and all that would do would be

THE LADDER IN THE SKY

to kill the lot of us quicker than jump! You don't want to get out of here alive, apparently—but I'll bet that the rest of you do! In twelve hours we can find out if there's a way."

"And if there isn't?" Dorsek said.

"How can we be any worse off than we are right now?" the doctor demanded.

"Six hours," Dorsek said suddenly. "That's all. Then we come in after you—clear? If you don't send him out to us."

The doctor blanched. He said, "I'll need—"

"You get nothing!" Dorsek cut in. "Except time. And six hours is a hell of a long time. Count yourself lucky. And I warn you, if you're lying, we'll settle accounts with you as well as with Kazan, understood?"

"I'll need the drugs that man was bringing me," the doctor said firmly.

"They got spilled," Dorsek said. "You can go sort them out of the dirt on the ground, if you like. He oughtn't to have struggled."

The doctor seemed to go limp. He said nothing, but turned and went back into the building with his head bowed. With a final glare at Dorsek, Rureth followed him.

"What are you going to do now?" he demanded when he and the doctor were inside again. All those waiting for the outcome of the argument with Dorsek tensed to hear the answer.

"I'm not beaten yet, by the wyrds!" the doctor said. "The smug gasbrained fool!" He drew himself up and looked at Kazan. "I'll have to use the oldest and most primitive technique still in the medical repertory, and *will* it to work."

As though to himself, he added, "You're intelligent, you ought to be a good subject. But I wish I had the right drugs to help you along."

"You mean me?" Kazan said.

"Yes." The doctor indicated a vacant chair which had been shoved into the middle of the room in front of Snutch's desk. "Sit there. Lean back. Close your eyes and relax completely. The rest of you, shut up. I don't want a sound to be heard."

Kazan obeyed. Clary rose from where she had been sitting

THE LADDER IN THE SKY

and peered anxiously forward, her hands clasping and unclasping.

"Make yourself comfortable," the doctor said. "That's right. Have you ever been hypnotized before by voice alone?"

Kazan shook his head, looking startled; his surprise was shared by all the others present.

"That makes us even," the doctor said with an attempt at gallows humor. "Relax, close your eyes—that's right. You feel comfortable, you're quite relaxed, you feel sleepy, you feel your eyelids getting heavy, now they're shut, you can't open them again, you feel sleepy, you feel relaxed and comfortable, relaxed and comfortable, your eyelids are very heavy and your body is getting heavy because it's relaxed and you feel sleepy."

He reached out, continuing his droning flow of instructions, and took Kazan by the wrist. He raised the arm to shoulder-height and abruptly stroked it for its full length.

"It's rigid!" he said. "You can't lower it, no matter how you try. Your arm is rigid!"

He let go. The arm trembled, and stayed where it was. A sudden bead of sweat trickled down into the doctor's eye, and he wiped it away mechanically.

"Fantastic," he said in a low tone. "It works."

"Four hours!" Rureth said. "And nothing! Nothing!"

The doctor fell wearily back into a chair, staring at Kazan. He said, "It's like a wall. It's as if he himself wasn't responsible for creating the force field—and yet he did! The memory of how he did it simply isn't there!"

"They're getting restive outside," Rureth said. "I went out to see a few minutes ago. Can't you do anything else?"

Wringing her hands, Clary said desperately, "There's got to be something! There's—Doctor! You just said maybe he himself wasn't responsible for the force field!"

A wild hope lit her face. The doctor glanced at her.

"The—the thing he always talks about!" Clary said. "The devil that appeared in the conjurer's ring! You haven't taken that seriously, but suppose it *was* real?"

"What do we do?" the doctor countered. "Even if it was!"

"Well—" She cast around. "Well, maybe he remembers

120

THE LADDER IN THE SKY

what the ring was like, what the conjurer did." Her voice trailed away, and she added defensively, "We haven't got much time, you know!"

"I'll try," the doctor said. He forced himself to his feet. "Kazan! Remember again, remember clearly. Go back in your mind. Go back to the time when the black devil appeared in the ring!"

Kazan's body was racked by a vast shudder. He said, "I—I remember."

"What was the ring like? What did the conjurer do?"

"He—I don't know. It was dark in the room. I didn't see."

"Remember!" the doctor insisted.

There was a sudden noise behind him, and he glanced round angrily, words forming on his lips to rebuke the person who was interrupting. He never uttered them. The noise was from Hego, still half unconscious in the corner, who was struggling to speak.

"What's happened?" Rureth said in a low voice.

"He's probably in a susceptible state," the doctor answered equally softly. "It often happens. I knocked him out with a heavy dose of the same drug I would have used to help Kazan go into trance if I'd had any more of it." He turned back to Kazan.

"You saw the ring!" he insisted. "You remember it, you remember what the conjurer did!"

"Yes," a thick voice said. "I saw the ring."

The doctor looked at Rureth with an expression almost of fright. Together they turned to look at Hego again.

The bully was struggling to get to his feet, and failing because his muscles were limp with the aftereffects of the drug he had been given. He could speak, though, and he was speaking, mumbling incoherently.

"The ring—I saw when the conjurer showed it to Bryda. Ring of copper and gold sliding like this." He made an indeterminate gesture. "Pictures on it. Carved on it. Pictures of things. I remember. I see it now."

His face was streaming with perspiration, and when he broke off his teeth started to chatter with terror.

The doctor closed his eyes for a moment, seeming to gather his strength. Then he said in a calm voice, "Can you

THE LADDER IN THE SKY

remember it so clearly that we could make one, Hego?"

"I see it now!" Hego insisted. "I see it right in front of me. Like there!"

He was staring now at a place on the floor in front of Kazan where there was nothing anyone else could see. Shaking, he raised his arm and pointed for a moment. Then he gave a tremulous groan and fell forward on his own knees.

"I think," the doctor said with much effort, "that something is happening. Here in this room. Do you feel it, Rureth?"

The tubby man nodded. Together and in silence, with those watching, they waited for whatever it was to be fulfilled.

XX

WEARY BEYOND endurance, weakened by lack of sleep and food and the pounding of the doctor at his mind, Kazan was yet almost unbearably aware. His consciousness burned like a white-hot star in the dark cloud of his body.

Under the doctor's commands, ever since he entered trance he had moved back in memory, out of the present and into the past, so that now his knowledge of time was tenuous and diffuse; *then* and *now* were arbitrary to him, and he had lost track of how long had elasped since he was hypnotized.

Since the ship's doctor had jolted him out of his lost apathy en route to Vashti, his memory had widened vastly in scope. The events over which the doctor now commanded him to return were close to reality in their vividness, and the sense of helplessness which possessed him when he struggled to remember how he had acted to save the ship crashing into the center of the settlement had the quality of waking nightmare.

THE LADDER IN THE SKY

And yet, little by little, the frustration was fading.

More than once he had almost shrieked at the doctor, the incessant questioning fraying his nerves to the breaking point. Somehow he had held on. Perhaps it was the conscious knowledge that the penalty of yielding was certain death which drove him so far. He had no energy to spare with which to wonder.

Now something had happened. As if a limit had been reached, beyond which the gap in his memory—made? willed?—must somehow be filled. He knew the shape of the gap, as it were; his fevered mind was hunting through everything he had ever learned for facts with which to fill it, and now he was finding them. Ghostly, they seemed to loom out of nowhere, irrelevant and yet meaningful. A physical law, barely noted, and a theoretical equation derived from a tenuous chain of logic rooted in that law. A table of figures, concerned with the properties of gases. Two seemingly unrelated statements about the nature of motion in a gravitational field.

That was—and it had gone again. Almost! Almost! And now he was lost from what he had been concentrating on before and there was mention of a ring and the black thing appearing in it and the vivid intensity with which he could now recall the past brought back the dark room, the blue-glowing circle, the thing in the middle with ember eyes, the voice like a gale piping on an organ of mountains.

Soon, the voice said. *Not yet. Not at once.*

There was a strangeness in Kazan's mind. A weighing sensation. As if he were being evaluated. And beyond that, the most world-shaking knowledge.

The black thing—the devil, if it was a devil—was as clear to him as though it were physically present. He doubted whether it was. He doubted if it had been before, if it was ever present anywhere as a solid form. He could ask it his questions. Or he could answer his questions for himself, using knowledge that he had just acquired. It didn't matter which. The effect was the same.

I have not been possessed? I have always been Kazan?

Kazan magnified. But Kazan.

But the year and a day of service?

THE LADDER IN THE SKY

When Kazan is ready. When Kazan-optimus is realized.
Why? What? How? Who? Who? Who?

The field in the ring, the web of forces (diagram, as it were: so and so and so my—this consciousness there—then) and effective identity. Intense, directed forces. (Nervous system.) Pass through the ring. (Nervous system resonating with the web of forces, glowing like lightning strikes, optimized, freed: brain, memory, reflexes, subconscious processes, the physical totality of human existence.) Consequence: perfect memory, immeasurable intelligence, reactions under stress beyond the human. Slowly developed. Made ready. Beneficial. (These concepts blended simultaneously in a flash of illuminating comprehension.)

Who? Who? Who?

I—black thing seen by you. (A glimpse of others. Very many others. A glimpse of power and intelligence as vast as the cosmos itself.) Called a devil, if you like.

The conjurer?

Service for a year and a day. Eventually.

Why?

Awe; disbelief; urge to understand; incredulous doubt; personal experience; conviction; possession; absence of penalties; benefits.

Kazan began to laugh. It was like the triumphant laughter of a child afraid of ghosts, emerging from a long dark passage into the daylight, mocking the absurdity of his own groundless alarm. His trance ended. He saw with total clarity. He saw it all.

Then he opened his eyes.

They were looking at him. Rureth, the doctor, Clary, Hego, those beyond who had waited tensely while his memory was scoured clean of facts that might perhaps have bearing on their predicament. They were very pale, so pale that even in the twilight gloom they could eye each other furtively and see that their faces were all bloodless and wan.

Rureth spoke first. He shifted, as if he had remained in one position for a very long time and was stiff in all his limbs. He said, "I—don't know what happened. But something did. Something important."

THE LADDER IN THE SKY

Seeming to come out of a daze, Clary shook her head to clear it. "Kazan!" she said. "Are you all right?"

"Yes," Kazan answered. He sounded very tired. "Yes, I'm all right." He didn't look directly at any of them, but kept his eyes straight ahead. He got to his feet and began to walk towards the door.

"Kazan!" Rureth said sharply, but the doctor laid a hand on his arm and shook his head.

Everyone else drew back slightly. Hego, crouched against the wall in the corner, kept rocking his head and making little moaning sounds, but that seemed to be the only noise in all the world.

When Kazan reached the door, Clary started forward after him, as though she would have caught at his hand. But she did not; she merely fell in behind, and in turn the others copied her.

Outside, in the fearful dusk, the workers from Berak were waiting in little knots of half a dozen, talking in low voices, occasionally falling silent as though oppressed by the weight of what overhung them. When they realized that people were emerging from inside the building they had surrounded, they gave a united sound halfway between a sigh of relief and a growl of anticipation, and began to move forward. By chance or design their groups patterned into a rough arrowhead shape, and among the foremost group was Dorsek.

He seemed to have aged in the past few hours. When he spoke, though a note of cracked triumph colored his words, his voice was hoarse and shrill at the same time.

"Kazan!" he said. "What are you doing out here? Come to beg for mercy?"

Kazan said nothing. He walked past him, towards his companions, who would have fallen back but perhaps felt ashamed to do so with so many eyes upon them. Foremost among them was a man who carried one arm limp in a crude sling, and grimaced at frequent intervals with pain.

Kazan put his hand on the splinted arm and walked on by.

"What'd he do to you?" Dorsek snapped. He looked puzzled, not knowing why he had let Kazan pass.

The man with the broken arm probed cautiously with the

THE LADDER IN THE SKY

fingers of his other hand. "It—doesn't hurt now," he said after a pause. "And say, look! I can move it without it hurting."

He raised it, shaking it free of the sling, and turned it this way and that. The doctor hurried forward, demanding to take a look at it. He peeled away the bandages holding the splint with a mutter of disgust at the primitive techniques he had been forced to use through shortage of decent supplies.

"You had a broken radius and ulna both," he said. "But you have a whole arm now."

"What do you make of that?" Rureth said in low tones to Clary beside him. Then he looked at her, and realized idiotically late that she was not where he had thought her. Nor was Kazan, he found when he remembered about him and raised his eyes to him.

"Where have they gone?" he said, and the people gathering to look at the miraculously healed arm suddenly remembered Kazan too.

"That way!" someone said, pointing towards the area which had been emptied of its people, under the sag in the center of the force field overhead. Everything else disregarded, they began to stride, run, limp or hobble in Kazan's wake.

They came upon him in an open space between three apartment blocks—one was the partly-ruined block where Clary and he had found refuge, Rureth realized. They would have gone close, but Clary had halted twenty paces from him and stood with her back to those who had followed, her arms outstretched in a kind of symbolic barrier. They did not attempt to pass the point where she stood, but paused uncertainly and asked random questions of each other without expecting answers.

"What's he doing? Why's he standing there? Is he going to get us out alive?"

And then—

"Look there!" somebody shrilled, flinging up an arm. All heads turned to the threatening down-bulging menacing weight above. Kazan was looking up at it, his face blind with a kind of exaltation, and his hands knotted into fists so hard that the muscles of his arms were like braided ropes.

There were grinding noises like ice breaking on a river at

THE LADDER IN THE SKY

the time of spring thaw; then sliding rasping sounds and heavy crashing sounds, so that people flinched as if from a blow and began to move together shoulder to shoulder. And last, there came cracking noises, crisp and sharp, to put listeners in mind of a giant snapping treetrunks across his knee for firewood.

"Look!" someone shrilled. "Look! Look! Look!"

The opaque dome roofing them was splitting apart; plates of darkness were riving off and falling, making way for the sight of evening sky and sunset and the first hesitant stars. When almost all the sky was clear again, there came a shower of fine white gritty dust, stinging the eyes and making the people spit. But rain to desert travelers could not have been more welcome than the dust to the imprisoned workers.

A cry of jubilation went up, and men and women started incontinently towards what had been the limit of the impenetrable vault. Already it could be seen that those outside on the landing field had realized what was happening, and were turning the brightest of their lights on the half-ruined settlement.

Alone, turned to a white ghost by the sifting dust, Kazan wavered where he stood. Clary stepped forward, putting her hand to her mouth, but before she or any of those who still lingered could come to him, Kazan had fallen prone to the ground.

He lay still, as one dead.

XXI

"In a minute," the doctor said. "I haven't let anyone see him except Clary. I don't know what he did, but I can tell you this. The energy to accomplish it came from his own resources, and when I picked him up afterwards he was as exhausted as if he were dying of starvation. Do you understand it?" he shot finally at Rureth.

THE LADDER IN THE SKY

The tubby man shook his head. He said, "Did Hego? It seemed it was his talking about the—the ring, you remember, which set Kazan off."

"He was scared," the doctor said. "Just scared. The evocation of that devil stamped itself deep on his mind. As to whether he had anything to do with triggering Kazan's reaction, how can I say? My guess is that it was the immediacy of what he said that counted, if anything did. Saying he could see the actual ring right in front of him. Perhaps that broke some barrier in Kazan's memory—but I just don't know."

"Dorsek?" Rureth said. His eyes roved the newly repaired walls of the room in which he was sitting. There wasn't much that could be done until relief ships came out from Marduk, but repair of the hospital had been the top priority, and gangs had labored at it with bare hands to weatherproof and restore it.

"You know some of the workers figured out that Dorsek had wanted to kill the guy who saved them in the end," the doctor said.

"Yes. I saw him. He didn't look pretty."

"He isn't. I'm keeping him alive, but that's all I can do. Hospitalization on Marduk for him. And Hego, too. And quite a lot of others. Including, and especially, Snutch."

Rureth was silent for a moment. He said, "Is it really that bad?"

"Worse." The doctor shrugged. "I have to admit I never realized how deep his sense of frustration went, though I had my suspicions when he hit Kazan without reason the day he was landed here. Remember?"

"Seems like an eternity ago," Rureth said. "What is his trouble?"

"Frustration. Simply that. He pledged himself to a five-year contract, and renewed for another term because he was afraid that in five years he would have been left behind in his profession at home, and he's been regretting the decision steadily more and more without being able to pluck up the courage not to renew for still another term. It just happens to have come to a head now, because he would soon have

THE LADDER IN THE SKY

had to decide whether to stay or leave on the expiration of the second term."

"Can you straighten him out?"

"Oh, yes. They'll root out the irrational fears which make him envious of everyone more intelligent or calmer than he is, restore his confidence in his own ability—the wyrds know, he has plenty. It won't take long."

He checked the time and got to his feet. "I'll call you in to see Kazan in a moment if he's strong enough," he said, and vanished through the door to the room where Kazan was recuperating. He only kept Rureth waiting a moment; then he was back. He beckoned Rureth to come in.

Kazan was resting in a deep chair with infrared lamps bathing the remaining traces of bruises on his chest. He looked a picture of health aside from that; his face was alight with vigor and the hand he gave Rureth was strong.

"The doctor said you might be too weak to talk," Rureth said, parodying disgust. "You're healthier than I am."

"He does it himself," the doctor said. Rureth shot a startled look at him and gave up the idea he had had of being jocular.

He said, "What I want to get straight—what for the love of life am I dealing with? Some—some super-mutation? Or am I crazy, and did I dream what I think I remember?"

The doctor heaved a sigh. He said, "Since I brought him in here I've disciplined myself against asking. If you want to know how I made it—"

His voice trailed away. Rureth said, "Go on."

"I was afraid to," the doctor said with naked honesty. "I don't know that I want to find out." He rubbed his hands together as if feeling his palms sweaty and uncomfortable. "I don't know that I want the truth."

"I do," Rureth said. "I'm prepared to listen to anything. I'm prepared to believe in devils. Kazan! Will you explain?"

"I'll try and explain," Kazan said. "I know, you see, but I haven't tried to put it into words. Some of it doesn't fit words, anyway. They can use words, but words can't be their normal means of communication—"

"They?" Rureth said.

"The black things. The devils."

THE LADDER IN THE SKY

There was a pause. Eventually Rureth said, "Carry on." He sounded grim.

"Even their location," Kazan said. "They have some appreciation of place and time as it appears to us, they know that we exist at physical distances from one another on various planets, but I had the impression that this too was foreign to their nature. And yet there is a vast amount in common between us. What they think of as intelligence has some resemblance to our idea of it. If you like, the fact that they and we both *think*, in whatever different modes, is a link. Well, they exist, and they have enormous intelligence and vast powers, and they have a drive like ours towards total understanding of the cosmos. We form part of their environment, so they want to comprehend us too."

"What connection has all this got with the wild stories Hego was telling about you being possessed by one of them, and raised from the dead, and being contaminated with an aura of evil?"

"Except for two things, the story is true. The aura of evil, as you put it, is of course nonsense, and I am not and have not been possessed."

The doctor jerked forward in his seat with a startled exclamation. He said, "But I was sure—!"

Kazan gave him an expectant look. After a moment he leaned back again, shaking his head. He said, "It occurred to me to check your genes when I had you here unconscious. I was looking for some clue to your talents. Finding nothing, I was thinking in terms of the influence of these devils," he ended in a somewhat disheartened tone.

"Influence, yes, but possession—not yet," Kazan said. "I get the picture, when I think about this, of a rough path being turned into a smooth road, so that what was formerly only fit for foot traffic becomes capable of carrying wheeled vehicles traveling at high speed. I think the image of a path is a kind of symbol for the nervous system of my body. It's being smoothed out, if you like. There were obstructions, and hindrances. Until they are all cleared away, the black thing does not want to enter into possession. Doesn't want to claim the year and a day of service which was its price for helping Bryda."

THE LADDER IN THE SKY

"For the love of life!" Rureth said with violence. "When are we coming to the facts in the matter? You're circling round them, never closing in."

"What sort of service?" the doctor said, after a glance at Rureth. "And why? Because from what I've heard, the black thing was willing to make a very fair exchange. It's giving you these powers; it kept the bargain it struck with whatever her name was who was Luth's mistress—Bryda, that's it."

"Oh, yes. It's an honorable bargain. I have no regrets; I consider myself enormously rewarded."

"Then what did this devil want for itself?" Rureth demanded.

"There's one thing about human beings that they can know nothing about, except vicariously," Kazan said. "And that is—dying."

"They're immortal?" Rureth said thinly.

"That wouldn't mean anything to them at all. Until they encountered human beings, they did not believe that intelligence could exist in a—how can I choose a word? Not *body*, that's irrelevant. That intelligence could exist in a perishable *context*. That awareness could be finite, if you like, and certain to terminate."

He closed his eyes, feeling an indescribable echo of the blended thrill which had gone through him when he understood what he had just reported for the first time. The awe, and the doubt, and the shivering disbelief, and the need to comprehend the improbable phenomenon at first hand by sharing the mental experience of a frail creature subject to death.

"They are looking for some clue to explain this thing which to them is a paradox," Kazan said. "Because their nature is so different from ours, they choose what seems to us a very strange procedure to enable them to do so. The man I took for a conjurer, who offered help to Bryda, was—as I now know—serving his promised year and a day in return for some favor granted to him previously, or to someone else. Before he was claimed for that period, he would have undergone the same process of opening out as I have done.

THE LADDER IN THE SKY

"For him, perhaps, it was less shocking and frightening. I can imagine that if you, Rureth, or you, doctor, were to experience it you would suffer very little. I came out of the Dyasthala on Berak, illiterate, superstitious to some degree, and incredibly ignorant about the universe in which I found myself. I was haunted almost to the brink of madness by fear of possession, not understanding what was happening to me; my new talents were virtually useless until I found ways to exercise them.

"The ring which the conjurer passed over me—I take that to have been a sort of generator of nervous resonance, which enabled the black thing to—not materialize; they aren't material—present itself at a particular location. When it was passed over me, it informed the black thing about me as an individual, and at the same time allowed the imprinting on my subconscious of the information necessary for me to carry out the service which the black thing had promised as its half of the bargain: the rescuing of Luth.

"That depended on a technique which I didn't attempt to understand consciously—the making of resistant areas in empty air, like steps. At the time when I was actually doing it, I was predominantly pleased, like a child who is proud of having learned to toddle and knows nothing consciously of placing one foot before the other, but simply acts automatically in imitation of adults. When I was able to consider what I had done, my overwhelming terror at being, as I believed, possessed of a devil set up such a barrier in my mind that I could not gain conscious access to the knowledge I had been given.

"When I saw the ore tub tumbling towards the settlement, and realized that I was probably going to be killed along with everyone else, what happened must have been different. I suspect that, as well as marking me as an individual, the conjurer's ring had another function: to impose on me the will to safeguard my life. After all, I was a rare and valuable person; I was pledged in due time to serve out my year and a day, and until that was fulfilled the black things wanted me to remain safe and sound. Reflex on a level below consciousness brought back the technique I had been taught, because it was applicable to the situation and enabled me

THE LADDER IN THE SKY

to protect myself, and incidentally the settlement, from disaster.

"By then, though, I had a very much clearer understanding of both physical and mental processes. I could then and there have undone what I had created; I had the facts! The only thing that stopped me was the irrational terror still governing my subconscious, the terror of being possessed. It was not until you had me under hypnosis, doctor, and regressed me to the time when the conjurer called up the black thing, that I was able to make—how shall I put it?—a new appreciation, a new *evaluation* of what had happened, in the light of all the information I'd acquired since then.

"At that point, of course, I broke free. I could reason out why I had failed to understand the true nature of what I had undergone. And I could use my knowledge."

"How"—Rureth's voice shook audibly—"how did you create that force field, and the steps in the air?"

"The black things aren't material. They have had to invent means of using material substances in order to communicate with and influence human beings. Some of the techniques that they have developed are alien to ours. The force field—as good a name as any, I guess—that's one of them. How would it appear to them?" Kazan frowned. "Like this, perhaps: it's strange that we human beings, thinking entities in material bodies, who can move our material limbs, cannot move material objects with which we are not in physical contact. Well, it is! Moreover, the fact that air—which is gas, a state of matter—is permeable is an accident due to temperature and composition. Change the way it's organized, and its properties change too. I could teach you how to do it, I think. But it would take me twenty years."

"It doesn't seem much," Rureth said. "It doesn't seem like a bargain at all, when you're pledged to die for them so that they can experience this unique event." His face was pale.

Kazan stared at him blankly for a moment, and then broke into a peal of laughter. He said, "But—oh, but you don't see it at all! I didn't say that what they wanted during the year and a day of service that they exact was to share the experience of *death*."

THE LADDER IN THE SKY

Rureth and the doctor exchanged startled glances. The doctor said, "But—"

"I said *dying*," Kazan cut in. "Do you see now? A creature in a material body is dying from the moment that it completes its growth. Simply to share the awareness of a human being is enough for them; during that time, if there are others among them who wish to claim the experience, they will teach the subject how to make one of the blue-glowing rings and how to find someone else to be pledged to service. But that's all. The adult human being is dying, to their minds; I am, you are, all of us. Lesser creatures die, too. What concerns them is the simultaneous existence of intelligent thought and the awareness of approaching extinction, nothing more. When they are satisfied, they depart. They leave behind whatever gifts they have bestowed, and after that there is perfect freedom."

There was silence for a while. Rureth broke it.

"What are you going to do?" he said in a strangled voice.

"Live," Kazan said. "But beyond that—" He let the words trail away, nodding slowly as though it had just come to him what he ought to do. Under his breath he added, "Yes, I can do that, of course. To move a thing at a distance, or a great many things. They think differently from human beings; that's why it seems such a roundabout operation, but it has a logic of its own."

"What did you say?" the doctor asked.

Kazan shrugged and got up out of his chair. The patched-up hospital walls, to start with, he thought; then the other buildings, and of course, the injured people. If he could turn the air into a solid barrier he could organize the molecular processes of living tissue, and had done so to distract Dorsek's attention from him, and when he had undone as much as possible of the harm which innocent people had suffered indirectly because of him, there was the whole galaxy before him.

On the point of leaving the room, another thing occurred to him, and he paused. It was bad that Rureth and the doctor, or anyone at all, should fear him. The black things did not harm each other, and where there was no conception of damage or destruction, fear could not exist;

equally, when there was no danger of damage or destruction, it was illogical for people to be afraid of his powers.

He reassured them. When he had done so, he went out of the room, and out of their lives, and out of their minds. For good.

XXII

THIS WAS the place she had been told to come to. She looked at the door for a long time before going in, as though finding the decision to enter a difficult one. Still, she felt so desperate, and the tales she had heard were so convincing.

She opened the door and went in.

Like most houses of the traditional Berak pattern, this one consisted of an open ground floor with pillars the bases of which formed cushioned seats, and another floor above. On one of the seats was a man in dark clothes, who looked up as she entered. He was quite young, she saw, and rather good-looking, although he had a certain air about him which made her sure at once that he was the man she was looking for.

She said, "Are you—are you the conjurer?"

"Some people call me a conjurer," he said with an ironical half-bow. "They bring their problems to me, and I help if I can."

He indicated a seat facing his own, and she moved to it, glancing about her. The house was well appointed; he was clearly prosperous, and he seemed quite affable—not what she had been subconsciously expecting.

"What can I do for you?" he said, leaning back on his own seat and studying her with a thoughtful expression.

"I need—I don't know what I need," she said. "I need out,

THE LADDER IN THE SKY

if you like. I was born here, in the Dyasthala, which has gone now."

"The thieves' quarter, they called it," the conjurer nodded.

"That's right. When it was cleared away, I went to work on Vashti for a while—five years. I had to get away because of a man; I thought I could make myself independent in that time. What I didn't consider was that I had only Berak to come back to. And things have gone wrong since my return, and I'm—oh, trapped."

The conjurer nodded. "Yes, Berak is no place—yet—for people like you. And it's not easy to get out of. The mines on Vashti don't recruit casual labor any more, do they? And there's little opportunity elsewhere on this planet. So you came to me. Why?"

She made a vague gesture. "I'd heard talk. About how you could help people change their lives even if they hadn't any special talent. I haven't, which is half my trouble. I'm too ordinary."

"No," the conjurer said. "Not ordinary."

"Thank you. But I know different. I wouldn't have thought about coming to you if I wasn't so hopelessly confused. I always used to scoff at conjurers and witches and people like that. In the Dyasthala they were all fakes, and everyone knew it, and only went along with the pretense because they used to squeeze money out of superstitious rich people, who were fair game. But there is one very odd story which you hear now. You aren't from Berak, are you?"

"As a matter of fact, I am," the conjurer said.

"Are you? I—well, then you know about Luth's rebellion." The conjurer nodded.

"The other day," she said, "I met a woman. I don't think she can have been old, but she looked old, and she talked so wildly I thought she was crazy. Now I think perhaps she was just drunk, but I'm not sure. She made the most extravagant claims. She said she was Bryda, who used to be Luth's mistress, and she told me about a conjurer who made Luth's escape possible." Looking doubtful, she broke off. "Was it nonsense?" she added after a moment's pause.

"No," the conjurer said.

"You aren't the same conjurer, are you?"

136

THE LADDER IN THE SKY

"No to that too," was the smiling answer. "But we're in the same line of business, you might say. And Bryda may have been drunk, and she may by now be crazy, even, but what she told you was true—Clary."

"How did you—?" she began, and could not finish.

Kazan got up, still smiling, and took from a nearby table a simple ring of gold and copper with a curious chased design around it. He said, "You'll know in a moment. I've been hoping that word would get to you. I've been waiting."

He did something to the ring which made it expand, and laid it down on the floor at Clary's feet. Then he came behind her where he could lay his hand on her shoulder reassuringly.

"Don't be afraid of anything," he said. "You used not to be afraid of devils. You don't have to be afraid now. There's much that I owe you, and I want to repay it."

"But—!" she said in a timid voice.

"Wait," Kazan said.

The ring on the floor began to glow with a faint, faint blue radiance. Darkness seemed to gather within the circle, and out of the darkness looked two ember eyes that were not at all like eyes.

"What world is this?" said an awesome voice like a gale in a range of mountains.

Kazan tightened his hand on Clary's trembling shoulder and replied.

Here's a quick checklist of recent releases of

ACE SCIENCE-FICTION BOOKS

35¢

- D-530 **THE DAY THEY H-BOMBED LOS ANGELES** by Robert M. Williams
- D-531 **THE OUTLAWS OF MARS** by Otis Adelbert Kline
- D-534 **DAYBREAK 2250 A.D.** by Andre Norton
- D-535 **THE SHADOW GIRL** by Ray Cummings
- D-538 **THE THOUSAND YEAR PLAN** by Isaac Asimov
- D-541 **SCAVENGERS IN SPACE** by Alan E. Nourse
- D-542 **THE LAST PLANET** by Andre Norton
- D-544 **SPACE STATION No. 1** by Frank B. Long

40¢

- F-123 **COLLISION COURSE** by Robert Silverberg and **THE NEMESIS FROM TERRA** by Leigh Brackett
- F-127 **WORLDS OF THE IMPERIUM** by Keith Laumer and **SEVEN FROM THE STARS** by Marion Z. Bradley
- F-129 **THE AUTOMATED GOLIATH** by William F. Temple and **THE THREE SUNS OF AMARA** by William F. Temple
- F-131 **THE BEST FROM FANTASY & SCIENCE FICTION:** Sixth Series
- F-135 **THE LONG TOMORROW** by Leigh Brackett
- F-139 **THE MAKESHIFT ROCKET** by Poul Anderson and **UN-MAN** by Poul Anderson

If you are missing any of these, they can be obtained directly from the publisher by sending the indicated sum, plus 5¢ handling fee, to Ace Books, Inc. (Sales Dept.), 23 West 47th St., New York 36, N. Y.